Xeriscaping for Florida Homes

Monica Moran Brandies

A Great Outdoors Book

Great Outdoors Publishing Company, St. Petersburg, Florida

Great Outdoors Publishing Company, Inc.
4747 28th Street North
St. Petersburg, FL 33714

Publisher's Cataloging-in-Publication Data:

Brandies, Monica Moran
      Xeriscaping for Florida homes / Monica Moran Brandies. -- 2nd ed.
          p.   cm.
      Includes bibliographical references (p. 175) and index.
      ISBN 0-8200-0418-9 : $18.95
         1. Landscape gardening—Florida—Water conservation. 2. Xeriscaping—
Florida. I. Title.
      SBR75.83.B73 1999
      635.9'5--dc20
                                       99-06691

Second Edition, 1999.
Printed in the United States of America.

Note: The word Xeriscape is a registered trademark of the Denver (Colorado) Water
        Department, the creators of the word and the original promoters of the concept of the
        system of seven basic principles of beautiful, water-conserving landscapes.

Dedication

To my sons Mike and John, who remember when the pump didn't work, when we had to go to the spring for water, and when the Lerches had to use the outhouse. To my children's children, the third and fourth generations, that they may have water to drink and to grow.

Acknowledgments

Special thanks to God who makes all things possible, to my family always, to the good people at the Hillsborough County Cooperative Extension Service and the Florida Water Management Districts, especially Lou Kavouras who answered my many questions, to my publishers and editors Jan and Joyce Allyn for their kindness and motivation, and to Betty Barr Mackey who first got me started in regional writing.

Contents

About the Author

Mrs. Brandies is a full-time, freelance writer whose work has been published extensively. She writes about gardening, landscaping, family life, handicapped children, religion, travel, self-help, crafts, how-to, parenting, food, nutrition, health, business, people, and the environment.

Once a regular contributor to the garden pages of the *Des Moines Register*, the *Muscatine Journal*, and the *Tampa Tribune*, she now writes and takes photos for the Grower's Guide pages of the *Brandon News*. Her weekly newspaper columns have appeared in various local newspapers for more than 21 years.

Books to which Mrs. Brandies has contributed include Better Homes & Gardens' *Step-by-Step Landscaping* and *New Garden Book*, Ortho Books' *All About Trees* and *All About Ground Covers*, among others. She is also the author of *Ortho's Guide to Herbs*. She and Lois Trigg Chaplin co-wrote *The Florida Gardener's Book of Lists* for Taylor Publishing Company. With co-author Betty Mackey, she wrote *A Cutting Garden for Florida*. Her *Florida Gardening: The Newcomer's Survival Guide* and *Herbs and Spices for Florida Gardens* are published by B. B. Mackey Books. Strawberry Hill Press published her very first book, *Sprouts and Saplings*. In 1997 she expanded her repertoire into autobiographical essays with *Bless You for the Gifts*, a delightful collection of stories about family farm life.

Mrs. Brandies' magazine credits include: *Better Homes & Gardens Ideas, Garden Planning and Products, Country Journal, Plantsman's Journal, Nursery Digest, Midwest Living, Family Circle, Woman's Day, Mature Outlook, Family Digest, Catholic Digest, House and Garden, Beautiful Gardens, Flower and Garden, Lutheran Digest, Twin Circle, Women's Circle, Home Life, Our Family, True Story*, and many others.

Introduction

Your Garden Can Look Like the Cover

The "pink streets" of Pinellas Point lead to the home of Mary Alice and Jim Harley, whose yard (pictured on the cover) shows the touch of the artist. This unique and unusually beautiful landscape gives the visitor not only a pleasant hour and a lasting memory, but also inspiration and a feeling of power to go home and replicate its success.

Like the pink streets, the seven principles of Xeriscape water-saving landscaping can lead you to your own low-maintenance, high value landscape — high value as in real estate, but even more important, in comfort and enjoyment.

The Harleys have lived in their Pinellas Point home for nearly 30 years, with Mary Alice gardening and improving the soil the whole time. Ten years ago she started to convert her yard to a Xeriscape garden. The shady areas made the transition neatly with some plant rearranging. "But where we had looked out on green sweeping lawn, there was suddenly dead grass, brown walks, brown beds that weren't yet finished. The grass I didn't pull out, I covered with black plastic. Then I cut holes to plant and covered the plastic with more attractive mulch. It didn't look so good in those two years of transition," she says.

"You really have ruined the yard," was husband Jim's first reaction. But she hadn't. She made it better, much better.

"I did one side of the yard one year and the other side the next. And I put wedelia [a fast-spreading

Wood carver Mary Alice Harley poses with one of her creations near the pond which separates oasis and drought tolerant zones in her garden. Her shady, tropical, Xeriscaped yard provides ample living and working spaces for her and her family. A rustic gazebo in the back yard provided the focal point for the garden wedding of a family friend a few years ago.

ground cover] in some of the beds just to fill them up until I got enough other plants together. I didn't spend much money, so it took more time."

Entering the Harleys' garden through arches of wisteria, one is instantly captivated by the colorful flowers under spreading trees. There seem to be no boundaries, just paths of brick or flagstone or pine needles leading from one lovely spot to another, cool and shady with a gentle breeze on a summer day, warmly sunny and exhilarating when winter lets more sun in through barer branches.

A tall, wood-framed greenhouse built by their son connects the garage and house, so that the garden goes right inside. Vines outline the Spanish architecture with controlled richness, never abandon. Perhaps sixty feet into this enchanted garden, you notice that the next section leads to a view of the Gulf of Mexico, with a bridge etching the horizon.

"At the pond, the oasis zone — which I water perhaps once a week — becomes the occasional watering zone, which just had its first drink in eight weeks," said Mary Alice on the last day of the driest May on record. "Nothing had wilted, but when we dug some volunteer palms, I realized how powder dry the soil was. Well, actually the lantana got a little droopy looking in the afternoon, but it always revived overnight."

This second section, open to the sun but still partly shaded, is mostly native plants. It is abloom with the rich golds of lantana, butterfly weed and necklace pod. A vine-covered gazebo stands on the edge of an expanse of lawn that never gets watered and looks just fine. A lawn expert might not think it perfect, but it suits this garden well.

"We never water our arid zone along the beach," says Mary Alice. Plants there, "whatever grows," are a bit taller, giving a reed and meadow look between the mangroves and creating a feeling of extended, almost endless space.

On the other side of the house are three separate fenced gardens of trees, shrubs, ground covers, and paths. The partly sunny one is a work yard, and a smaller, sunnier garden teems with roses and herbs. Swings hang from trees and benches invite rest in various nooks and crannies.

Many of the plants that were moved from the oasis zone to the occasional watering zone, especially daylilies and ferns, have done just as well with much less water. The only plant lost in such a transition has been elderberry.

Jim rakes pine needles from various places to keep the paths covered. "They decompose quite a bit in the summer," says Mary Alice.

About once a year, when a big storm piles seaweed on the shore, Mary Alice brings it up to mulch beds and paths, covering it with more pine needles and watering well to flush out the salt. She feeds most plants only once a year, prunes seriously once or twice a year. Most of her gardening is done on an everyday, little-bit-at-a-time basis.

She disconnected the automatic sprinkler system and now waters by hand and hose-end sprinkler, only as needed. A shallow well and pump provide water at reasonable cost.

Her yard is a Certified Wildlife Habitat and she thoroughly enjoys the birds, squirrels, and other creatures that come to call. Three hummingbirds stayed for almost a week when the cardinal spear bloomed. She admits to feeding the raccoons. One raccoon mother, when she is between litters and more friendly, will come out to get Mary Alice in the evening and remind her to fill the feeder, sometimes even eating out of her hand.

In spite of severe water restrictions, anyone in Florida can create such a magical garden with a minimum of work by following as many of the common sense suggestions in this book as suit each situation. Using less water does *not* mean that we must give up beauty and practicality in our homes and gardens. Landscapes designed and maintained using Xeriscape principles are *more* attractive, productive, and comfortable than those most Florida homeowners currently have and, once established, they require *less* time and money for upkeep than a lawn.

Use this book as a resource and catalyst to create the most hospitable, colorful and efficient garden possible. The environment will benefit and so will you.

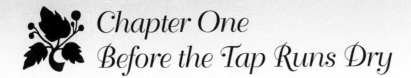

Chapter One
Before the Tap Runs Dry

Many Florida homeowners can remember either living in or visiting in houses with no running water.

As children, my sisters and I were thrilled to spend the night with family friends who kept a large bucket of water on a stand in the kitchen. There was a dipper in it from which we drank. Sometimes we'd get to refill the bucket from a pump in the yard. Mrs. Craycraft heated water on the stove for washing dishes, people, or clothing. Needless to say, she wasted nary a drop. Probably she did not find her privations as exciting as we did, but she never said so.

She also had a beautiful garden.

We had running water at home, but our water heater only worked at night and when the day's ration was gone, we had to heat any more that we needed in the teakettle. No one in our house took long showers or deep baths and we took none at all on wash day.

As young married people, we twice had the pump go out in our well and went as many as three days without water. Cooking, washing, drinking, and watering the family cow took on new meaning in those days. Luckily, there was a spring nearby and we had ten-gallon milk cans in which to bring home the precious H_2O.

One of our family funnies (now) is remembering the time we were visiting my parents, whose water was piped from a spring and therefore rationed by nature. A teenage daughter was in the shower with her long, blond hair full of shampoo when the water stopped, to start again an hour or so later. Brigid was furious for some time after that, mostly at me, for I had taken a shower before and certainly used up her supply of water.

The Water is Running — Out

It is no joke that today we are using and abusing the supply of water that we should be conserving for our grandchildren and future generations. There are fewer and fewer of us who remember when water was not relatively cheap and plentiful at the turn of a tap. As long as the water runs, too many are content to use it at will. Some find conforming to water restrictions a dull discipline. Let the water people worry about it, they think, as they take their second twenty-minute shower of the day. And even as I nag my teenagers, I realize how much water I put on my garden when dry times threaten.

One third of the people in the world today do not have access to a safe and reliable source of drinkable water[1]. Famines are most often caused by lack of rain or irrigation water to raise crops. Wars are caused by disagreement over water rights where water is scarce.

We will think differently when the tap stops running.

And it will.

During the summer flood of 1993, the entire city of Des Moines, Iowa, had no running water for more than a week, and no drinkable running water for a month. There are 300,000 people along the flood plain who will never take water for granted again.

Florida Water Management Districts

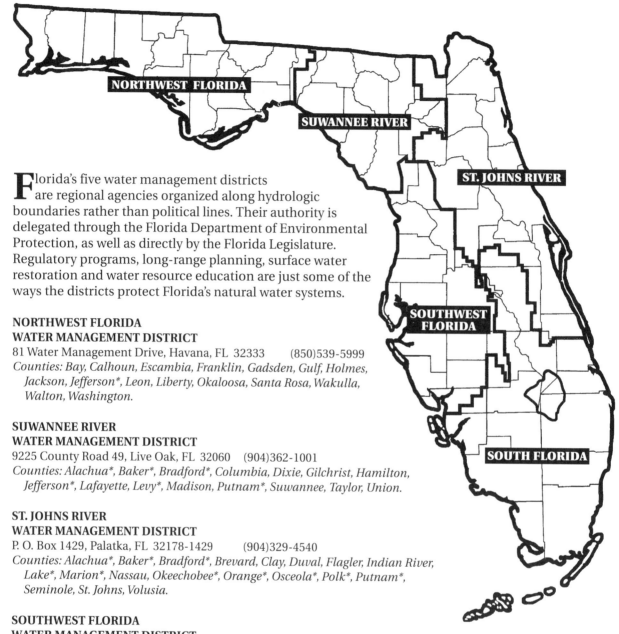

Florida's five water management districts are regional agencies organized along hydrologic boundaries rather than political lines. Their authority is delegated through the Florida Department of Environmental Protection, as well as directly by the Florida Legislature. Regulatory programs, long-range planning, surface water restoration and water resource education are just some of the ways the districts protect Florida's natural water systems.

**NORTHWEST FLORIDA
WATER MANAGEMENT DISTRICT**
81 Water Management Drive, Havana, FL 32333   (850)539-5999
Counties: Bay, Calhoun, Escambia, Franklin, Gadsden, Gulf, Holmes, Jackson, Jefferson*, Leon, Liberty, Okaloosa, Santa Rosa, Wakulla, Walton, Washington.

**SUWANNEE RIVER
WATER MANAGEMENT DISTRICT**
9225 County Road 49, Live Oak, FL 32060   (904)362-1001
Counties: Alachua*, Baker*, Bradford*, Columbia, Dixie, Gilchrist, Hamilton, Jefferson*, Lafayette, Levy*, Madison, Putnam*, Suwannee, Taylor, Union.

**ST. JOHNS RIVER
WATER MANAGEMENT DISTRICT**
P. O. Box 1429, Palatka, FL 32178-1429   (904)329-4540
Counties: Alachua*, Baker*, Bradford*, Brevard, Clay, Duval, Flagler, Indian River, Lake*, Marion*, Nassau, Okeechobee*, Orange*, Osceola*, Polk*, Putnam*, Seminole, St. Johns, Volusia.

**SOUTHWEST FLORIDA
WATER MANAGEMENT DISTRICT**
2379 Broad Street, Brooksville, FL 34609-6899   (352)796-7211
Counties: Charlotte*, Citrus, DeSoto, Hardee, Hernando, Highlands*, Hillsborough, Lake*, Levy*, Manatee, Marion*, Pasco, Pinellas, Polk*, Sarasota, Sumter.

**SOUTH FLORIDA
WATER MANAGEMENT DISTRICT**
P. O. Box 24680, West Palm Beach, FL 33416-4680   (561)686-8800
Counties: Broward, Charlotte*, Collier, Dade, Glades, Hendry, Highlands*, Lee, Martin, Monroe, Okeechobee*, Orange*, Osceola*, Palm Beach, Polk*, St. Lucie.

* Indicates only part of the county is included in the district.

Source: Florida Water Management Districts brochure.

Currently, the rest of us are using an average of 110-150 gallons of water per person per day. Some Greedy Guses use 500 or 600 gallons. This does not include water used in agriculture, industry, mining, or for recreation as on golf courses.

One study showed that people who have their own wells used an average of 27% less than people on city water[3]. We are fortunate to enjoy modern technology, but that does not justify our using more water than all the generations before us put together. Or after us. Nature is not geared for the water waste we are wrecking today.

Sensible St. Petersburg
St. Petersburg, Florida, was the first major city in the country to reuse all of its wastewater and discharge none to surrounding waterways. People there can hook up to a dual water system that includes reclaimed water at about 30% the cost of drinkable water. Lawns so watered require less fertilizer[2].

The fact is that, although 70% of the world's surface is water, 97% of that total is salt water unsuitable for people or plants. Of the rest, approximately 2.6% is locked deep in the earth or in icebergs. Of the tiny 0.4% left, there is none to waste, yet we are all wasting it at alarming rates.

Right now, roughly 50% of available, treated water in Florida is being used for landscaping. Not agriculture. Ornamental plantings. Having spent my working life writing about horticulture, I am not about to say "Stop landscaping." The trees, shrubs, and lawns that surround our houses are not quite as important as the food we eat, but almost. They are food for the spirit. In many cases, with edible landscaping, they can be food for the family as well, especially here in Florida.

There is good news. We do NOT have to give up the gracious outdoor living for which Florida is famous. We can have beautiful yards and save water, too, with Xeriscaping.

The word Xeriscape is a trademark of the Denver (Colorado) Water Department, which has been active in defining and promoting it since its inception. It comes from the Greek word *xeros*, meaning "dry." You will hear it pronounced zir-i-scape, zeer-a-scape, or zair-a-scape. I find that the first pronunciation meets with the fewest frowns. But the word will be one of the buzzwords of the next few decades and soon be as common in our language as "ecology." It already rolls from the tongues of children who are learning about it in school.

The Xeriscape concept sprouted in the early 1980s in Denver, Colorado. It quickly spread to the desert Southwest, where water bills can run $1000 or more a year. Mothered by necessity, it was also inspired by the garden traditions of Spain, North Africa, and the Mediterranean countries. It quickly spread to dry California. Florida grasped it as a lifeline, for her water resources are dwindling in the face of rapid population expansion.

Xeriscaping Can Be A Large Part of the Solution

You May Already Be Halfway There

Xeriscaping is actually a very down-to-earth, common sense approach to beautiful and productive landscapes. Some of its principal practices you and I have been doing for years: improving soil, using mulch, cutting lawns down to size. One writer terms this "nothing more than landscaping with a conscience."[4] It does refine and define horticultural practices to a sharp saving edge where water use is concerned.

Like all good ideas and practices, Xeriscaping begins with attitude adjustment. It is first a state of mind, then a plan of action. It is going to become the guideline for all thinking, drinking people.

Already this sound idea is spreading rapidly through the rest of the country. Xeriscape landscaping or Xeriscaping involves natural or ecological planning. It does not require any more work or expense. In fact, it saves greatly on these, as well as water. *With it, homeowners find they can have beautiful yards and still use 30% to 80% less water.*

Every gallon of water we save
will help keep the supply flowing longer
and make the world a little better ❦

Xeriscaping can also reduce fertilizer and herbicide use by reducing runoff. A study in Novato, California, showed that it reduced water use by 54%, herbicide by 22%, and fertilizer by 61%[5].

Xeriscaping is so important a concept that I have felt duty-bound to mention it in every book I have written on any garden subject for the last several years. Yet many people, even horticulturists, have never heard of it. But more and more homeowners are adapting its principles every day. Wise architects and contractors are planning new homes accordingly. In Florida, new public buildings are required by law to use Xeriscaping.

Established landscapes can gradually be converted to this common sense solution (see Chapter 5). It is my hope that this book will help good gardeners who have been using some of its principles for years to intensify their efforts. Writing it has surely done that for me.

What Xeriscaping is Not

Xeriscaping does not in any way preclude the lush green that we enjoy in Florida landscapes almost all year round. Quite the contrary, it makes the lushness easier, more certain, more productive of flowers and fruits. It will lead to more success and fewer failures in our yards and gardens. And it will mean less work, less wasted water, energy, money, and time.

For all of our benefits, life is very complicated these days. The only way to succeed, indeed to survive, is to set goals and priorities. Xeriscaping does that for landscaping chores. It makes life simpler and landscaping success more certain, and it takes away the stress and strife of wasted work and failure.

Some people hear a bit about Xeriscaping and visualize yards of stone and cactus. Even in Arizona that isn't necessary, and certainly not in Florida. Xeriscaping does not rule out plants, watering, or green, green grass. It only rules out foolish waste.

What You Do Can Make A World of Difference

Can the simple, common sense things that you do in your own home and garden make a difference in one of the world's most important problems? You will be pleasantly surprised at how great a difference you yourself can make. At first you may see only a saving in your water bill and an increase in your yard's beauty and production. And you will have a well-deserved sense of accomplishment in knowing that you are becoming ever more a part of the solution instead of a part of the problem.

But at the same time, your good example will gradually spread. No one ever does something good without its having a ripple effect. It took twenty years for my older children to appreciate that some of my weird ways were also wise. Now they brag about the same things they used to laugh about. "My mother has been gathering mulch for years," they tell their friends who have suddenly become "environmentally aware."

If every household does its little part, the good effects can be multiplied by millions, and the result can be a turnaround in thought and action that will keep the taps running for decades longer and keep the cost of pure water lower. And in the meantime, experts well may solve the bigger problems that are beyond household solutions.

How We Can Turn Off the Water Waste

Here are the basic steps in the Xeriscape process. If you've been doing many of these things for years, now you can feel twice as virtuous and accomplished and move on to do more.

1. Design for Conservation

Careful design has always been considered crucial to the long-term enjoyment of our yards. A Xeriscape considers two principal elements: the site analysis and the planting plan. The first stresses such water-use conditions as slope, drainage, north-south orientation of permanent structures, and the location of native plants that control shade and sun exposure.

It is possible to significantly reduce water needs by capturing all possible rainfall and runoff instead of letting these overflow the sewers. To do this, we must sometimes change grades to channel this water to the landscape plants rather than into the street. Certain plants therefore would be placed in shallow basins, others on berms. Of course, drainage must be adequate, for very few plants will live in waterlogged soil. But given good drainage, any extra rainfall will then sink into the homeground for later use and then back into the aquifer for Mother Nature to recycle.

Windbreaks can greatly reduce wind velocity and water loss. Walls, fences, hedges, trees and shrub borders are windbreaks that you may already have in place. Plan your plantings to take maximum advantage of what you have and then add more where needed. See Chapter 3 for more details on planning and design.

∞ How Is Your Family Doing Waterwise? ∞

Look at your last water bill and see how many gallons you are using. Our bill for the month of May, before the rains start and the time when I use most in my garden, was $50.23. I don't have the other figures. The next, rainy month, the bill was only $22.78. We used 9400 gallons in July. We had five people living in the household. That was also after I'd put the buckets in the showers and the garbage cans under the leaks in the spouting, in other words, after we all became aware of the need to save water. That comes down to 62 gallons per person per day. It was also a bit lower than any other month of the year, even though we had a college daughter at home then who was away during all the months before May. Such checkups can let you know if you're making progress.

Lest we brag, my son's household of three was using only about 24 gallons per person. No one is home for much of the day. Short hair takes less for shampoos.

Even though we are way down on the average, water consciousness says, "You can do even better." We use water copiously. What must the people who balance the average the other way be doing?

2. Select Appropriate Plants

Xeriscaping stresses the need to use more native plants or plants that are appropriate and that are sure to thrive in our Florida climate. Most of us want to try a few exotic treasures, but they take extra work and water and are least likely to thrive. We don't have to give these up, but neither can we expect to grow a whole yard of imports. It isn't wise to be willful and insist on picking out all our plants ourselves. We'll have a more beautiful yard if we heed Mother Nature's suggestions.

Keeping microclimates (see pages 29 and 33) and your own needs and desires in mind, place plants in the areas which are best suited for them. Therein group them according to water needs. In most xeriscapes, there are three planting zones. Close to the house, within range of the hose and also of the eye, are *oasis zones* for the showy plants which require frequent irrigation. These areas include the entryway, the grass areas, vegetable gardens, and some flowers and fruits.

For the most distant areas with less traffic and visibility, use plants with low water and maintenance requirements. These may be called *natural* or *xeric zones* and they may never need watering once established.

In the transition or *drought tolerant zone* between go plants that take occasional, but not constant watering.

Grouping plants in this way not only saves water, the need for more hoses, plants, and energy, but it also assures that each group will get what it needs. None will be overwatered or underwatered because of its neighbors' requirements. The child will not have to wear the sweater because the parent is cold. See Chapter 4 for more help with plant selection and Chapter 12 for some sample Xeriscaping plans that are working.

3. Improve the Soil

If you've done any planting in Florida soil, you know that our soil is some of the world's worst. It holds up the plant, according to Tampa nurseryman Robert Perry, but you have to do all the rest. So you undoubtedly have been adding organic matter already, to increase the water retention capabilities, whether your yard is composed of sand, muck, or marl. Humus makes any soil more friable and easier to work.

Building up the soil with cover crops and constant additions of organic matter in every form becomes a habit for those who understand its importance and simplicity. Instead of filling up our landfills or polluting our waterways, we can just as easily recycle our kitchen scraps, grass clippings, leaves, newspapers, pine needles, and anything else that came from the soil and will return as it rots.

If this sounds indelicate to you, do make an effort to overcome your prejudice. What is definitely smelly after a few days in the trash can is not nearly as unpleasant when buried daily in a compost pile or simply spread over the ground and covered with a more attractive layer like pine needles or wood chips so it can compost on the spot. Once you realize this, and see what a difference it can make in your soil and the success of your crops, you will be like me and rescue every single banana skin thrown in the trash by visitors who don't understand the value of "garbage husbandry."

Chapter 6 gives details for various forms of soil improvement, including seed inoculation, the control of nematodes, and the use of enzymes — all practices that may be unnecessary elsewhere but can make an important difference in a Florida garden.

4. Mulch as Much as You Can

Mulch is an uppercrust way to improve soil. Instead of digging it in, you just lay it on. In a dry season, naked soil cakes and cracks as it dries out. When rain or the watering gardener comes, the water runs right off the top. An hour later, the dust returns. Florida sand is less

❧ Xeriscape Zones ❧

Oasis Zone:

Nearest to the house and hose, this zone contains showy plants which require frequent irrigation to look their best. Vegetable and annual beds also belong in this category, since they are more likely to contain new seedlings or unestablished plants. Keep the number and size of your oasis zones small to maximize water savings.

Drought Tolerant Zone:

Plants that need occasional watering during dry times or in addition to natural rainfall go in this zone. Areas of your landscape which are visible, but not focal points of activity, are good choices for this zone.

Natural Zone:

Ideally, the natural zone will not need watering at all once its plantings become established. Their low water consumption also means they will require less maintenance. Choose areas with low traffic and visibility for natural zone plants.

likely to crack or to rise up as dust, but still both water and soil are lost through runoff and wind erosion.

Rain that falls on mulch soaks in and keeps the soil and the roots cool and moist for days longer. It saves the soil, the water, the plant, and eventually, the grower's energy and expenses.

Mulched, "humusy" soil encourages earthworm and beneficial microbial activity, thereby enlisting these helpers in the growing cause. Chapter 7 deals with methods of mulching to the maximum advantage.

5. Use Turf Wisely

"Grass uses more water and requires more maintenance than any other part of the landscape," say the water conservation experts. "Grass should be concentrated in areas used for recreation and leisure." Its use for looks only should be minimized. Lawns should be shaped for maximum ease of mowing and edging or replaced with ground cover plantings, decks, patios, walkways or meadows. More and more landscape designers are using grass as a design element rather than as a cover-up for any place that has no other planting. Chapter 2 explains why and how to cut down lawn area and replace it with more interesting, less guzzling, less time- and work-consuming plantings.

6. Irrigate Efficiently

If only it would rain enough, you'd hardly have to irrigate at all. Actually, Florida is a desert where it rains a lot for three months of the year and very little during the rest. Even in Florida's rainy summers, there are dry days when some plants need watering. For the months from September through May, irrigation is essential for many plantings. If you use a rain gauge, you can expect to water oasis zones whenever the rainfall is less than one inch a week. If you water in the early morning or in the evening, evaporation will be minimal. Watering with trickle, drip, or soaker hoses or irrigation will cut water loss even more, though they take more equipment to water less space.

Water deeply, and that often means slowly also, so the water sinks in and doesn't run off. One good way is to let the hose run slowly around trees and shrubs while you do other garden chores. Just remember to move it as needed. For young trees, a ditch about four inches deep and six or more inches wide around the drip line will capture water where it can do the most good and hold it until it can sink into the soil for the deepest roots.

Check the efficiency of your watering. Either dig down with a spade or use a coring device to see how deep the ground is really soaked after you finish. Or use a wire, like an unbent coat hanger. It will penetrate the ground easily only as far as the water has. See Chapter 10 for more on irrigation systems.

7. Practice Proper Maintenance

In a Xeriscape, this means such practices as raising the lawnmower blades to get a higher cut and to encourage the grass roots to grow deeper, thus making the lawn more drought tolerant. Keep the mower blades sharp; a clean cut heals more quickly and loses less water than one made with a dull blade.

When water becomes limited, fertilize less. New growth increases water needs. As a last resort, let the lawn use nature's own protection and go dormant. It will green up again when the rain returns.

Strive for minimum weeds and pests, but remember that the fewer poisonous chemicals we use, the less contamination there will be of air and water. Natural controls are becoming more and more effective. The eye of the gardener is the best guard against pests; an insect plucked and stomped the first day it enters the yard may preclude a serious infestation.

Mulching keeps down weeds and also makes it easier to pull those that do occur. Keeping weeds to a minimum saves water, too. Why let weeds use the water your chosen plants need?

You'll find more details on water-saving methods of gardening in Chapters 11, 13 and 14.

References:
1. Postel, Sandra. *Last Oasis*, page 21.
2. Postel, Sandra. *Last Oasis*, page 135.
3. Ipswich, Massachusetts study, mentioned by Roger Swain in article "Well Watered" in May 1992 *Horticulture*.
4. Jerald Hyche, Tampa *Tribune* staff writer.
5. Postel, Sandra. *Last Oasis*, page 159.

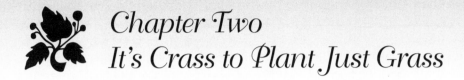

Chapter Two
It's Crass to Plant Just Grass

The modern concept of lawn usage is neither eternal nor infallible. As short a time ago as the turn of the century, Florida country homes were surrounded by sand that the housewife raked or swept. This kept it neat and also kept the area around the house free of material that could ignite from a stray spark and cause a serious fire. One of my professors in college, Louise Bush Brown, co-author with her husband James of *America's Garden Book*, worked for the Florida Extension Service in the early 1900s. One of her favorite stories was how she told her people about grass lawns and their reply was, "I can't imagine having a yard I couldn't sweep."

Grass lawns started as a status symbol among a pastoral people to celebrate their coming up so far in the world that they could afford to have one pasture "just for nice" with nary an animal in it. It developed further in Britain, where it rains almost every day so grass grows well. You can be sure that in days before modern mowers, no one had too extensive a lawn. But riding and self-propelled mowers have let us get carried away.

The most important step you can take to save water in the landscape is to reduce the size of your lawn. In the meantime, cut down on the water you give it.

Lawns in the United States cover more land than any single crop — more than corn, beans or wheat. We have an area roughly the size of Pennsylvania in turf grass.

If people spent half the money, time, and fuss on their gardens that they spend on their lawns, they could grow most of their family's food and be surrounded by flowers.

What plant, other than grass, would anyone plant if they knew it had to be pruned every week?

The Florida Crackers had better sense, and even today, lawns in Florida tend to be less ridiculous in size than in other parts of the country simply because they take more care and cutting here.

I have seen very attractive yards in Florida today where there was no grass at all. In one, for instance, the front yard was small and taken up with driveway, parking area, shrubs, and flowers in planters for color accents. The rest was in groundcovers and mulch. In the back the pool was surrounded by patio, gravel paths, and shrubs and trees with mulch or groundcovers beneath. The owners had happily given away their lawnmower.

Most of us want some green grass. But we can learn to live happily and graciously with much less.

Why You Should Limit Turf Areas

American lawns have been using every year more gasoline, fertilizer, and pesticides than India uses for food crops. People who say "I haven't the time for a garden" could easily make the time if they had less lawn. They'd end up with a more interesting looking yard and much more interesting and less exhausting work caring for it. I interviewed Armando Mendez, whose Tampa yard has little grass and so much fruit that he gathers some every day of the year. "What takes more work, the fruit or the grass?" I asked him. "The grass," he answered, without a moment's hesitation.

If you are a Florida homeowner, you have been slaving or paying through the nose to have grass cut at least once a week all summer and every other week in the winter. Lawn care is a big industry here and I don't mean to take anyone's job away. But lawn care people can just as well and just as cheaply care for other plantings. With less work and less water, you can have a showplace instead of the same spread of plain green that every other house has.

How to Go About the Decrease

If you are planning the landscape of a new home, alone or with the help of a professional, make lawn limitation a priority. Make it a design element instead of a cover-up. For years I have been trying to let islands of groundcovers, mulch, gardens, and mini-woods crowd out our lawn area. Only recently have I finally crossed over the line to visualize a better plan. If you are starting from scratch, you can start from the beginning to use islands of grass among other plantings.

This landscape looks lovely — but it's not for the conservation-minded. The container plants, impatiens, and lawn are all thirsty choices, effectively making the entire yard an oasis zone.

Kinds of Grass

The kind of grass you plant can also make a big difference in water use. None of Florida's grasses will have as fine a texture, withstand as much neglect, or exhibit the comeback power that northern grasses do. But on the other hand, none of our Florida grasses are brown for nearly as much of the year, winter or summer.

St. Augustine

About 80% of Florida lawns are St. Augustine grass, but Florida's most popular grass is also its thirstiest. We have St. Augustine in our front yard and bahia in the back. We have lived in Florida since 1987 and never watered the lawn. And it has been a better green than we ever had except for a few months of spring in the north for all of those years except for perhaps three weeks total while it recovered from frosts.

I do see St. Augustine lawns turning brown and dying out. Rejuvenation is very expensive and consumes much time, energy and water. It is better to water the lawn you want to keep than to let it die. But dryness alone seldom kills. It may weaken the turf for the pest invasion that does kill. Perhaps we have just been lucky so far.

Bahia

The only warm season grass usually planted by seed, bahia is less dense and less lush looking. It has the disadvantage of going to seed every several days in the summer rains. Improved varieties like Argentine make fewer, shorter seedheads less often and have a finer blade. Variety Pensacola is coarser and used mainly on roadsides. On the other hand, bahia has the advantage of roots that go 15 to 30 feet deep. It also has comeback power. After frost or in extreme drought, the grass goes brown, but soon turns green again when warmth or rain return.

The bahia in our back yard is easier to walk through than the dense St. Augustine in front. I've heard people call it a pasture grass and felt apologetic about it until I heard the Xeriscaping experts recommend it. Now I see it with new eyes. It has always been easier to live with. It doesn't climb the shrubbery with its runners. It is more open to weeds, but it is also more tolerant of neglect and resistant to pests and diseases. My neighbors have bahia in their entire yard, mow it weekly in the summer, and it is quite presentable at all times. I'm ready to stop apologizing and start appreciating bahia.

Other Grasses

Zoysia grasses are more tolerant of salt air and often used on the coasts. St. Augustine and Bermuda grasses are also salt tolerant.

Bermuda grass is used on golf courses but takes too much care and constant feeding and watering for most homeowners.

Carpetgrass does well in acid soils and the shade of pine trees, but it turns brown in the summer.

❧ Connect Lawn Areas & Avoid Isolating Little Bits ❧

Whatever lawn you keep should be connected, if necessary with grass walkways, so that you can mow it easily without diving under trees or having to turn off the mower to cross mulched areas.

Try to keep such grassed walkways near oasis zones so that they get sufficient moisture without having to overwater nearby plantings. One terrible example of Xeriscaping looked very nice at first glance (right). But each planting was surrounded by a border of grass too narrow for a mower swath, and the grass needed more water than the drought resistant shrubs. Lawn areas which will be watered automatically should be as wide as a sprinkler head reaches, or should be included in the sprinkling of an oasis zone.

Eliminate turf first in any hard to mow areas like slopes, narrow passages, and around tree trunks. The smaller the perimeters of turf areas, the easier it will be to edge, mow, and water efficiently.

☙ Use Xeriscaping Principles on Existing Lawns ☙

❦ *Don't over water. Automatic irrigation systems are great, but they are also much like riding mowers. They make it easy to overdo. If you are going to water, follow water restrictions. You will find that watering lawn areas 15 minutes twice or three times a week is quite adequate.*

❦ *Keep irrigation system in good working order and check it often. See Chapter 10. Use a shut-off device to turn off the automatic system when it is raining. Adjust it for less water in cooler months.*

❦ *Remember, plants don't waste water. People do.*

❦ *Before planting new plugs, seed, or sod, amend the soil with humus such as peat moss or compost. Check drainage. If necessary, break surface tension with a pitchfork and apply a mixture of water and biodegradable dish soap. Correct grade where needed. Water well the day before planting.*

❦ *After planting grass seed, sod, or plugs, apply half an inch of water every day the first week in two or more applications to keep the root or seed area constantly moist. In weeks 2–3, apply half an inch every other day. By weeks 4–6 a watering of 0.75 inches twice a week should do, and after that water only as needed.*

❦ *If you have been watering and plan to cease the practice, condition your lawn first to help the grass form deeper roots. Apply one inch of water at a time. This will go down as far as 12 inches in sandy soil. Then do not water again until the first signs of wilt appear: the grass turns a bluish-gray, footprints remain long after being made, and many leaf blades fold in half lengthwise. Continue to water only when the lawn wilts, and hopefully at longer and longer intervals, for up to six weeks and your lawn will be ready to go it alone except in the most severe or long lasting drought.*

❦ *Cut grass higher, to about 3 inches, especially in the summer, to encourage deeper roots. This also forms a living mulch that shades the roots, and thus reduces evaporation. Cut grass less frequently in shady areas.*

❦ *Cut grass often enough to remove only one third of leaf length at a time.*

❦ *Keep mower blades sharp to prevent tearing.*

❦ *Decrease fertilizer, time it appropriately, and use controlled-release fertilizers to prevent flushes of growth which can increase water requirements.*

❦ *Beware of thatch. It can build up, especially in St. Augustine grass, to the point where water cannot penetrate. This also promotes chinch bug damage. Treat for thatch as necessary. Hire or rent a verticutter every few years if needed.*

❦ *Use pesticides only when definitely needed. Beware of lawn care companies that promise to apply everything every month. Such regular applications are not needed and only leach away and add to ground water pollution.*

Centipede grass does well in parts of northern Florida but suffers from nematode damage in the rest of the state, has a medium green color and needs mowing only every ten days in the summer. But it does not tolerate drought, salt, or heavy traffic, and it turns brown in winter.

Winter Grasses

Every winter I notice a few yards that stand out for their constant new spring green. This is the result of sowing winter grass seed right over any of the perennial types mentioned above. Annual rye grass sown in October or November will stay that green until it dies out automatically in May. Sow it at the rate of five to ten pounds per 1,000 square feet. You can also use Kentucky bluegrass at the rate of two pounds or one pound of bent grasses for shady areas.

Beside the lush green all winter, this has some advantage in keeping weeds out of the warm season lawn. But be aware that this will take water to become established and possibly additional irrigation during the normally dry months. What is more, it will mean mowing every week all winter as well as all summer. If you really want it, it will be much easier in a smaller lawn area.

How Much Can You Shrink Your Lawn?

I have been whittling away at my yard for six years now. Much of the grass has been replaced with gardens and shrubs and trees surrounded by mulch or groundcovers. I have made definite headway, but not as much as I'd like. Spouse wants me to get the lawn, once half an acre, now perhaps three-eighths, down to at least half its present size before the last teenager grows too old to need the money and therefore mow the lawn. Spouse doesn't mind the exercise himself, but a little goes a long way.

We once had professionals mow and were amazed at how well they trimmed, edged, and left everything neat. They charged no more than we paid our children, did not complain in our hearing, and did not need room and board.

We do not water our lawn — ever. In theory, this is not what I would recommend for a lush Florida yard. But we aren't too particular about our lawn and it works for us. So I don't feel quite the pressure to reduce our lawn quickly that I otherwise would.

Still, the common sense that before said "Cut the lawn area in half," is now saying, "Cut it to at least an eighth of an acre, or a quarter of the total yard — or less."

We do not have automatic irrigation and do not plan to get it in the near future. When we do, we'll get it for the gardens first, the lawn last, if ever. One writer, Marianne Binetti, in her book *Tips for Carefree Landscapes*, suggests that you stick your sprinkler into the middle of your lawn, turn it on high, and then keep whatever gets wet for your lawn. Around the edges, set in drought resisting groundcovers or mulch. Binetti lives in the Pacific Northwest where it is almost always rainy. Her advice is that much more sensible for our rainy desert in Florida.

Where Grass Means Most

I have been following the above advice in our front yard. Unless your front yard is very small, you will probably want some lawn area there because that is what we have learned to value. It will allow your home to fit into the pattern of the neighborhood, though large areas of shrubs, trees, and groundcovers around the turf area will only make it look better.

Never stint on driveway, parking, or turn around space. This can be a matter of life and death if you live on a busy street or highway. It is a matter of great convenience no matter where you live.

On the other side of our drive we may eventually replace the grass with mulch for parking. We now often have one or more cars there on the grass. This is not good for turf.

Nothing is quite as good as grass for carpeting a play area. It absorbs falls, does not track into the house nearly as much as sand or mulch, and stands up to the wear and tear well.

Grass also reduces heat reflection, noise, and water and air pollution. It is second only to virgin forest in its ability to harvest water and recharge ground resources. Xeriscaping does not mean to do away with lawns, only to promote a better balance between lawns, hardscapes, and tree and shrub plantings.

In our back yard I am trying to establish native plants and wildflowers among the trees on the half that is farthest from the house. Eventually we will not mow this at all. Around the pool I will keep some grass as a play yard for grandchildren and a volleyball area.

How to Go About Changing Turf to Something Else

There are several ways to accomplish this:

- You can build a deck, patio, path, pool, extended driveway or parking area over the grass and cover it in the process. Remember that porous hardscapes are better for the ecology (see Chapter 3) and are also usually less expensive. To make them more lasting and maintenance free, you may want to use mulching cloth (see Chapter 7).

- You can use a product like RoundUp™ to kill off the turf completely. This works where you are going to put in a garden or groundcover planting, perhaps with trees and shrubs, as soon as the herbicide label says planting is possible.

Many people find that they use an outdoor living space like this deck more often than the grassy area it replaced.

- You can use newspapers and mulch to smother the turf (see details in Chapter 7) and plant the same day or within several weeks. This mulched area will not be permanent, however, and if you don't plant it, you'll have to add more mulch and remove some weeds occasionally, especially around the edges, or it will revert to grasses, often weedy ones. I am doing this a little at a time and keep a few such areas available ahead of my planting for spreading groundcovers, native plants, and wildflowers as they multiply. But doing too many areas or too large an area at a time by this method could be wasted work. Even with mulch cloth underneath, and even when I have used old carpets, the weeds move in from the edges unless curtailed.

- You can use a tiller and plow up areas of lawn for immediate garden use or other plantings. If you don't have a tiller, you can rent one or hire someone with one to come in and till where you want. I had a working tiller when we first moved and used it a good bit for the first gardens and plantings. It has since died and only a resident son can keep it going. Since I no longer have resident sons and the mulch method works so well for me, I do not mind. I once was going to hire a tiller, but I had so many small, tight, isolated spots, that I realized his rig was too big for my job.

Groundcovers Instead

Groundcovers add so much in color, texture, elegance, and ease that I'd want them to cover some areas of my yard even if they weren't such a water wise solution. In Florida we have a wide selection and most are evergreen. They can be flowering, fragrant, drought resistant, pest-free, and perfectly delightful. Some of them will take a bit of foot traffic. In others you can put stepping stones or paths of pine needles.

Groundcovers, like any other plants, take a bit of watering until they become established. This takes about six weeks for most. Use the same watering scale as for grass plugs and sod (see sidebar page 20). Plant them at the beginning of the summer and most of the watering will be done for you. However, you may have to water them even more than once a day for the first day or so, then at least daily for the next week if it doesn't rain. Half a day dry in summer heat and sun can kill newly planted groundcovers in that first week.

To save water without sacrificing beauty, replace areas of your lawn with drought tolerant, flowering ground covers like this verbena.

Spread mulch first and improve the soil as much as you can. Then weed the new planting roughly as much as you would a flower garden for the first few seasons. This will diminish to only a small bit of hand weeding as the plants spread and crowd out the competition. Groundcovers will grow and prosper where grass will not, as in shady places.

The distance you put the plants apart will also determine how soon they will fill an area. It is a good idea to do a section at a time. As that fills in, you can transplant some of the divisions or runners to the next section and start there. This will take less water than planting widely apart over a larger area.

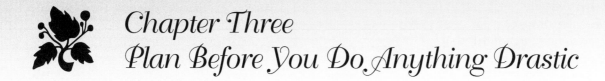

Chapter Three
Plan Before You Do Anything Drastic

I've written, and you've probably read, a great deal about making landscape plans. And always we face the same problem: reality.

Sure, we should all plan carefully and on paper before we do anything major, irreversible, or expensive in our yards. Planning saves money, mistakes, months to years of growing time, and a great deal of energy. Talk about common sense! Planning ahead is obviously the only thing to do.

But come on. How many people are making plans on paper? I have a college degree in landscape design, training in drafting, and publications to prod me. And so I have eventually drawn plans for the landscape of every house in which we've lived for more than a few years. But it usually took me a few years to get around to it.

Mental vs. Paper

I have met a few homeowners or gardeners who were working from paper plans. I salute them. But I have to say that planning in the head, while not nearly as good as planning on paper, is a whole lot better than not planning at all. And making a poorly done, crudely drawn plan on paper is much better than making plans only in the mind. Try making a plan of only a small area, like the dooryard or entrance area. That may prove to you how much it helps and how easy it is once you are determined to do it.

Get the Help You Need

There may already be a map of your property that includes the house and driveway or hard surface. If you can't find it with your deed, check with the builder or architect or with your mortgage office. The town or county building department may have a property survey on file. Check any of such plans for accuracy.

With or without this, you can call in professional help. Tell them from the first that you are interested in a Xeriscape. Many nurseries will draw up plans for you — free — with the understanding that you will buy a certain amount of plant material from them. This could be as little as $100 worth or as much as $300 over a number or years. At either price it is a bargain. I realize now that my first few trips to nurseries after we moved to Florida would probably have gotten me such a service had I thought to ask.

When you want casual landscaping from your nurseryman, it is best to either make an appointment or arrive on a weekday morning when he or she is not so likely to be busy with other customers. Bring any photos of your house or yard and measurements of your beds.

Some nurseries have consultants who will come to your house to answer questions for as little as $20 for the trip and about an hour's time. Should you move into a new home and not know which trees, shrubs, or plants are choice and which are weeds, this would be an excellent way to find out.

One landscape designer explained that they charge $100–$200 for just a plan, depending on the size and complexity of the yard. Then, if they do the work, this is deducted from the total cost of the landscape installation. Don't be afraid to call around and ask for the price of the help you need. And if you aren't sure of what you need, ask for some general ideas. The landscape designers, contractors, nursery people, and architects listed in the phone book or advertising in the local paper will be glad to help you. They will even give you references if you want to see some of their work before you make a commitment.

Don't worry that professional help will mean that the landscape is someone else's idea rather than your own. Explain your needs, desires, and ideas in full and tell your designer whether you want a detailed plan that needs no changing, a general one on which you can fill in the details, or a step-by-step plan to implement over several years' time.

Do-It-Yourself Measuring

Even if you must start from scratch, it takes less than an hour to do the first step: the outdoor measuring. It will go more quickly and you'll enjoy it more if you have someone, even a child, to hold the tape and keep you going until you finish. If you are working alone, use an ice pick or a large rock to hold the tape end. Use the largest measuring tape you have.

Pace It Off:

To measure your pace accurately, measure a strip 50 or 100 feet long. Walk this at your normal stride and count your steps. To convert paces to feet, divide the 50 by 20 or however many steps to get, for instance, 2$\frac{1}{2}$ feet per step.

Or measure your stride and pace off the perimeters. Record all measurements in a notebook on a rough sketch of the house and property lines.

Locate the house by measuring from each corner perpendicular to the two nearest property lines. Then place all other structures, walks, driveways, tree trunks and tree spreads (roughly), and any other plantings you expect to keep. You will want to mark the windows and door for views and access, the depth of the eaves, location of downspouts, location of meters and utility and water lines, irrigation heads, and anything else that may influence your plan. These could be done later, but it is just as easy to do all the measuring at once.

When you get back inside, sit at any flat surface and turn the rough sketch into a true picture, drawn to scale. There are two ways to do this. One is to work on graph paper and let every square be one or two or five feet. Most yards of up to half an acre can go on a page 18 to 24 inches square. Tape several pages together or buy large sheets of graph paper at an art supply store. If your yard is very large, you may want to make separate, enlarged plans of special areas eventually, but all that can be easily done from your base measurements.

You can use a T-square and a scale if you have those drafting tools. Be sure to mark the scale on the plan for future reference: $\frac{1}{4}$ inch=1 foot, or 1 square=2 feet, for example.

Make the base plan as soon as possible after measuring, while all the numbers and marks are fresh in your mind. Otherwise, you'll wind up making trips back outside.

To Find Underground Cables:

Before you plow them to pieces, call your phone and/or TV cable company. They will be glad to come and show you where the cables are and will also help you mark these with a dot of paint on the fence or turf or with little flags that will be permanent. This is less embarrassing than having to call them later to dig and mend, I found. You will not be charged directly for a broken cable, but the costs get back to all of us eventually.

This scale drawing will not take long to do, perhaps another hour. There are no decisions to make at this time. Mark the north point to help you remember where the shadows will fall during different seasons. Details that you would otherwise never notice suddenly become clear — like how far that oak tree actually spreads, how much of the yard is under utility lines where you don't want to plant tall trees, how the driveway, parking areas, and turnaround may well take up as much room as the house, or more.

Once you have your base plan, it is a good idea to have several copies made. On some of these, or on tracing paper laid over the base plan, make any notations that seem appropriate, especially any changes in grade.

Evolving Your Xeriscape Plan

You can measure and make a base plan easily in an afternoon. But both on paper and on the TV screen of your mind, a landscape plan must evolve. Save any big decisions until you have lived with a yard for at least a full cycle of seasons. And in Florida, there is good reason to take longer, because seasons can vary greatly from year to year.

Meanwhile, you will want to consider all the options for outdoor living: patios, paths, pools, and all the special Florida conditions like salt tolerance, hardiness to winter cold, summer heat and humidity. All of these are treated in detail in *Florida Gardening: The Newcomers' Survival Manual.* You will also want to consider the special needs of your family now and in the future. If the play area will probably become a pool when the children get older, be sure to leave access room for needed equipment. You can take down a fence, but you can't move a tree.

Check Under the Eaves!
Many Florida houses have wide eaves and anything planted beneath them never gets rainwater at all. Often plants with roots along the dripline rot away from excess water. It is best to keep all plants outside the dripline. If you have windowboxes under the eaves, the watering is up to you.

Sun and shade patterns can vary also. Because the sun comes in at a lower angle in the winter, some plants under the eaves may have plenty of sun then, but none at all in summer.

Privacy is one of the most important aspects of comfortable outdoor living. Consider which views you will want to frame and which to screen, both from the indoors looking out and from the street or neighbor's yard looking in.

Hands-On Learning

By all means, enjoy your yard while the plan develops. Plant all you want of flowers, vegetables, small fruit, even shrubs and trees that are small enough to move if you change your mind.

This is also a good time for container growing. Even trees grow well in Florida in large tubs or half barrels. You can move pots of herbs or vegetables so that they get more or less sun as the seasons change, bring the mango into the garage if frost threatens, or move the kumquat to the entranceway when it is blooming.

By working with container-grown plants, you will become more aware of sun and shade patterns which change with the seasons, and come to realize that a certain spot that doesn't get a shadow in the summer also doesn't get enough sun to grow vegetables in the winter. Instead of straining your brain to remember all of these details, they will sink into your soul as you work and be second nature by the time you finalize your plan.

∾ Evaluate Your Existing Plan ∾

Don't be too quick to eliminate. The tree that is already there, perhaps hiding among other weedy ones, may well be just what you need, or at least what you want to keep until you can replace it with something better. Take samples of tree foliage to your Cooperative Extension Service office or call in an expert to help you identify them. Then go to books on trees at the local library to help you evaluate what is choice and what is not. Living with the trees will usually tell you much, but if Florida has a bad year weatherwise, it may take longer to appreciate a truly fine plant. Many plants freeze to the ground and come up to bear fine fruit only a few years later because the root systems and grafting point are unharmed. Sometimes a grafted tree will come back from the roots but will have thus reverted to its inferior rootstock variety — for example, you might get sour oranges instead of navels.

Don't Wait for Shade!

Shade is so vital everywhere, but especially in Florida sun, that this is the one exception to the waiting rule. If you need shade, buy at least two of the largest trees you can afford as soon as possible. Envision them full grown. Check for utility lines. Then plant them far enough away from the house, 10 feet for trees that will stay small, 15 to 40 feet for trees that will grow tall and spread — like oaks — so that the canopy will shade and cool the house but not threaten or collapse it. Luckily, firm-wooded trees like oaks grow quickly in Florida, as much as 5 feet per year with proper care.

In other places where you need quick, temporary shade, consider vines. Choose them carefully and they will serve you well and give shade in a few months instead of years. When your trees get large enough, you can pull the vines out.

Hardscapes

Hardscapes, as the term is used by landscapers, indicate the areas of driveways, paths, patios, pools, decking, gravel, or stone where no plant materials grow. Part of our water problems come from the fact that house roofs and non-porous hardscapes direct rainwater runoff into storm sewers. Before development, that same rain would have sunk directly into the ground and returned, unpolluted, to the underground reservoir to maintain the water table.

So a deck is better for the environment than a cement patio. A flagstone or gravel patio is preferable to solid cement as well. When our children were in the tricycle stage, they once compared our old house with our new one according to the paths of cement available. But paths of stepping stones near the house, and beyond that pine needles far enough out to prevent their being tracked indoors, are more ecologically sound. You probably want your driveway surface to be hard, but consider making the extra parking area of mulch, gravel or lattice cement blocks with grass or groundcover plants growing in the spaces.

The water that percolates into the ground will replenish the water table. But first it will replenish the moisture levels of your garden and cut down on some water needs. Where you must have nonporous surfaces, direct the runoff onto your lawn or garden whenever possible.

Make Note of Microclimates

You will soon discover and appreciate the microclimates of your yard: the protected pockets where borderline fruit may survive a frost, the windy spots that dry out first, low areas that collect water and are ideal for elderberry or banana but cause rot for citrus or death to papayas.

You will get acquainted with your soil type and begin to improve either sand or clay with all the humus you can work into it. On plots that you think you'd like to plant later, a cover crop now will yield rich rewards.

Have your soil tested for pH at your extension office or note its acidity by the color of the leaves on acid-loving plants like azaleas and gardenias. If they yellow, the soil is too alkaline. Most of Florida's sandy soils are in the 6.5 to 7.5 (almost neutral) range. Clay and muck generally test 5.5 to 6, more acid. Man-made soils, often found on canals and waterfronts, are usually very alkaline. You can amend the soil with lime to make it less acid, sulfur to make it less alkaline. But Mother Nature will revert to form. You will find it much easier to choose plants that thrive in your soil type, pH range, and natural conditions such as wetlands or dry.

If you are building a new home, putting the long axis of your house on an east-west line will save energy on heating and air-conditioning. This will also give you maximum room on the south side for plants of borderline cold hardiness.

Xeriscaping Considerations

The Xeriscaping concept takes landscape design one step further. By incorporating Xeriscape principles into the design from the beginning, water will be used wisely and plants put in their proper places. There will be less maintenance, more growth and production, fewer failures, and therefore less frustration and lower costs.

One of the most important of these principles is putting each plant in the correct water zone. Those that need most water are often also those that make most color impact and should be nearest the house and the hose. But perhaps not too near, for what is under the windows will not be seen from inside, while what is a few feet away will be in the frame of view. These plants are said to be in the *oasis zone.*

Usually just a bit farther away, in the *drought tolerant zone,* are plants which need to be watered occasionally, once every 10 to 14 days if there is no rain. There are few times of the year in Florida that this occurs. Spring and fall, before and after the summer rains, when it is still quite hot, are the most likely times. This could also include some fruit trees that will need watering during their times of bloom and bearing.

The *natural zone* is at the farthest reaches from the house and the hose. In it go the plants that will thrive with only natural rainfall, once they are established.

The less maintenance you want, the smaller should be the oasis zone and the larger the natural zone. In fact, you can make your whole yard a natural zone if you want.

Another important aspect of Xeriscaping is using turf as a design element rather than as a cover. In former times, we aimed for islands of planting among the grass. In a Xeriscape, we aim for islands of grass among the planting, mulched areas, and structures. Because grass is the thirstiest plant in the landscape it should, in truth, only go in the oasis zone. (See Chapter 2.)

Completing Your Plan

Little by little, make notes and changes on a copy of (or a tracing over) your base plan. You may decide that you definitely want a flower garden, a vegetable garden, plantings of fruit, a wildflower meadow. You can make cutouts of these and move them around on the plan. Try several different arrangements. Always keep in mind soil conditions and shade patterns.

Your access areas, paths, and play areas will probably develop naturally over the first year. For little children, the play area should be in view of the kitchen, study or patio, where adults can supervise without interfering too much. You may want to encourage that development from the start by placing the swingset or sandbox accordingly. Such things can be moved if you come up with a better plan.

Within a year you should have enough of your ideas in place to complete the plan. My current working plan still says such things as: *sunny flowers, shade garden, fruit, keep lawn open for volleyball.* But it shows all the existing buildings and trees and works as a good map for where I am going. I feel a hundred times better about my yard, about any new plants I get, and about the future harmony of my efforts for having even such a general plan.

Keep Your Plan Updated

Every landscape plan, like every road map, needs to be updated occasionally. If your trees grow as you hope, some parts of the yard that are sunny now will be more and more shady. If you get too much shade, a problem I used to dream of in the north but often see in actuality in Florida, you can have the branches of the trees trimmed higher for more light and air circulation. Or you can gradually remove the less choice of your trees.

As your children grow or you yourself get older, you will have different needs. These can be easily worked into a landscape plan. Even a stone wall can be moved, if that's what you really want. But if you make a good plan from the start, revision will usually be only a minor chore.

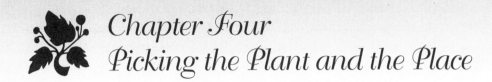

Chapter Four
Picking the Plant and the Place

One of the most important secrets of success with any landscaping project is to put the right plant in the right place. This escalates in importance when planning to save water or work. And it involves one of the most fascinating and frustrating parts of gardening: decision making.

This is the place where each of us can be most creative and expressive. But it takes some study even for people like me who are fairly familiar with many plants. I've made more poor placements in my time than I can count. The number decreases with experience, but it is still part of the picture. I have learned to dig up, discard, rearrange, or replant as needed. The more you plan first, the more of that you can avoid.

My worst scenario is having a bundle of plants arrive from a mail order nursery and not having the slightest idea where to put a one. This happened several times, the last one the day I was in labor with child number seven. Son Mike heeled in the new plant arrivals, but it was weeks before I got them planted where they should be. So I made a firm and fast rule: decide where to plant it *before* you order it. Life is much easier that way.

After all, selection is a function you can do from your easy chair by the fireside or in air-conditioned comfort with no back strain at all. It is very good for developing your powers of imagination. So view it as a challenge rather than a problem.

When you have relaxing time, make it even more pleasant by poring over garden books and catalogs. Make your wish list. Check the charts and lists in this and other Florida books. Then decide if a particular plant will fit into your plan.

What Makes a Plant Drought Tolerant?

A drought tolerant plant, by definition, is one that does not lose moisture at a high rate. This can be because it has woody stems and deep roots or small, thick or waxy leaves. Trees and shrubs are more drought tolerant than perennials, annuals, or vegetables because they have much more extensive root systems and because wood evaporates less moisture than green growth.

Some trees and shrubs are so drought tolerant that they will usually survive with natural rainfall. Many need occasional watering, most often during Florida's spring when the hot weather has arrived but the rains have not come yet. Although April and May are the biggest water-use months in Florida landscapes, be aware that extra watering can be needed during any dry times, and that these can come to sandy soil even in the rainy summer with only a few rainless days.

> **Important fact:** *Any plant that will grow in your section of Florida can be a Xeriscape plant if it is planted in the appropriate zone for its water needs.*

Florida climate can vary fairly widely from year to year. In a warm winter, plants will transpire much more than in a cool one. So drought tolerant plants may also vary their behav-

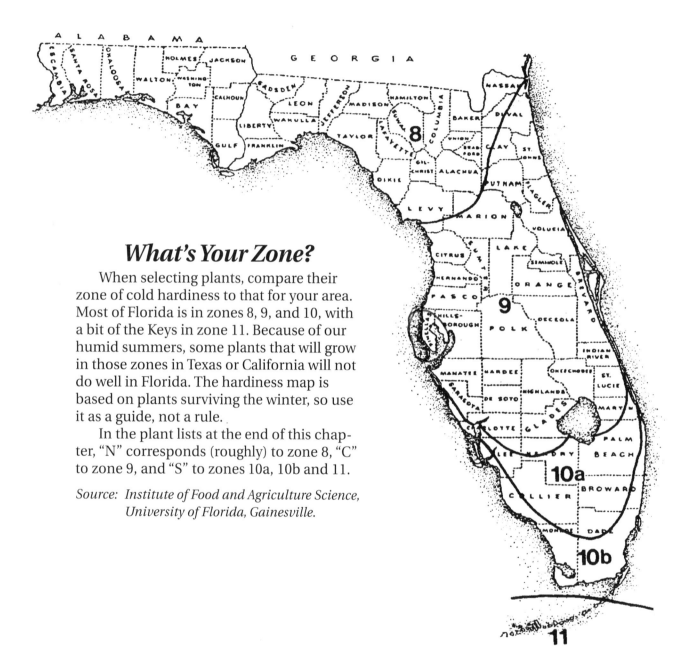

What's Your Zone?

When selecting plants, compare their zone of cold hardiness to that for your area. Most of Florida is in zones 8, 9, and 10, with a bit of the Keys in zone 11. Because of our humid summers, some plants that will grow in those zones in Texas or California will not do well in Florida. The hardiness map is based on plants surviving the winter, so use it as a guide, not a rule.

In the plant lists at the end of this chapter, "N" corresponds (roughly) to zone 8, "C" to zone 9, and "S" to zones 10a, 10b and 11.

Source: Institute of Food and Agriculture Science, University of Florida, Gainesville.

ior. The oak trees may lose more leaves earlier in the year. In a very dry winter some plants will grow more slowly, or bloom and bear less, or go dormant longer and more completely. But drought tolerant plants will survive and most will continue to look reasonably attractive. Other plants may look better at the beginning of drought conditions but soon avoid the drought by dying away.

As a rule, plants with larger leaves, or more of them, need more water. Fuzzy, grayish, or finely-divided foliage is often a sign of drought tolerance. Prostrate plants need less water because they stay out of drying winds and have less foliage for transpiration. The aromatic oils in highly scented plants like herbs and silver dollar eucalyptus often keep such plants from drying out as quickly as others.

Consider Soil and Site as Well

Besides drought tolerance, you must consider other plant needs, like amount of light. Most fruits and vegetables need as much sun as possible, but they also may tolerate more shade in Florida summers than they would elsewhere.

Soil type is also important. Some plants — dogwood, azaleas, blueberries, gardenias and others — like acid soil. Most Florida soils are slightly acid to nearly neutral and have a pH just below 7.0. Close to a new house, on man-made ground near the water, or in the Florida Keys, soil may be quite alkaline with a pH of 8.0. (See page 57 for more on soil pH.)

Soil tests and advice are available from each county's Cooperative Extension office. So are the instructions for gathering samples. You can also buy a home testing kit, follow instructions, and test your own.

You will do best to select plants that will be happy in the natural pH of your yard. You can amend the soil, adding lime to make it less acid, sulfur to make it more so. But in time it will revert to type and you'll be fighting a losing battle. If you want to grow acid lovers and your soil is not low in pH, try growing them in containers where the soil will hold its amendments longer. You'll still have to add some every several months as they do leach out with watering. Joe DaPonte of Brandon, Florida, has had much greater success with his blueberries since he put each bush in a half barrel.

Climate Is Not an Option

Many plants will not grow in some parts of Florida because it is too hot in the summer or too cold in the winter. Some of the northern fruits don't do well here because they need chilling hours to set fruit. However there are varieties, even of apples, that will grow in the central to northern sections. Every 100 miles north or south can make a difference in how well even *those* apples do. Proximity to water also affects climate. St. Petersburg has many thriving plantings that will die out in Tampa, and growers only 10 miles east of

> ### Microclimates Can Make a Difference
>
> ❧ *In every yard there are areas unprotected by buildings or trees. These therefore get more wind and dry out more quickly.*
>
> ❧ *Plants that like the beach (sea grape, sea oxeye daisy, saw palmetto, beach verbena) will do well in the above places in sandy soil.*
>
> ❧ *Low lying areas will collect more rainfall and stay wet longer. Plant water lovers like bananas and elderberry there, but not plants like citrus or thyme that are likely to rot in dampness.*
>
> ❧ *The south side of every house is the warmest, so put fruit trees or other frost tender plants there. Florida growers for the most part learn to gamble with cold and take losses of a few plants every several years in stride. Many, like citrus in the central and northern areas, come back from the roots.*

the Tampa airport (on Tampa Bay) learn to subtract 5 to 10 degrees from the lows predicted there.

Other plants that take heat and drought very well and thrive in California or Arizona will rot in our wet humid summers. Lillian and Arnold Stark of Tampa manage to get some herbs sensitive to humidity through the summers by growing them in wide, upright sections of drainpipe. But this takes more water the rest of the year. So you see, we Floridians have to keep many points in mind and select carefully.

Preserving Natural Beauty

For years, people took over a property and immediately changed it completely. Pioneers cleared the land in an effort to make it functional for them. The native plants, trees or prairie grasses were considered the enemy to be subdued at all costs.

For a long time after that attitude was practical or necessary, it still hung around. If nothing else, changing the terrain showed a measure of control. We often went overboard in this and developed yards of lawn, clipped hedges, and shrubbery that needed constant pruning.

Choose native plants like this beauty berry for minimum maintenance and maximum drought tolerance.

Homeowners no longer need to clear land to raise livestock and our "crops" are usually limited. We can often preserve much of the natural beauty of the land on which a new home is built, especially if it is on a wooded lot. The state and city forestry departments of Florida are fortunately so aware of this that in many places you must have a permit to remove trees or native plant material. If this includes rare or grand trees (very large and old trees of choice species), you may be required by law to adjust your building to preserve the trees.

Developers and builders of commercial sites sometimes fight this, but most homeowners appreciate the great benefits. Some cities, like Tampa, will send a city forester who will tell you which trees are choice and which are not.

With shrubs and flowers, we are more on our own, but the philosophy of preserving good specimens which might take years of growing to replace is still valid.

Using Native Plants

This new movement in gardening may well be one of the most important swings of the pendulum since the invention of the lawnmower. But it isn't always easy to understand. Most of us are not readily aware whether a plant is a native of Florida or not. The charts in the appendix are one of the easiest places to find that information.

There are a growing number of Native Plant Societies throughout the state where you can learn more about native plants, often obtain seeds, cuttings, and plants in a raffle or other giveaway, and enjoy the company of like-minded people. Look in the garden section of your newspaper for meeting times and places. You are welcome to attend the first time as a guest, and you may want to check out more than one meeting before you join.

Even a seasoned gardener can feel overwhelmed at such gatherings the first few times. I did. But then I also felt

> ### What IS a Native Plant?
> *A native plant is one that has been growing in a place for thousands of years — for so long no one can remember that it originated anywhere else — and as such has learned how to cope with the unique conditions of its environment. In other words, it is a plant chosen by Mother Nature for a particular locality.*

✑ Things to Consider When Selecting a Plant ✑

What will it do?

❧ *How tall and wide will it grow? Watch out for overhead power lines, windows, paths, and property lines.*

❧ *When will it bloom and what color will it be? What else will be blooming at the same time?*

❧ *What will it drop? Fruits, leaves, twigs? Does it matter where it is planted? What is fine for mulch on a garden may be a disaster on a patio.*

❧ *Can it withstand summer sun and winter cold?*

What does it need?

❧ *Does it prefer sun, shade, or some of each? Many plants that need full sun elsewhere will do best with some summer shade in Florida. Shade gardening takes less water and there are many shade-loving flowers and shrubs for color.*

❧ *Wet soil or dry? Should it go on high ground, or in the hollow that collects the most water?*

❧ *Which Xeriscape zone? How often will it need watering once it is established?*

that way at my first meetings of the Rare Fruit Council when I had just moved to Florida. The people might almost as well have been speaking a foreign language. After a few meetings I began to understand some of it, and now I find them "more fun than God ought to allow" as well as always teaching me some new and exciting ideas. Like all aspects of Florida gardening, you must never give up too soon or you miss the best part.

You can, of course, learn about native plants on your own. Get all available information on them from your Cooperative Extension Service. Then read books like *Requiem for a Lawnmower* and magazines like *Wild Garden* (see sidebar at end of this chapter). We can't grow all the plants mentioned by Texas author Sally Wasowski, we can use her ideas and those plants that are native here as well.

Notice what grows wild, under what conditions of sun or shade, moist or dry ground. Notice what other plants grow with it. Most native plants have adapted to local conditions. They thrive on natural rainfall and survive all but the most unusual freezes. Selecting a plant native to Florida is only a first step. It is important to try to match the conditions in each section of our yards with the natural preference of each plant. Some plants are native to bog areas and require a great deal of water. But many others grow in areas much like your own yard. Like learning to knit or to roller blade, choosing native plants seems difficult at first but is soon both easy and fun.

If you use them in a similar setting in your yard, native plants will do remarkably well. Some will also provide food and cover for wildlife and thus help preserve the native habitat that is so threatened by our urban sprawl.

Fitting Natives into Your Present Plan

It is important to know that learning about and using native plants doesn't mean starting over from scratch or eliminating non-native plants that we have and enjoy. I still grow my bananas and rare fruits. In fact, I find I have more time to give them when the rest of my yard is more self-sustaining.

"My philosophy has always been to use what works," writes author Wasowski. "My landscape is only 50 percent native. The rest is composed of naturalized plants and a few cultivars of more exotic origin." I agree wholeheartedly. And I find that what does work for me usually turns out, upon checking, to be either a native or a plant that has adapted so well that it behaves like one. Be wary of plants like the kudzu vine and the melaleuca tree that have adapted so well they would take over if we let them. Again, knowing what a plant will do is the first step in deciding where to plant it.

Like Wasowski, you can make a gradual changeover to native plants. She replaced plants that perished in her own yard with natives that would thrive in the same conditions that killed the others. Moreover, she forced the issue in some cases by cutting her watering back drastically. What did not survive the cut was replaced with natives.

Where and How to Get Native Plants

There are more and more nurseries offering native plants, which is a blessing. Seeds are also available in many nursery catalogs. Seeds or cuttings can be taken in the wild, as long as they won't deplete the plants or the planting. You wouldn't want to take anything — even seeds — from a threatened or endangered species. It is often safer to buy plants that are already well started. (See Appendix B for nursery and catalog sources.)

If you have permission, you can sometimes collect plants from property where they will be lost otherwise to new building or road construction. But wildflowers do not always move easily.

People who grow native plants are often willing to share, as the members of the Native Plant Societies do.

Be Aware of Invasiveness

Some drought resistant plants, because of their durability, can run rampant if put where they have more water and less competition. The same is true of non-natives brought to places where their natural checks do not exist. The charts in the appendix tell whether a plant is invasive or not. If it is, be aware of that; it is best to select another. If you must have that false roselle or ficus, plant it in a pot on the patio, a container sunk into the ground to corral roots, or in an area confined by pavement or some other physical barrier.

Some plants (mint and buddleia, for example) that are considered invasive in the Midwest are subdued by Florida summers and quite well behaved. Some, like bamboo, spread by underground runners and can crop up across a driveway. My neighbors just spent days of hard labor to remove a bamboo hedge that was eating up their yard. Yet bamboo in a contained area decorates one of Tampa's bayside restaurants very nicely.

Other plants, like Chinese tallow and asparagus fern, are spread by birds eating and then dropping the seeds and can come up anywhere. If you find volunteers in your yard, take them to the Cooperative Extension Service or to a plant clinic, or ask a knowledgeable friend for identification. Check them out before you transplant or nurture them. Birds can give us treasures, and not all potentially rampant plants are bad. But we need to know how to handle them before putting them into our plan.

Placing vs. Pruning

Many plants, both native and non-native, that are excellent choices for one part of your yard may be invasive in another part simply because of their size. Place trees, shrubs, vines, and even flowers where they have room to assume their natural shape. Plants that need constant pruning, like pittosporum under a window, not only mean extra work, but they are never given a chance to develop fruit or flowers. By being aware of a plant's ultimate height and spread, you can give it room to grow.

Mulch around young plants will help them grow more quickly with less water. Plant annual flowers or vegetables in bare spaces until surrounding woody plants reach maturity. Well chosen plants grow so quickly in Florida that "the unfinished look" is not long a problem.

Finding and Redefining Favorites

Many people come to Florida after years of gardening in other climates and then experience a period of adjustment. During this period many formerly great gardeners give up and quit. If you are one of these: Quit if you like — there is an extensive industry of lawn and garden care here that will gladly take over.

But if you still want the fun, exercise, therapy, and sense of accomplishment that gardening gave you for years, and if you want a landscape that is truly personal and distinctive, it is well worth learning new methods, plants, and timing. My book *Florida Gardening: The Newcomer's Survival Manual*, was written to ease and hurry the learning time.

Many of us will still want to baby a few old favorites. I have two lilacs, varieties "Blue Skies" and "Princess Pink," especially recommended for warm climates with little winter chill. One is in an almost-natural zone and doing well. The other is in a drought tolerant zone and doing perhaps a bit better.

POSSIBLE PROBLEM PLANTS
Do not plant these species. They are particularly invasive:
Bischofia javanica   Bishopwood
Casuarina spp.   Australian pine
Melaleuca quinquenervia   Punk tree
Schinus terebinthifolius   Brazilian pepper tree
Ficus retusa 'Nitida'   Laurel fig
Cinnamomum camphora   Camphor tree
Sabium sebiferum   Chinese tallow tree
Asparagus densiflorus   Asparagus fern

But other plants I was sure I could coax into becoming Floridians steadfastly refused to cooperate (delphiniums and foxgloves). Rhubarb agreed to become only a winter annual, and corn refused to grow except in the cooler months. Some (horseradish, grape hyacinths) cooperated for a while but slipped out of the plan the first chance they got. Others (most daffodils, tulips) would bloom fine if I took the time and trouble for special handling (starting bulbs in the refrigerator to artificially chill them, for example), but they seemed not worth the extra effort.

For every plant we give up by moving to Florida, there are ten to take its place. Once we adjust our outlooks, we'll like them just as well or better.

Understanding Salt Tolerance

People who live on or near the coast find that salt spray limits their choice of plants. But salt problems are moving inland because as we deplete the underground aquifer, salt water can intrude. Many homeowners are finding their well water salty, a taste that is obvious at 500 parts per million (ppm).

If this happens to you, take a water sample to your Cooperative Extension Service to determine just how salty it is. With up to 1,000 ppm, water is still suitable for most landscaping. See the sidebar on the next page for plant tolerances.

With water above 2,000 ppm, it is best to water with half an inch of the salty well water, then with half an inch of fresh rainwater or city water. Be sure to use the fresh water last to wash any salt off of the topgrowth. Watering at night reaps the additional benefit of freshwater dews.

If you live right on the coast, you can still plant salt tolerant plants in salty soil. Plant after heavy rains or fresh water soakings to leach the salts out of the root zone. Most of these soils are sandy and need as much organic matter as you can add. Select wind and salt tolerant

❧ Salt Tolerance in Landscape Plants ❧

Plant	Salt level tolerated
Orchids	Below 500 ppm (parts per million)
Succulents	Below 1200 ppm
Bird-of-paradise	Below 1200 ppm
Crossandra	Below 1200 ppm
Florida heather	Below 1200 ppm
Gardenia	Below 1200 ppm
Foliage plants	Below 1500 ppm
Bahia turf	Below 1500 ppm
Azaleas	Will survive 1500 ppm — rinse with fresh water
Blueberries	Will survive 1500 ppm — rinse with fresh water
Marigolds	Damaged at 2000 ppm
St. Augustine	Can survive as high as 4000–5000 ppm
Roses	Can survive as high as 4000–5000 ppm
Snapdragons	Can survive as high as 4000–5000 ppm
Stocks	Can survive as high as 4000–5000 ppm
Beets	Can survive as high as 4000–5000 ppm
Cole crops (cabbage, broccoli, etc.)	Can survive as high as 4000–5000 ppm
Cabbage palm	Can survive as high as 4000–5000 ppm
Wax myrtle	Can survive as high as 4000–5000 ppm

plants, and use berms, dunes, fences, or walls to block both wind and spray as much as possible. Fertilize with natural organic products, as they are lower in salts than most chemical fertilizers. Use containers and purchased potting soil for salt sensitive plants and guard them from spray and wind. Wind along the coast or inland during storms can cause damage that is much like salt damage. Sometimes they work their woe together.

Some Trial and Error is Part of Gardening

I find a good bit of "survival of the fittest" in my garden evolution. After a few seasons, this will prove true in most Florida landscapes.

Drought tolerant plants are any that you have thriving in your yard and haven't watered much or at all. Pentas are not native plants, but mine have bloomed 365 days a year in all parts of my yard that are watered occasionally to rarely. Luckily they multiply easily by air-layering, division, or cuttings. So I am spreading pentas around the outlying areas and enjoying their reliable color.

Actually, I had also spread various pentas around my inlying areas. So as I improve my Xeriscape plan, I will move them from the oasis zone to the drought tolerant zone and then have room to pamper something else.

Plants that thrive and grow and produce fruit or flowers no matter what the weather may not start out as our first choices. But they win that place by good behavior. Aim to make such plants the backbone of your landscape. I am aiming for 60% natural zone plants because I enjoy and need (for my writing) to experiment and try new plant challenges. Luckily a privacy fence around the entire and fairly large back yard allows me to do this without visits from neighborhood committees of protest.

If your landscape also has some high risk areas and plants, plan to keep them in low visibility until you find the keys to their success.

Planning Cuts Way Down on Disappointments

The charts and lists in Appendix A and following this chapter will help you evaluate your plants either before you plant them or as you move and regroup them according to water needs. The charts are from the materials developed by the Water Management Districts of South Florida, Southwest Florida, Northwest Florida and St. Johns River and are reproduced with their kind permission.

Other helpful books are listed in the sidebar on page 44 and in the bibliography.

Herbaceous Plants: Flowers, Herbs

The charts in Appendix A give full and useful information about woody plants for Florida and even some herbaceous ground covers. In other words, they cover all permanent plants well. But annuals in Florida are a more complex and often a more colorful subject. Actually, many annuals can thrive on far less water than is needed for turf.

Pentas, easily propagated by cuttings, are fairly drought tolerant and have colorful pink, white, or red flowers which attract butterflies. They bloom year round and prefer full sun. Some varieties grow to four feet; others reach no more than a foot in height.

You will find annuals offer a wide variety of flower and foliage color, texture, and adaptability to every season and soil condition.

Some will thrive right through the summer heat, humidity and heavy rains: like verbena, periwinkle, torenia or Florida pansy, gomphrena, portulaca, marigolds, zinnias, melampodium, and chrysanthemums.

Others do well if planted in fall. Some will bloom within weeks. Others like Ammi or Bishop's flower will grow slowly and vegetatively through the first part of winter, and then burst in full and abundant bloom with the first hint of spring. But many of these die out from the heat by the end of May or June.

Cool season annuals are pansies, violas, alyssum, larkspur, rudbeckia, poppies, stocks, snapdragon, calendula, dianthus, feverfew, sweet peas, nasturtiums, poppies, coreopsis, and cornflowers. Annuals that need little water — like celosia, cosmos, gaillardia, marigolds, nicotiana, petunias, portulaca or purslane, and verbena — can be grown starting in September until they die out from the heat in April to June.

A few annuals can be grown any time of the year, like the salvias, jewels of Opar, sunflowers, marigolds, globe amaranth, and true amaranths.

All of the plants listed in the following charts grow in some areas of Florida. Chances are that if you have never seen a particular plant in your area of the state, then it's not hardy there. If you've seen only a few, it may be borderline. Even natural zone annuals will do better with an occasional watering in April and May.

ANNUALS

Natural Zone

BOTANICAL NAME	COMMON NAME	AREA*	HEIGHT
Catharanthus roseus	Periwinkle	NCS	1 – 3 ft.
Cleome hassierana	Spider Flower	NCS	4 – 5 ft.
Coreopsis tinctoria	Golden Coreopsis	NCS	2 – 3 ft.
Eschscholzia californica	California Poppy	NC	8 – 18 in.
Gaillardia pulchella	Blanket Flower	NC	1 – 2 ft.
Geranium carolinianum	Carolina Cranesbill	S	2 ft.
Geranium sanguineum	Blood-red Cranesbill	NCS	1 ft.
Gomphrena globosa	Globe Amaranth	NCS	8 – 20 in.
Helianthus annus	Sunflower	NCS	4 – 8 ft.
Helichrysum bracteatum	Strawflower	NCS	1 ft.
Heterotheca subaxillaris	Camphorweed	S	3 ft.
Kalanchoe spp.	Kalanchoe	NC	1 – 2 ft.
Lepidium virginicum	Peppergrass	S	2 ft.
Linaria canadensis	Toadflax	NCS	42 in.
Matriacaria maritima	Scentless Chamomile	NCS	6 in.
Monarda punctata	Horsemint	NC	3 ft.
Pentas spp.	Pentas	N	2 – 5 ft.
Petunia hybrids	Petunia	NCS	1 ft.
Portulaca oleracea	Common purslane	NCS	3 – 5 in.
Rudbeckia hirta 'bien'	Black-eyed Susan	NCS	1 – 3 ft.
Salvia coccinea	Tropical sage	NCS	30 in.
Tithonia rotundifolia	Mexican sunflower	NCS	2 – 5 ft.
Triodanis perfoliata	Venus' Looking-glass	S	3 ft.

Drought Tolerant Zone

BOTANICAL NAME	COMMON NAME	AREA*	HEIGHT
Alyssum lobularia	Alyssum	NC	3 – 6 in.
Amaranthus caudatus	Tassel flower	NC	2 – 4 ft.
Ammi majus	Bishop's Flower	NC	3 – 6 ft.

* N=North, C=Central, S=South

ANNUALS

Drought Tolerant Zone *(continued)*

BOTANICAL NAME	COMMON NAME	AREA*	HEIGHT
Begonia spp.	Begonia	NCS	1 ft.
Calendula officinalis	Pot marigold	NC	1 ft.
Celosia cristata	Cockscomb	NCS	1 – 3 ft.
Centaurea cyanum	Bachelor button	NC	1 – 3 ft.
Coleus hybrids	Coleus	NC	1 – 3 ft.
Cosmos spp.	Garden cosmos	NCS	3 – 4 ft.
Dianthus armeria	Pinks	NCS	6 in.
Dyssodia tenuiloba	Dahlberg Daisy	NC	6 – 12 in.
Gypsophila elegans	Annual babysbreath	NC	10 – 18 in.
Iberis spp.	Candytuft	NC	9 – 18 in.
Limonium latifolium	Statice, Sea Lavender	NCS	1 – 2 ft.
Melampodium paludosum	Melampodium	NCS	2 – 3 ft.
Papaver spp.	Shirley and Iceland Poppies	NC	1 – 3 ft.
Perilla frutescens	Beefsteak plant	NC	1 – 3 ft.
Torenia fourniera	Florida pansy	NCS	1 ft.
Tropaeolum majus	Nasturtium	NCS	1 ft.
Verbena hybrids	Verbena	NCS	1 ft.
Viola spp.	Pansies	NCS	6 – 12 in.

Oasis Zone

BOTANICAL NAME	COMMON NAME	AREA*	HEIGHT
Ageratum houstonianum	Flow Flower	NCS	1 – 2 ft.
Antirrhinum majus	Snapdragon	NCS	6 – 36 in.
Capsicum annuum	Ornamental Pepper	NCS	1 ft.
Eustoma grandiflora	Prairie Gentian	NC	1 – 2 ft.
Impatiens walleriana	Busy Lizzy	NC	1 – 3 ft.
Lathyrus odoratus	Sweet Pea	NCS	1 – 5 ft.
Matthiola incana	Stock	NC	1 – 2 ft.
Molucella laevis	Bells of Ireland	NC	1 – 2 ft.
Nicandra physaloides	Shoofly Plant	NC	2 – 4 ft.
Nicotiana alata	Flowering tobacco	NC	1 – 2 ft.
Tagetes spp.	Marigold	NCS	6 – 36 in.
Zinnia elegans	Zinnia	NCS	1 – 3 ft.

PERENNIALS

Natural Zone

BOTANICAL NAME	COMMON NAME	AREA*	HEIGHT
Aletris lutea	Yellow colic root	C	2 – 3 ft.
Achillea filipendulina	Fernleaf Yarrow	NCS	3 ft.
Anemone canadensis	Meadow anemone	S	s ft.
Aralia nudicaulis	Wild sarsaparilla	S	1 ft.
Arenaria lateriflora	Sandwort	S	8 in.
Artemisia stellerana	Dusty Miller	NCS	1 – 3 ft.
Asclepias tuberosa	Butterfly Weed	NC	1 – 3 ft.
Aster linearifolius	Linear-leaved Aster	S	12 – 18 in.
Baptisia lanceolata	Pineland Baptisia	NCS	3 ft.
Catharanthus roseus	Periwinkle	NCS	1 – 2 ft.
Centratherum intermedium	Manaos Beauty	NCS	1 – 2 ft.
Chrysanthemum parthenium	Feverfew	NCS	1 – 2 ft.
Digitalis purpurea	Foxglove	NC	2 – 5 ft.
Echinacea purpurea	Purple Coneflower	NCS	2 – 4 ft.
Euthamia tenuifolia	Flat-topped Goldenrod	S	1 – 3 ft.
Gillea spp.	Standing Cypress	NCS	3 – 6 ft.
Gazania rigens	Treasure Flower	NCS	8 – 10 in.
Hedyotis caerulea	Blues	S	7 in.
Hypericum perforatum	St. Peter's Wort	S	2 ft.
Hyssop officinalis	Hyssop	NCS	2 – 3 ft.
Kalanchoe spp.	Kalanchoe	CS	1 – 3 ft.
Liatris punctata	Gayfeather	NCS	2 – 3 ft.
Lilium philadelphicum	Wood Lily	S	2 – 3 ft.
Oenothera spp.	Primrose, Sundrops	NCS	1 – 2 ft.
Pentas spp.	Pentas	CS	2 – 5 ft.
Solidago speciosa	Noble Goldenrod	NCS	3 – 6 ft.
Verbena spp.	Clump or moss verbena	NC	6 in.

Drought Tolerant Zone

BOTANICAL NAME	COMMON NAME	AREA*	HEIGHT
Hibiscus abelmoschus	Musk-Mallow	NC	1 – 3 ft.
Anthemis tinctoria	Golden Marguerite	NCS	2 – 3 ft.
Aster dumosus	Aster	NCS	2 ft.
Beloperone guttata	Shrimp Plant	NCS	1 – 4 ft.
Coleus hybrids	Coleus	CS	1 – 3 ft.
Delphinium hybrids	Delphinium	NC	1 – 3 ft.
Dianthus plumarium	Pinks	NCS	9 – 18 in.

* N=NORTH, C=CENTRAL, S=SOUTH

PERENNIALS

Drought Tolerant Zone (continued)

BOTANICAL NAME	COMMON NAME	AREA*	HEIGHT
Dietes vegeta	African Iris	NCS	1 – 2 ft.
Dischorisandra thrysiflora	Blue Ginger	CS	2 – 5 ft.
Hemerocallis spp.	Daylilies	NCS	2 – 4 ft.
Lavendula	Lavender	NCS	1 – 3 ft.
Malva alcea	Hollyhock Mallow	NC	2 – 4 ft.
Pelargonium spp.	Common geranium	NCS	1 – 3 ft.
Tradescantia ohiensis	Spiderwort	NC	1 ft.

Oasis Zone

Coreopsis gladiata	Tickseed	CS	3 ft.
Chrysanthemum spp.	Mums	NCS	1 – 2 ft.
Chrysanthemum x *superbum*	Shasta Daisy	NC	1 – 2 ft.
Gerbera jamesonii	Transvaal Daisy	NCS	1 ft.
Lobelia cardinalia	Cardinal Flower	CS	3 – 6 ft.

VINES

Drought Tolerant Zone

Ipomoea tricolor	Morning glory	NC	10 ft.
Tecomaria capensis	Cape Honeysuckle	CS	6 – 20 ft.

HERBS

Drought Tolerant Zone

Aloe vera	Chives	Garlic	Shallots
Anise	Coriander	Hyssop	Tansy
Borage	Cumin	Lavender	Tarragon
Caraway	Dill	Parsley	Thyme (all)
Chamomile	Fennel	Rosemary	Winter Savory
Chicory	Feverfew	Sage (all)	Wormwood

Oasis Zone

Basil	French Sorrel	Mints	Summer Savory
Chervil	Leeks	Sweet Bay	Watercress
Comfrey	Lovage	Sweet Marjoram	Winter Cress

∽ For Further Reading ∽

Requiem for a Lawnmower, **by Sally Wasowski.**
This series of excellent essays reads almost like a novel and will explain much of the native plant movement and how you can best use native plants for an easy-care, low-water-use landscape. The title comes from one section that tells how the author quit watering, raking, and eventually mowing, and wound up with a much more interesting and beautiful yard.

The Water-Thrifty Garden, **by Stan DeFreitas.**
This covers all areas of the country, especially the south and west. Cross reference lists cover Florida specifically.

Taylor's Guide to Water-Saving Gardening **(edited).**
This is also written for the country in general so you have to overlook many plants that don't grow in Florida — that can be difficult if you're not sure which those are. (The lists in this chapter and the appendix can help you.) But Taylor's does cover flowers and has excellent color plates so you can easily put the right names with the right information.

Water Conserving Gardens and Landscapes, **by John M. O'Keefe.**
No color pictures here but good descriptions of trees, shrubs, vines, perennials, grasses and vegetables. Again, many plants listed will not grow in Florida, but each has area indicated.

Waterwise Gardening, **by the editors of Sunset Books and Sunset Magazine.**
This has much good information, but a West Coast slant.

Xeriscape Gardening: Water Conservation for the American Landscape, **by Connie Ellefson, Tom Stephens, Doug Welsh.**
This large, well-illustrated book has a wealth of excellent information, most of it for the entire country in general. There are, however, some excellent sections on plants for Florida.

Chapter Five
How Does Your Yard Measure Up?

If you've read this far — even skipped and skimmed this far — you have already made some giant steps toward a water-wise landscape. At the risk of repeating, it all begins in attitude and progresses from there. And most of the process is fairly painless. You'd be doing your yard work or paying someone else to do it in any case. With Xeriscaping, you will do less or pay less and enjoy more.

Few people manage to turn their yard into a Xeriscape overnight. But making yours measure up can be a fascinating project.

The first step is learning as much as you can about Xeriscaping. The basic principles are simple common sense, but I am finding the details more and more exciting the more I learn. I've studied and condensed the information in many books to write this one, also adapted it to our special Florida conditions, so I will be so bold as to say this is all you need to proceed. You can skim other information just to check for newly developing ideas, but mostly it is now a time for action.

If you don't have your landscape plan drawn to scale, read Chapter 3 again and make yourself a goal: "By (DATE) I will get down on paper what I have already."

That is to give you the broad picture.

Listing Your Plants

This is not only easy but fun. Go out with a notebook or sit in the window (or sit in an airport and remember). Write down the name of each plant in each bed. You can use common or botanical names. The latter will help you identify more precisely, but it is not necessary.

If you have a computer, you can list your plants on a simple word processor program or database program. Using a computer makes it quicker and easier to update your list, and makes it more permanent, but it is not really necessary either.

I love these jobs that are better done badly than not at all. That adds much to the sense of accomplishment.

Check in the charts and write down, for sure, that the asparagus fern is very drought tolerant, the beauty berry will grow in the natural zone, the dracaena also natural, etc. Also make notes, if you wish, of colors, time of bloom, height, and whatever other details you may want to keep handy.

My own front garden includes Italian cypress, melampodium, portulaca, chrysanthemums, abelmoschus, crape myrtle and pittosporum.

45

This listing will take some time. Treat it like a crossword puzzle and make it fun. Most of it will come easily from the charts. Some of your plants may prove difficult or impossible to find. In that case, use your own experience and judge accordingly. I have yet to find pentas listed, but they've grown for me with both occasional and hardly any watering and both have done equally as well, so I rate them natural.

Just Having The List Will Help

This listing will help you in two ways. First, you will see how you need to regroup for a really efficient Xeriscape. No one expects you to go out and do this all at once. But over the next several seasons, you will naturally work that way.

∞ **Sample Personal Plant List** ∞

My Own Yard When We First Moved In:

Laurel oak, *Quercus laurifolia*, natural
    4 small and 1 large

Pittosporum, *P. tobira*, drought tolerant
    Planted around foundation.
    Needs pruning too often to keep under windows

Pampas grass, *Cortadenia selloana*, natural
    Planted under eaves, gets roof runoff

Dwarf holly, *Ilex crenata compacta*, drought tolerant
    or *Ilex vomitoria "Schillings,"* natural

Plumbago, *P. auriculata*, drought tolerant

St. Augustine grass, *Stenotaphrum secundatum*, drought tolerant

Bahia grass, *Paspalum notatum*, natural

The place didn't look too bare, but it had little interest and needed plenty of care with all that grass and pruning.

My Own Front Border as Planted at the Moment:

All of the above except Pampas grass, which overdosed on water

Lantana, *Lantana camara*, natural

Blue Daze, *Evolvulus glomeratus*, drought tolerant

Carolina Yellow Jessamine, *Gelsemium sempervirens*, natural

Pentas, *Pentas lanceolata*, white, natural

Blue Sage, *Salvia farinacea*, drought tolerant

Aloe, *Aloe barbadensis*, very drought tolerant, but grows much larger with occasional watering than with none.

Shrimp plant, *Justicia brandegeana*, drought tolerant

Abelmoschus, *Hibiscus abelmoschus*, drought tolerant

The list may help you decide now where you eventually want to have oasis zones, drought tolerant zones, and natural zones. For most people the first will be the most colorful and closest to the house for maximum enjoyment and minimum maintenance, and the rest will progress accordingly. But yours may vary.

For instance, the bed by my front door, though it is front and center in the spotlight and a high priority in my efforts, is not an oasis zone. I just don't remember to water it often. My oasis zone is near the rabbit cages, where I have to turn on the hose every day or so for them.

I keep putting plants in the front bed for high color that lasts as long as possible with little trouble. Doing this has forced me to water it more often for new plants. So now it is at least in the second zone. Just knowing that will guide me in placing new plants or new divisions of old plants.

If you are planning to move up from hose watering to any kind of irrigation system, this will also influence the placement of zones. So don't make any permanent decisions until you read Chapter 10. But once you get your overall plan on paper, either get copies so you can mark them up as you go, or else put layers of tracing paper over the original to try various arrangements.

You'll Automatically Water More Wisely

Also, knowing the needs of each plant will guide me when I am watering with the hose. I'll just stand longer by the oasis plants, water the drought resistant ones perhaps every second watering, and pass over the natural ones unless they are new or pining. When I carry the bucket from the shower (see Chapter 14), I'll empty it on either new plants or oasis ones.

Turf Decisions

How much time, water, fertilizer, and money are you spending for the upkeep of your grass? Chances are good that you can cut all of these down drastically.

Any book or article you see on Xeriscaping will emphasize that the best move you can make is to cut down your turf area. Most of us want some lawn. You probably already have in mind which section is most important: a part of the front yard, or the section where your children play. I am planning to save one of each, but even those I can reduce greatly with areas of mulch and groundcovers.

Few of us will go to the extreme that Samm Philmore did to change St. Augustine grass to bahia (see Chapter 12). But it is good to know that you not only can, but such a move may be a definite improvement, a gift to the planet. I changed my attitude completely about the bahia grass in our backyard. It moved up from second best to first choice in my mind and therefore I enjoy it much more. I don't feel guilty that it is easier to cut and needs mowing less often. I feel downright virtuous for being smart enough to appreciate that.

There may be sections of your yard that you can quit watering and worrying about. Let the turf live or die as it will and if it chooses the latter, you can replace it with something better.

Start Some Groundcovers

Look over the lists of groundcovers in the charts, the ones that are growing in your neighbors' yards or in public gardens you visit. Then, on your next trip to the nursery, buy one or two pots of whichever ones you like, as a test. Plant them in your first enriched soil, right among your flowers or vegetables if they like sun, or in shade if that is their preference. Let them start spreading.

By the time you have your landscape plan settled and your lawn area ready to convert, you will know which of your chosen ground covers will grow best and spread fastest for you and will also have a good start on your planting stock.

Divide or take cuttings of the original plants and plant a small area at a time for the least expense. I did this with ajuga, striped liriope, blue daze, society garlic, and beach sunflower.

They have since grown into fine patches. Some still need transplanting from the flower beds to better places, but I have plenty of plants now with which to work.

Also watch for a neighborly gardener thinning an overcrowded groundcover planting, and ask for starter plants that would otherwise be thrown away. Or don't bother to wait until you catch him thinning. Ask. If he has a good stand, he'll usually be glad to share some cuttings at least or some starts at best.

It is also extra fun to have patches of plants that bring back memories of special people or trips. When I went to visit my

Curving beds of groundcovers can soften the sharp angles of a house. Once established, this juniper and the other plants use less water than a lawn.

friend and coauthor Betty Mackey in Pennsylvania, I came home with a bag of cuttings and starts. She had at least a third of her fairly hilly yard in handsome groundcovers. I found that the goutweed will only live in Florida for the winter months and then die out in summer. Sweet woodruff did much the same, but I may find a way to save that eventually, since I really want it. But English ivy, vinca minor, and even pachysandra are living happily in the shade of an oak in my occasional watering area, and the ivy and vinca are spreading slowly.

Another source of groundcovers and native plants are volunteers that show up in your yard. Some of these come from seeds dropped by birds, others are blown in by the wind. I left in Iowa an asparagus fern that I treasured since it was one of the few survivors in a planter given me by my daughter Brigid. In Florida, the birds gave me more. In fact it threatens to take over a bed that I had almost covered with ajuga. Most volunteers can be invasive. Check in the charts and decide when you first see them if you want to welcome them, banish them, or keep them in controlled areas.

What I'm Already Doing Right:

- 🐛 *Recycling grass clippings as mulch.*
- 🐛 *Using other mulches.*
- 🐛 *Selecting plants that will need little pruning.*
- 🐛 *Letting grass grow taller, about three inches.*
- 🐛 *Improving the soil with garbage from the kitchen.*
- 🐛 *Pruning and weeding as needed.*
- 🐛 *Keeping irrigation system in repair.*
- 🐛 *Directing water onto grass rather than the street.*
- 🐛 *Using pesticides and poisons sparingly.*

Give Yourself Credit

Whatever you do, don't let Xeriscaping be a guilt trip. It can come to that. One of my writing friends says, "I know so much about the need to save water that I feel guilty every time I flush a toilet."

Most serious gardeners have always tended to use water with some measure of wisdom simply because they know its value. Non-gardening homeowners can quickly adopt this knowledge and attitude. Chances are your water bills will go down just as a result of your reading this book and beginning to practice the simplest of its suggestions.

Chances are, also, that you are already doing many things right. Check back in the book and list these. Your list might look like the sidebar at left.

As you read further, your list will grow in length and intensity. Read each chapter and absorb the information. Some of it you will put into practice at once and automatically. The rest may take you some time.

I've been at this for years and still have a long way to go, but I'm enjoying the trip. My yard is looking better. I now have flowers for bouquets, and fruit and vegetables to pick and eat almost every day of the year. Of course, I want the yard to look great instead of just passable (and sometimes it stretches to be just that). I want cascades of color and enough fruit to ship north to my children. But I am confident that will come in time. In the meantime, I feel better about what I am doing. And I'm saving the water bills so I can keep tabs on our progress. Like the scale, those bills naturally go up and down with the seasons and reasons. It is important to take all that in stride and not get unduly upset.

It may be years before you get the soil improvement you want or the irrigation system. What we do may seem like little enough. But if many people make small improvements, the resulting water savings will be astounding. As all of us, together, make more small improvements and a few big ones, we can make a definite difference. It may seem that we take two steps forward and one backward, but as long as we are making some progress in the right direction, we can feel proud.

Learn As You Go

If all else fails, read the instructions. In this case your list is part one and this book is part two. Too often it is only after a plant succeeds or fails that I ask myself Why? Often the answer is because it is in the wrong watering zone.

With trial and error, success takes years to develop and wastes much water and effort in the process. If your plants, like mine, are often trying to tell you something, by all means take note. But both before and during this learning experience, take charge.

Your plants are much like teenagers. There are many things they aren't telling you. You'll have to find out about their light, temperature, soil, water, and nutritional preferences by reading, talking to other gardeners, and by making careful observations. Learning more about your plants' requirements will make you a better caretaker and you will be rewarded with a more beautiful and productive garden.

Granddaughter Amy with a bouquet from the garden.

Improve and Update

There is no perfect plan. The best landscape plan ever drawn still needs to be updated as the trees grow and change the sun/shade patterns, as families grow and needs change.

Planning, selecting, improving the soil, using mulches, watering wisely, saving free water, accumulating irrigation equipment and keeping it in order, and sensible maintenance will make a remarkable difference in your landscape and in your life. It may not improve your marriage or increase your salary. But it may be an important part of what you do with the bit of earth God has put into your care. And it may be one of the most important gifts you give your children and your grandchildren.

Chapter Six
Soil Improvement: Getting Down to Earth

Living with any soil is much like living with a spouse. You have to study its ways and learn to work with it. But you will never understand it completely. It will sometimes disappoint you, but at such times it leaves you with a niggling notion it may have been your own fault. When soil does its job well, and that is amazingly often, you are never sure why or how to repeat the success. After a time you learn to depend upon the mysteries and powers hidden therein.

I've lived with three different kinds of soil. We had hard clay in Ohio and had to use a pick to loosen it enough to dig a tree-planting hole. I dreamt of moving to a place with rich, wonderful soil that would magically solve all my garden problems.

Then we did exactly that, quite by chance. My husband's job moved us to Iowa where the soil was superb. But it still didn't magically solve all my problems. I didn't have to use the pick anymore. But the soil was too rich to grow nasturtiums and some other things I loved. It was hardly ever necessary to fertilize except to offset the nitrogen that got the upper hand from all the manure from our livestock. I suddenly realized that I'd done just fine in that hard Ohio clay.

When we moved to Florida, I was warned by Tampa nurseryman Robert Perry that the sandy soil does nothing more than hold up the plant. The grower must do everything else. I couldn't believe that until I started digging. Our yard was like a sandbox. Most of what I first planted died. I got the message. But I couldn't wait until I had improved all that sand to start growing.

Solutions for Soil Problems

There are plants for every soil and climate and solutions for every soil problem. Since soil is such a basic and important part of growing everything, a little basic understanding is in order. Luckily, just as we don't have to know all about nutrition to eat or about the combustion engine to drive a car, we don't have to understand all about soil to use it wisely. But there are three very important things to remember about any soil:

1. You can't change its basic nature in any area larger than a planter.

2. It is a duty of every property owner or user to be a steward rather than a miner — to use what we find and leave it better rather than take all it will give and leave it spent. I feel I can truly tell my Maker on judgment day that I left a lot of good soil behind me.

3. Whatever kind of soil you have, humus will make it better.

Soil Structure

The more sand (larger particles) in the soil, the more quickly it dries out, and the more quickly nutrients leach or wash through. Both clay particles and humus slow leaching, but sand has balancing advantages: it takes less water to irrigate sandy soils and you can work in and plant in them sooner after a rain. There is no mud in a sandbox. Don't work in clay soils (made up of smaller particles) after a rain until a ball of soil, squeezed tightly, is dry enough to break apart easily if you drop it.

How To Grow While Improving the Soil

Now that I am older and wiser, especially about Florida gardening, I tell people to keep much of their planting in containers the first year — not all, but much. Container growing outdoors in Florida is not at all like growing house plants indoors other places. You still are working with Nature, using her humidity and rainfall and beneficial insects.

It's best to grow plants which develop extensive root systems, like this Ficus tree, in containers in order to keep them from interfering with sewer lines, swimming pool plumbing, or other underground utilities. Use a sturdy pot and check periodically that no roots have made their way through the drain hole and anchored themselves in the ground.

Container vs. Ground Planting

Fruit grower Armando Mendez of Tampa has planted two similar fruiting trees, one in a container and the other in the ground, and had the one in the container bloom and bear first. Another grower, Charles Novak of Plant City, admits that in the long run, and all other things being equal, he finds that plants grow better in the ground than in containers. But frost protection may well keep you growing some plants in containers long after you've improved your soil enough to put most hardy plants in the ground.

I find that soil, even Florida sand, covers a multitude of my sins. Pots fall over or root through the bottom into the soil anyway. The limited amount of soil in pots is less forgiving if I forget to water or feed it often enough. But still I grow tender plants in containers so I can bring them in or turn them over when frost comes. I grow many seedlings in containers until they are past the intensive care stage, and I grow some others in pots to rotate them to the house or spotlight of the garden when they are looking their best.

You can fill your containers with good soil mixes of peat moss, compost, well-aged manures or harmless ones like rabbit, potting soil, vermiculite, and/or perlite. To this you can add sand where it won't make the containers too heavy to move.

For small pots that will be in hot sun, you may want to mix in a water retainer. See Chapter 13 for details. These can cut watering in half.

Start with Some In-Ground Planting

As I said in Chapter 3 on landscaping, plant needed shade trees as soon as possible. Trees grow fast in Florida and they can get a good start while you improve the soil around them. Most of their roots will go deep enough to find whatever they need. Mulch them well (see next chapter).

Then plant annual flowers and vegetables in small beds and improve the soil as you go.

For a general purpose potting mix, use:
1 part potting soil
1 part humus (peat, compost, manure), and
1 part sand

How To Start Improving the Soil

Whatever type of soil you have, there are two ways to improve it, and both involve adding all the organic matter you can get: cover crops and bringing in humus. You can use both methods at once on different sections of your yard.

Cover Crops

Are you planning future beds of flowers or vegetables? Do you want to eliminate the lawn area for other plantings, but need not do the actual planting for six weeks or more? Then plant a cover crop there and grow large amounts of "green manure" on the spot. This can be done at any season in Florida, though the choice of crops may vary. Even if you aren't sure where the beds will go, you can't go wrong planting cover crops. If you decide later to put turf back there, it will grow better with less water in the improved soil.

We live about 10 miles from Plant City, which is the strawberry growing capital of the country. We go there to see the Reds in spring training and pass fields of strawberries being picked. Later in the spring, we go to those same fields for the best pick-your-own I've ever enjoyed: 4 quarts for $1 and large berries easy to pick from elevated rows.

Over the summer we see those same fields planted in cover crops, sown, and then cut and tilled into the soil. This is not wasted effort. When you till or spade this "green manure" crop into the soil, you add more pounds or tons of organic matter than you'd ever care to haul from the nearest horse stable.

✺ Florida Soils Vary from Place to Place ✺

Gray and black flatwoods soils are found in much of central Florida, the eastern coastal counties, and some of the northeastern counties.

Gray and black flatwoods soils over lime materials are found in parts of many of the eastern and southern counties.

Muck and peat soil predominate in inland pockets of southeastern Florida and in a few other narrow bands in eastern counties just south of central.

Red and yellow clay soils, overlapping from Georgia, are common in northwestern inland counties.

Red and yellow sands of the central ridge are in several broad areas of the western counties north of Gainesville.

Red and yellow sands of the central hammocks are in narrower slivers of the same area.

Swamps, scrub, or dry sand are in the western lower tip and in a few other pockets throughout the state.

I was appalled when I learned that some parts of South Florida have a soil that is so rock hard that an auger must be used to dig holes for planting trees or shrubs. Such is the soil in the Homestead area, and during Hurricane Andrew many of the trees popped loose like corks out of bottles.

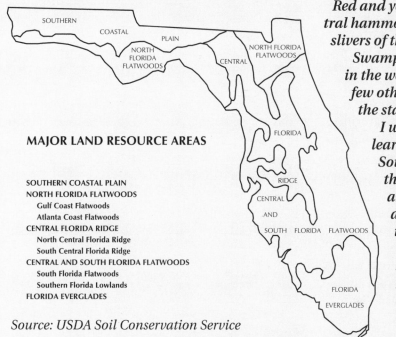

MAJOR LAND RESOURCE AREAS

SOUTHERN COASTAL PLAIN
NORTH FLORIDA FLATWOODS
   Gulf Coast Flatwoods
   Atlanta Coast Flatwoods
CENTRAL FLORIDA RIDGE
   North Central Florida Ridge
   South Central Florida Ridge
CENTRAL AND SOUTH FLORIDA FLATWOODS
   South Florida Flatwoods
   Southern Florida Lowlands
FLORIDA EVERGLADES

Source: USDA Soil Conservation Service

You can plant cover crops in any spots that are empty in your garden and destined to remain empty for a few weeks — in any season. Summer is the best time, because cover crops grow quickly and vegetables and many flowers do not grow at all, so their spaces would otherwise be empty. But get some cover crop seed (from local suppliers or Mellinger's catalog), keep it in the freezer, and get in the habit of planting cover crops in any garden spots that would otherwise be empty for a few weeks or more.

Cover Crops Around Trees

You can also plant around young trees. Keep the soil directly around the trunk, especially of citrus trees, bare. Just beyond that you would not want to turn under the crop and disturb the roots, but can cut the crop and rake the topgrowth out beyond the dripline of the outer branches where you can safely till. This tillable area will shrink as the trees grow. You can then cultivate under citrus and mulch under other trees with the green material you have growing just beyond their branches.

This growing of an additional crop keeps weeds from taking over. It means that you don't have to mow unsightly grasses that would otherwise sprout or mow close enough to young tree trunks to injure them. Cover crops add mostly humus, but also some nutrients to the soil. Legumes like peas and beans add nitrogen especially.

Cover Crop Culture

Cover crops need the same nutrients, water, and care that any other planting needs. So your first ones on unimproved soil will not grow as lush as they will later. They will grow better if you till the soil well, feed, weed, and water as needed.

If you don't have a tiller you may spade the area by hand, kill off the turf with Round Up™ or a similar herbicide, or use the "Mulching Instead of Tilling" method described in Chapter 7. With Round Up™ and with small seeds in mulch, there will be some delay in planting the crop. There are some cover crops, like rye grass, that can be sown directly over other grass in the fall. A good raking before planting will help seeds make contact with the soil and germinate better. Then the cover crop and the grass can grow together until you are ready to turn them under. The taller the crop and the grass grow, the more green manure you'll have to turn under.

Again, if you don't have a tiller, you can mow off the cover crop a few weeks before you want to plant something else. Leave the green leaves as mulch. Put newspapers over the top and proceed as described in Chapter 7 under "Mulching Instead of Tilling."

Once you plow down a green manure crop, you should wait two to three weeks before replanting. In that time the soil microbes can turn the green material into humus that will make your soil easier to work and allow it to catch and retain much more water for longer periods of time. This will enable the soil to use more nutrients longer also, for the fertilizers will not leach through so quickly. Richer microbial life will also make more nutrients available.

❧ Cover Crops for Florida ❧

Summer:

beggarweed	legume	*Desmodium tortuosum*	
cowpeas	legume	*Vigna sinensis*	
crotalaria	legume	*Crotalaria mucronata*	
hairy indigo	legume	*Indigofera* spp.	
peanuts	legume	*Arachis hypogaea*	
sorghum	grass	*Sorghum vulgare*	
sudan grass	grass	*S. vulgare* var. *sudanense*	Very productive.
soybeans	legume	*Glycine max*	
velvet beans	legume	*Stizolobium deeriangum*	

Fall through winter and spring:

beans	legume		Sensitive to frost.
oats	grass	*Avena sativa*	
amaranth	amaranth	*Amaranth* spp.	
buckwheat	buckwheat	*Fagopyrum* spp.	Sensitive to frost.
hairy vetch	legume	*Vicia villosa*	One of the best cover crops. Inoculate (see page 59).
millet	grass	*Panicum* spp.	Does well on poor, dry soils.
peanuts	legume	*Arachis hypogaea*	
rye	grass	*Lolium* spp.	Dies out in warm weather.
soybeans	legume	*Glycine max*	May be killed by frost.
weeds		Can be a cover crop, but if they go to seed, they could come back to haunt you.	

Dual Purpose Cover Crops

For twice the benefit, plant cowpeas or any kind of beans, including edible varieties of soybeans. Fertilize as you would for any vegetable crop, at planting time and about every three weeks through the growing time. Then harvest whatever you can use and plow the rest into the soil. These legumes take nitrogen from the air and settle it in the soil by means of nodules on their roots. So if you plant a late bean crop and frost comes before you can harvest, you still have grown a valuable cover crop.

The first time I planted a cover crop, in that horrible, beloved Ohio soil, I felt better than I did the first time I planted a tree. A cover crop seems less selfish, although the benefit still reverts to the planter. It just doesn't show, like a silent virtue.

In Ohio, I once planted plain old oats from my father's granary on March 1, when we planted our early garden. By May 15, when we planted our late garden, I had 12 to 14 inches of growth to turn under. In Florida, where crops grow faster, I would have had more.

Humus You Can Buy

There are several forms of humus you can buy. Canadian peat moss is one of the best because it takes a long time to break down and disappear from your soil. This can hold up to 20 times its own weight in water. Michigan peat is further broken down but still very good for your soil. Peat usually comes by the bale, but it is not as heavy as it looks.

Treated cow manure is available by the bag. There are soil conditioners like Erth-Rite that contain minerals and beneficial bacteria in addition to humus. Most potting soil and seed-starting soil mixes are rich in humus. You may be able to buy topsoil that's richer in humus than what you have, but be wary of judging soil by its color alone. The blackest of soil may be no better than what you have, and may not even be as good.

There are other soil conditioners that are natural but are not actually humus. Gypsum, vermiculite, and perlite are longer lasting than humus because they do not break down so quickly. They hold water and air in the soil and improve its structure. However, most Florida soils need more help than most people will want to buy.

Bringing in Free Humus

Besides what you grow yourself, or buy, there are great quantities of humus going to waste in your own neighborhood. They are filling up our dumpsites and will continue to do so, to a lesser degree, in spite of new laws and increased charges for hauling. Some people are neater than they need to be.

It can be a bit embarrassing to gather the goodness so wasted at first. But you can be sure that:
1) anything left out for trash collection is legal plunder, and
2) the trashmen will bless you for every bag you take.

I have an understanding with my neighbors, and provide an empty lawn cart whenever they mow their lawn. This saves them the trouble and cost of bagging and makes distribution easier for me. They can't believe that I always want their grass clippings, but they are kind and go along with "this crazy lady." I felt duty bound to tell them how much the clippings would help their own yard, but they preferred to buy wood chips instead.

I also have developed a method for collecting more. I wait until workers and school children leave on trash day and then set out. Within three blocks I can gather 30 bags of leaves or grass clippings, or, best of all, mixtures of both, depending on the season. Some places put out bags of pure pine needles, a great looking mulch.

One man sat with me beside his beautiful garden and said, "If all the organic matter I put on this garden had stayed, it would be higher than a house by now." It doesn't stay. You have to keep gathering, buying, or growing it all the time.

What do you do with it when you get it home? The easiest thing is to spread it as mulch. More about this in the next chapter. Empty the cart as soon as possible or grass will start to decompose, especially with rain, and get much heavier and harder to spread. This is also hard on the cart, but I admit to delaying much too often. (See sidebar on page 65 on garden carts vs. wheelbarrows.)

Composting

You can also use the gathered material for compost. I was recently with a group of market gardeners who were discussing the problem of visiting the horse stable first to bring home the bedding, and then having to stop at the school or the post office on the way home. If someone in line is a bit odorous, there may be a very good, earth-enriching reason.

There are dozens of ways to make compost and you can't do it wrong, only more slowly. You can compost on the spot by letting organic mulch rot into the ground around your plants. It looks neater to cover a bucket of vegetable scraps from the kitchen with grass clippings or leaves.

In a compost bin or pile, mix layers of dry and green material and add manure, compost activator, or something with nitrogen like cottonseed meal or cheap dog food. You can also improve the quality and speed the process with such amendments as rock dust, wood ashes, milled oyster shell, bone meal, or dolomitic limestone. These add minerals to the soil and aid beneficial organisms. Lime may be needed in small amounts for this even where it is not needed to change pH.

The heat of the pile will destroy many harmful bacteria and weed seeds and will hasten decomposition. Water and air are necessary, so put your compost pile near your oasis zone and remember it when you are out with hose. Turning adds air and puts the material from the cooler sides into the hotter center, but this labor is not necessary for the pregnant, the infirm, the oldster, or the lazy (I gladly share my collected excuses). As an alternative, you can shovel finished compost from the bottom while you add new layers to the top. The finished product takes from a few weeks to a few months, depending on the season, the composition, and how much you turn, add amendments, and water the pile.

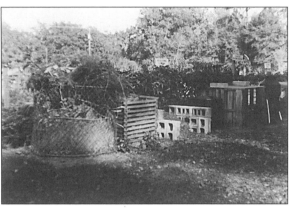

Compost bins constructed of various materials lined up at a Cooperative Extension Service exhibit.

Smaller pieces will also decompose more quickly. You can bring the lawnmower up and down over a pile of weeds or leaves and thus chop them. If you don't have a shredder, make a place behind a bush to pile branches and such.

If you want to build a compost bin or a series of bins to turn the material from one to another, one of the cheapest and easiest ways is to simply pile up cement blocks with some air spaces between. Leave an open front.

Understanding Soil pH

The soil pH is a measure of its alkalinity or acidity. A pH of 7.0 is neutral. Numbers below 7.0 indicate the degree of acidity, those above, alkalinity. Most flowers and vegetables grow best in a slightly acid to neutral range. Trees and shrubs vary in their needs. Dogwoods, camellias, azaleas, hollies, and gardenias prefer acid soil.

Although virgin Florida soils can range from pH 3.8 (very acid) to pH 8.0 (quite alkaline), most Florida soils have a slightly acid to nearly neutral pH. If the soil is high in limestone or seashells, close to a new house, man-made ground near the water, or in the Florida Keys, it may be quite alkaline.

Important Fact: *Large amounts of organic material will bring any soil closer to neutral, correcting soil pH no matter which way it is wrong in the first place.*

Soil tests and advice are available from each county's Cooperative Extension Service for about $2 per sample. So are instructions for gathering samples. You can also buy a home testing kit, follow instructions, and test soil yourself.

To tell the truth, I seldom test soil. Testing certainly makes for more exact feeding, higher yields, and fewer problems. It would definitely be a good idea to have your soil tested. But if your plants are growing well, the pH must be in a suitable range. If it is not, you will soon know by their decline.

Fortunately, most of the land-scape plants that grow in Florida aren't too particular about the pH of the soil they grow in. Those that do exhibit a preference usually like an acid soil; a low pH level helps plants absorb nutrients.

Acid-Loving Plants

Azalea	Gardenia
Begonia	Hibiscus
Bougainvillea	Irises
Camellia	Ixora
Coleus	Ligustrum
Coreopsis	Lilies
Crape Myrtle	Magnolia
Ferns	Oaks (some)

Plants for Alkaline Soils

Joewood (*Jacquinia keyensis*)
Pineland Allamanda
    (*Angademia berterii*)
Spider Lily
    (*Hymenocallis latifolia*)
Marsh Elder (*Iva frutescens*)
Seacoast Beach Elder
    (*Iva imbricata*)
Twin Flower
    (*Polianthes geminiflora*)
Florida Boxwood
    (*Schaefferia frutescens*)

If the leaves of the gardenia turn pale or yellow, this is a sign that the roots need more acidity. Often, watering with a product like Miracid™ will make a remarkable difference in just a few days. But such treatments will need to be continued indefinitely to maintain unnatural pH levels. It is far easier, and takes less water as well as energy, to grow what thrives in your soil.

Pine needles, oak leaves, and peat moss make an alkaline soil more acid, but it takes huge amounts to make much difference.

Some Ways to Correct pH

Chipped sulfur will make soil more acid much more easily. Bette Smith, who writes the garden page for the St. Petersburg Times, has a lovely yard on the edge of Treasure Island. She uses chipped sulfur in a whirly-bird thrower to keep the pH down to a work-able level. Two treatments a week apart can last for years, she says.

A temporary home remedy for overly alkaline soil is to add a tablespoon or two of vinegar to each gallon of water used for irrigation.

Ground limestone, dolomite, or lime in any form makes soil more alkaline.

You can estimate a soil's pH by noticing which plants grow well in it. If your neighborhood or yard features flourishing azaleas, blueberries, strawberries, or the other acid-lovers listed above, this indicates an acid soil. If these are conspicuous for their absence, alkaline soil may be the reason.

One very good plant to use for indicating soil pH is the common or "blue" hydrangea. Florist's hydrangeas sold as Easter plants are fine for this purpose. The flowers and bracts react to soil pH by changing colors. Oddly, the effect goes contrary to the coloration of litmus paper. Where the soil is acid enough for azaleas, the hydrangea flowers will be blue. Where soil is neutral to alkaline, blooms will be pink. The hydrangea is a very thirsty plant, however, and should only be planted in your oasis zone. It also needs heavy fertilizer and is often potbound when sold. So pull the roots apart before planting.

Maintaining Fertility

While organic matter will greatly improve the texture and water retention of a soil, will feed the microbes and earthworms and make the nutrients already there more easily avail-able, it does not add sufficient nutrients to do away with fertilizing. It sometimes did in Iowa. But it never does in Florida.

So it is very important with Florida soils, heat, summer rains, and humidity to fertilize all plants on a continuing basis. Whether you use regular chemical fertilizer or slow release organic fertilizers or coated pellets like Osmocote™, you will still have to add more as needed. That could be an average of a pound a month per banana plant, more in the summer during rapid growth and less in the winter during slow growth. Vegetables can bear feeding every three weeks. Feed citrus three or four times between mid-March and the first of November.

A balanced fertilizer is usually best. Sometimes I put on enough compost and manure (high in nitrogen) to think I need less of N and more of P (phosphorus) and K (potassium). But other gardeners who use great amounts of compost do not find any imbalance. Watch plants for signs of deficiency (see Chapter 11), and occasionally use a fertilizer that includes minor or trace elements.

Watch growth for signs of under- or overfeeding. Like every good thing, feeding must not be overdone or it will result in fast, often weak growth susceptible to breakage, cold damage, and pest problems. Overfeeding will also increase the amount of water needed. Most landscape trees and shrubs will thrive with two or three feedings each year.

Friendly Organisms

I had always heard of living soil, but assumed before that most of this life was invisible. Most of it is. But my Florida soil is so full of insects that it literally seethes beneath my spade when I dig about six inches deep, mostly with pill bugs. I manage to grow many things well nonetheless.

Most of the soil organisms are invisible. I found a fascinating little book at the library, *Your Florida Garden Soils, 500 Questions and Answers*, by Seton N. Edson, published in 1963 by University of Florida Press at Gainesville. Therein he says: "Soil, very much alive, is teeming with the largest collection of creatures from the animal and vegetable kingdoms, more so than any other medium. A thimbleful of soil can contain 2 billion bacteria, about 20 million fungi, and perhaps 200 thousand protozoa." These usually include a balance of harmful and beneficial organisms. There are several ways to contribute to tipping the balance in your favor.

Earthworms

Most gardeners have learned to appreciate these visible helpers. Early in my Florida gardening I sent to a worm farm and bought a box of worms. I put most of them under the rabbit cages to multiply, but I also put some in various sections of the garden.

This did no harm and certainly did some good. But I realize now that it was unnecessary. Earthworms migrate and will soon show up when the soil is sufficiently improved. Until then, there are other kinds of soil organisms we should be adding.

So if you find some worms in your soil, it is a very good sign. And certainly, once there, they will continue to help the process along.

Make an Earthworm Box:
For a container use a wooden box, a garbage can, or a plastic bucket with holes in the bottom for drainage. Order, buy, or collect a start of earthworms or fishing worms. Put them in the box and add soil to fill it halfway. Keep this moist and add your kitchen scraps every day. Cover scraps with soil and the box with a cover to keep out light. You can also add wood ashes, manure, and sawdust in small amounts. This idea comes from Marian Van Atta. She takes a bit of soil out of the bottom to put into planting holes, thus adding worm castings and worms to enrich the soil.

Inoculants

Whenever you buy legume seed, you should also buy a legume inoculant, which comes in a little packet for the homeowner, of live bacteria. There is a specific inoculant for every legume, but most seed catalogs offer a home gardener's packet that will do peas, beans, soybeans, sweet peas, etc. You need to get a new one every year and they are not expensive.

I gardened for years before I ever heard of this. I used it in Ohio when I was desperate and crops did much better. I didn't always use it in Iowa where there was plenty of bacteria and crops thrived in any case. But I just learned that it is especially important in Florida because the moisture and temperature deplete the bacteria in sandy soils. In fact, we should use two to seven times the amount of inoculant that is recommended for other states.

To apply, just before planting, moisten the seed well and then pour off the excess. You just want every surface to be wet enough to make the black, bacteria-laden compost cling. Some people use Karo syrup, but it is messy and not really necessary. Then add the inoculant and stir or shake gently to coat each seed. Plant as usual.

Enzymes

I'd heard of enzymes in canning and freezing vegetables, but I'd never heard much about their action in the soil until just lately. I went on a tour with the members of the Pinellas County Organic Matters garden club and we got to talking about crop failure and problems.

"The one thing that made the most difference in my garden was when I started to use enzymes," said Naomi Kerr, who runs Garden Goodies Health Food Store in Clearwater and grows an acre of produce that she sells there. "They are especially important while you are building up your soil."

Another member agreed. A third member, Bill Adrian, sells these products and sent me further details.

Extra Nitrogen Needed:

Common advice I'd long heard and ignored was that adding mulch or large amounts of organic matter to the soil should be accompanied by an extra application of nitrogen fertilizer. This is needed to feed the microbes and if not provided, they will take it from the plants. I've mulched for years without doing this and without noticing any sign of nitrogen deficiency on nearby plants — no pale or yellow leaves. But when I added enzymes, the beans turned pale until I added the nitrogen. So be prepared to add extra nitrogen, either automatically with the mulch, sawdust or enzymes, or quickly at the first indication of need.

In the meantime, I found on my shelf bottles of Help™ and Spray-N-Grow™. Help describes itself as a vitamin enzyme complex that restores the microbiology of the soil, making it able to absorb water better, resist disease and creating an environment for the micro-organisms necessary for growth to flourish. It is supposed to make soil more alive and make it hold water like a sponge. Spray-N-Grow is a micronutrient that increases microbiological life in the soil. I have tried both of these, but inconclusively so far. I am currently trying some of the products made by ByoTron of Port Richey, which are highly recommended by the members of the Pinellas Organic Matters garden club.

My dictionary describes enzymes as any of numerous proteins produced by living organisms and functioning as biochemical catalysts in living organisms.

I've long been looking for magic. When these products described themselves as magic, I didn't believe it. If they weren't nutrients, what were they? Now I am beginning to understand and appreciate enzymes.

Nematodes

Nematodes are microscopic roundworms present in most soils, and are often a problem in Florida. There are also beneficial nematodes, but when you pull out sickly-looking beans and find swollen, knotted, gnarled roots, you are seeing a common kind of nematode damage. Nitrogen nodules on the roots of a healthy legume crop will easily rub off.

There are several ways to control harmful nematodes. They are less prevalent in soil that is rich in humus, so adding plenty of organic matter may solve or at least stave off the problem. Very susceptible plants such as figs can be mulched knee high and do quite well. Mine have.

Nematodes are less likely to be a problem near a walk or the foundation of the house. I recently saw a group of red cordyline, also susceptible, thriving near walks in a school planting with every leaf perfect, while mine are sulking, and that's why.

In open ground they are most prevalent in the top 12 to 15 inches of soil. One grower, Dr. Celso Gomez-Sanchez of Lutz, Florida, plants his figs in large, bottomless pots that he fills with very rich organic soil and sinks into otherwise normal planting holes. The sides of the pot form a mechanical barrier that prevents most nematode damage. The open bottom lets the roots spread deeply into the soil.

Some plants are not bothered by nematodes, and some varieties of susceptible plants are more resistant to them. A fig rootstock of *Ficus coculafolia* is more resistant to nematodes but less so to frosts, but a bank of soil and mulch above the graft will protect the plants from winterkill.

Marigolds, impatiens, and many native plants seem resistant, and sweet potatoes seem to repel nematodes. Most other plants are affected to some degree. The damage may be minimal your first year, but increase in subsequent years.

Solarization

Many gardeners used to use Vapam to treat soil for nematodes and mourn its removal from the market but to me, it always seemed to belong in the category of drastic measures. I have used soil solarization as an alternative during the warm months. This involves preparing the soil as if for planting, raking it smooth, and watering it so that it is moist two feet deep. Then simply cover the area with 2- to 6-mil clear plastic and seal the edges well with soil, rocks, or such. A cheap plastic paint dropcloth may not be quite as good, but it will do.

Gaps or air pockets will retard the heat buildup, though they are just about impossible to do away with completely. So will pockets of water, which you may drain away with a small hole where needed. Allow four to six weeks for treatment, longer if a cool spell comes. Afterwards allow the soil to dry to a workable texture.

This method was developed in Israel and has been used extensively in California. Consider it if you have soil empty now or a new plot in mind to till. In four to six weeks, soil can reach temperatures sufficient to kill many nematodes, weed seeds, and soilborne fungi. You might try this one year and cover crops another.

Cooking the sod without tilling is safer around buried underground cables. Solarization works on small or large plots anywhere where the summer sun is hot enough, actually in most of the country. It is safe, inexpensive, nonchemical, leaves no plant-injuring residues, and is simple to apply. It kills many soil pests and brings favorable physical and chemical changes to the soil itself.

For better or worse, it does not kill everything. It can therefore be used around trees and shrubs without doing any damage to the roots.

Solarization kills nematodes without harmful chemicals. Florida's hot, humid summer months are an ideal time to perform this treatment.

Soluble nutrients such as calcium, nitrogen, magnesium and potassium proved more available for plant use after treatment. Several beneficial soil microbes either survived the treatment or recolonized the area soon after. The net result was increased plant production that lasted for several years.

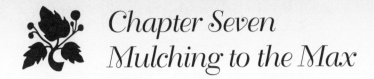

Chapter Seven
Mulching to the Max

I gardened and farmed for at least eight years before I knew about mulch. In my two years of horticulture school, I learned what it was and how to use it. But it wasn't until I read Ruth Stout's wonderful book *How to Have a Green Thumb Without an Aching Back* that I began to really appreciate it.

Now I tell people without hesitation that:

> *Spreading mulch is the easiest, cheapest,*
> *and most important garden practice*

. . . and Xeriscaping considerations underline its value.

What is Mulch?

Mulch is anything that covers the ground between plants. Mother Nature uses it in *all* cases. She never leaves ground bare. If nothing else, she will see that weeds grow on any bare ground. But in the timbers she uses leaves and pine needles. In the desert she uses sand or rock.

Long-time mulchers tend to separate garden mulches into two categories. Organic mulch is any material that originally came from the earth and has not been so altered that it won't, eventually, rot back into the earth.

Truck farmers often use such inorganic mulch as strips of plastic. Once, in Iowa, I had a 10-foot square of black plastic in one corner of my garden for four years. Through the slits cut in this material I planted tomato plants and cucumber vines, crops that needed a great deal of space but only a small area of contact with the soil. There was no way that weeds could grow through that plastic and it worked very well with no plowing, tilling, or hoeing. I don't recommend that for Florida because the soil needs organic matter added more often. The strawberry growers routinely use raised rows covered with black plastic, but they alternate strawberries with cover crops to add organic matter every year.

One grower I know, Gordon Bemis, has his own 40-acre experimental station near Brooksville, and about 20 of those acres are covered with old carpets turned upside down. This adds both organic and inorganic matter to the soil. It works so well for him that he is able to handle much more land and planting than he otherwise could. I've gathered some carpet scraps and used them myself. Florida weeds will grow right over small pieces, coming in from the sides eventually, but until then they work just fine.

Organic mulches:
Grass clippings, leaves, straw, hay, peanut shells, peat moss, newspapers, hortopaper.

Inorganic mulches:
Black or clear plastic, old carpet, landscape fabrics or mulching cloths (the latter two let water through).

Benefits of Mulch:

- *Cools soil in summer — Warms soil in winter*

- *Soaks up moisture*

- *Prevents evaporation*

- *Prevents soil caking, cracking and hardening*

- *Prevents soil erosion and water runoff*

- *Reduces stress on plants*

- *Increases microbial life in soil*

- *Increases earthworm activity*

- *Improves soil structure*

- *Reduces weed growth*

- *Reduces disease and insect problems*

- *Can add eye appeal*

Last year my son left the mat from a discarded car in my back yard, and I placed it around the roots of a shrub that had been bent on taking over. Once the shrub was in leaf, the mat disappeared under the foliage and made it possible to get to my clothesline without a machete.

In some cases you may use both organic and inorganic mulches together: a layer of plastic under a layer of stones, for example. The plastic makes a thinner layer above it more efficient.

What Does Mulch Do?

Mulch insulates the soil, keeping it cooler in summer and warmer in winter. Mulch makes the most of rainfall or irrigation water by soaking it up like a sponge, holding it in place and allowing it to penetrate slowly. When it pours, particularly in the summer, much water will otherwise run right off dry, hard ground, causing erosion. On exposed ground all evidence of rain may be gone in a few hours, while on mulched areas the soil will stay damp much longer. Especially in a dry season, mulched plants will do much better, and Florida has a dry season most years from September until June.

I first suspected that mulch would offer a haven for bugs and pests. This proved false. Because mulched plants tend to be healthier, they suffer much less from pests and diseases. On the other hand, beneficial bacteria and earthworms, a gardener's greatest friends, thrive under mulch and contribute further to soil and plant improvement.

Mulch improves soil structure because roots and rainfall can more easily penetrate loose, damp soil than hard-baked, dry, cracked soil.

Mulch makes weed control much easier. If the layer is thick enough, it will block out the light and prevent most weed seed from germinating. Any weeds that do come through are easily pulled from the soft earth if they are single. If they come in a multitude, you can destroy them by stirring or turning over the mulch.

Mulch reduces mud in clay soils and allows you to walk on its carpet even after a rain. Beans, lettuce, and strawberries stay cleaner and are easier to prepare in the kitchen. Because there is less splashing of rain drops, disease spores are less likely to spread and cause such problems as black spot on roses. Cucumbers, unstaked tomatoes, and other vegetables that sprawl on mulch instead of on bare ground suffer less from mildew, mold, and rot.

So why don't more gardeners use mulch?

I can't figure that one out myself. A few may be like I was in my teens and just

Exhibit at Hillsborough County Cooperative Extension Service showing various types of mulch.

haven't heard of it yet or gotten around to trying it. But others seem to find it offensive to their sense of neatness.

So ingrained is the idea of bare ground around select plants that when my neighbor spread hay around her uncle's roses in a moment of generosity, she later returned to find it "all cleaned away." Some of my own relatives find the whole idea of mulch as foreign to their natures as throwing trash on the floor.

I will admit that some mulches look neater than others, and if neatness is your goal, you can use the better looking mulches, even such expensive ones as white stones or bark chips on the top layer with less attractive material like newspapers and plastic underneath. This can be very important in the front yard. In our vegetable gardens, most mulchers tend to see the usefulness as more important.

I've been spreading wood chips for years. My children have sat and played on piles of wood chips. To my surprise, we've never gotten so much as a splinter from those wood chips that I consider treasure. I've

> ## ∽ How to Haul Mulch ∽
>
> *To get it home:*
>
> 1. *Pick-up truck or trailer. Many organic gardeners have these specifically for that purpose.*
>
> 2. *Car. Use bags, boxes, plastic bins or garbage cans to contain it. Drive directly home and unload immediately. I once loaded up on my way somewhere, to beat the trash truck, and left hot grass clippings in a hot car while I did a morning's work at church. Big mistake — it took months to get the odor out of the car.*
>
> 3. *Hire the hauling. Some people will deliver wood chips or other mulch at a reasonable price. Check price before hauling.*
>
> *To move it around once home:*
>
> 1. *Wheelbarrow. We used to wear out one of the cheap aluminum ones every year. An expensive model lasted a little longer. There are places where a wheelbarrow will go that a cart won't.*
>
> 2. *Garden cart. We bought one (major investment) over 16 years ago, have used it hard, left it out in rain and snow, and are still using it.*
>
>
>
>   *I recommend carts highly, but if I ever buy another, I'll get one with a front panel that opens.*

gardened with mulch and without mulch, and believe me, "with" is better and results in fewer problems with bugs and pests, not more.

Mulch can add to the attractiveness of your yard even beyond its growth enhancing characteristics. You can use mulch that picks up and accents colors, or adds textures to the scene. I've seen coal used as a mulch that was quite striking, though I admit I still don't know what effect it would have on the soil. It no doubt had plastic underneath. Coal does come from plant material, compacted by the centuries, so it would be probably be harmless. The plants around it looked good. Bark and wood fiber mulches come in shades of browns and reds.

Rock can be anything from white to gray to almost black. I find anything that keeps out weeds and makes plants grow better with less water quite attractive.

Dark-colored mulches will absorb the sun's rays and reduce heat reflection, while white material will reflect heat. This could be a factor in air conditioning costs here in Florida, as well as comfort in your garden.

Where Can One Get Mulch?

One aspect of mulching that stops some people is the matter of accumulation. The fact is, you can find a great deal of mulch right around the home and yard. Even pulled weeds, as long as they have no seeds, can be added to layers of mulch. I am careful to place pulled weeds with roots on top of other mulch where they will dry and die, not in contact with bare soil where they could recover and grow again.

Beyond these materials, the acquisition of mulch becomes a great adventure. Many of your neighbors will probably be glad to save their grass clippings and leaves for you. (See "Bringing Home the Humus" in Chapter 6).

If you have a lawn service, ask them about saving grass clippings for your garden. More and more people are using mulching mowers these days, but as long as some people prefer bagging yard clippings, they are better used by gardeners than added to the landfill.

A great many mulches, by-products of some other activity, are free. Most people who have stables or rabbit pens will be glad for you to come in and haul away the used bedding and manure. The wood chips I used to get free now come with a small cost for hauling, but at any reasonable price, mulch is a bargain.

When I was a green horticulture student just beginning to work on the estates around Philadelphia, one eccentric owner asked if I needed some mulch for the daylilies. I'd already learned that you can never get too much mulch, so I said, "Yes, of course."

"Fine," she answered. "I'll have John (the chauffeur) climb up on the roof and bring us down some baskets of peanut shells."

I was stunned. I had thought peanuts grew in the ground, not on trees. Much later I solved the mystery. This lady bought peanuts in 50-pound bags and fed the squirrels out the window

---

∽ Mulching Tips ∽

∾ *The visual impact of mulch is often greater in the water-conserving garden because plants are not as close together and more of the mulch color and texture is visible.*

∾ *Many landscape fabrics are made of a polypropylene that is permeable to water and air. Covering this with a thin layer of organic mulch keeps it in place, improves the appearance, and makes it last longer by blocking the sunlight.*

∾ *Use a spading fork or pitchfork to make small holes in plastic for rainwater to seep through.*

∾ *Do not use gravel or light colored mulches under deciduous trees or the leaves will look messy. Fallen leaves can blend and add to organic mulches such as wood chips or chopped bark.*

∾ *Do not allow gravel or stones to touch plant stems or the reflected heat may burn the plants.*

---

of her second floor sitting room. The squirrels dropped the shells on the garage roof. I learned much in that garden besides the source of peanut shells. The only thing we didn't use for mulch was a "bad" weed, a type of bindweed that came back to life unless burned.

The Rare Occasions When It Is Best Not to Mulch

Around citrus trees: I had to learn not to mulch around the base of citrus trees because they are very susceptible to root rot. This rule can be bent during very dry times. As long as you keep the trunk and an area about two feet in diameter around it open for air circulation, I believe it is better to mulch the rest than to let weeds grow there. My lawn-mowing children make no distinction between citrus and other trees and may dump a bag anywhere. I am so glad to have both the lawn mowed and the mulch most places, that I have not discouraged this but just rake it back from the trunk of the citrus.

Some experts will throw up their hands at this advice and say it is dead wrong. But both Marian Van Atta and I have mulched some of our citrus very carefully and find it works. I have never killed a tree with mulch yet, while other trees that got less attention have died.

When clippings are contaminated: Mulch of grass clippings from a lawn recently treated with herbicide could still contain enough of the chemical to cause some damage to certain sensitive plants. I have faced this problem when gathering from unknown sources. Once I even found an herbicide label included in the bag. So I don't put any questionable grass clippings on irreplaceable plants. I put it instead where I want to kill off the weeds or turf in any case. Or I pile it up and let the rains wash through it for a few weeks. In the long run I think the organic matter is worth the risk.

In cold weather: In very early spring, you may want to rake the mulch away so the sun can reach the soil and warm it sooner.

Around new seedlings: When seedlings are planted in very moist earth, dampening-off can result from poorly ventilated soil. Either do not mulch at all, or else pull mulch well away from tiny seedlings until the soil dries a bit and the plants become established.

In too-wet areas: Do not mulch a wet, low-lying, poorly drained area, especially with leaves that could mat down and add to the sogginess in damp seasons. During a dry season, use a light, airy type of mulch on these spots, such as loose hay or straw.

On top of perennials: Keep mulch back a little from the centers of clumps of perennials, especially in prolonged wet weather, to prevent crown rot.

Around tree trunks: Pull wood chips or sawdust back about four inches from tree trunks to discourage gnawing of the bark by mice.

How to Use Mulch

Just spread it around your plants or over the area where you plan to put plants. As mentioned above, a layer of plastic is appropriate under expensive or purchased mulches to make a thinner layer work better. A layer of newspapers is always appropriate under mulch, except where you plan to sow seeds. This is a good way to recycle newspapers yourself and you will find that they break down quickly wherever they are kept wet. Avoid using them where a lawnmower may catch the edge and uncover them.

If you are going to sow seeds, you may want to simply pile the mulch between the rows or around the edges of the plot until the plants have emerged and are tall enough to keep their heads above the mulch.

Wind and rain will shift mulch around. If you are planting small plants in deep mulch, it is a good idea to put something like a milk jug with the bottom removed over the plant to keep the mulch from covering it until it is well enough established not to be buried.

How Much Mulch Should You Use?

A light mulch, half an inch or less, will hold in enough moisture to get crop seedlings up and growing quickly, ahead of the weeds. Most plants can grow right through such a layer so it can stay in place. Add a thicker mulch between rows or between larger plants, 6 to 10 inches. This will save hours of backbreaking work hoeing and weeding and gallons of water, not to mention time holding the hose. Any weeds that do come through can be easily pulled from the loose soil.

Trees and shrubs, especially those that are susceptible to nematodes (like figs) and that are heavy feeders and drinkers (like bananas), can benefit from a mulch knee-high.

Organic mulch is constantly breaking down and adding humus to the soil, thereby improving its structure and increasing its water retention ability.

Mulching Instead of Tilling

If you have neither a tiller nor young muscles, you can carry the mulching method one step further and never have to till the soil. Spread newspapers over the sod, overlapping them so weeds can't creep in through the cracks. Over this, spread a thick layer of grass clippings or leaves or both. After watering well you can plant at once, by pulling the mulch back to the newspapers and adding soil around the roots of individual plants or over the top of seeds as needed. Holes for large plants can be dug through the newspapers: remove the bits of sod to the top layer of mulch, then pull the mulch back up almost to the trunk after planting.

This method, perfected by ECHO (Educational Concerns for Hunger Organization) for use in third world countries, works very well for Florida gardeners. I have used it extensively for three years. The roots will penetrate the newspapers when they need to. Meanwhile, the newspaper tends to keep the moisture and nutrients at root level and slow down their leaching through the sand. It also keeps the nematodes away from any roots formed in the mulch, blocks out weeds, and within a few months rots into the soil as humus.

The only problems with this method involve getting the soil to add on top, mulch sometimes smothering tiny plants, and eventual reentry of some weeds, especially grasses. For soil you can use purchased potting soil or mix any combination of soil, compost, peat moss, perlite, or vermiculite that you would use in containers, and it does take less soil than for container growing. To prevent shifting mulch from burying small plants, cut the top and bottom from cardboard milk cartons and place one around each plant after pulling the mulch back slightly from the stem. Using this method, you'll find that the weeds that enter are few compared to unmulched soil.

Chapter Eight
A Water Miser "Waters Wiser"

Until I came to Florida, I considered watering to be Mother Nature's job. We often had summer droughts in Ohio, Pennsylvania, and Iowa when her lack of cooperation was evident. Still, it never occurred to me to take over the chore myself. For one thing, it was quite impossible — my largest gardens were often far from the house and from sources of water.

I had been gardening for decades before I also noticed that there were many dry days during the spring, a season there known for its rainy, cloudy days and damp, cold soil. Seeds did not germinate well in dry soil, cold or warm, and the idea to water-where-I-could changed from a vague notion to definite action.

Understanding the Florida Climate

It was not until we visited California in 1985 that I was struck like a blow to the face by the fact that many people in many places must supply most of the water needed to grow their plants. About time I learned, and none too soon. Two years later we moved to Florida, and since then I have been one of those people in one of those places.

"You'll see," people told us with oracular certainty and importance. "It rains in Florida every day of the summer about 4 o'clock. You can almost set your watch by that rain."

Don't you believe it. Not only can you not set your watch, you can't set your irrigation system or your gardening by these "certain" rains either. I've seen it go ten days in the summer with no rain. And even after a good, soaking rain, our sandy soil is dry two days later. The summer humidity helps many plants to survive. It also helps to fool those who are not paying attention (or perhaps are visitors who have no plants to lose).

Important Fact: *Florida is a desert where it rains three months of the year. If you want to grow vegetables or fruit or anything other than the most drought resistant plants, YOU MUST WATER. And even those drought resistant plants will need water to get started.*

The heat and humidity also serve to overwhelm some plants that we cannot grow here at all or must start again after the summer is over (rhubarb, petunias, nasturtiums). Many plants that will grow fine in southwestern climates where it is always fairly dry will not do well here. When my daughter Mary lived in California, there was a field of asparagus behind her house, so I thought it would surely do well in Florida — before I understood about the humidity. Asparagus will survive here, but it will not thrive.

We had greater heat in Iowa (eight days one summer over 100°) and what we thought was high humidity, so I figured the corn that thrived there should grow fine in Florida. It does in the fall or spring, and some crops can extend a few weeks into one end or the other of the summer, but corn cannot take both high heat and humidity for months at a time. Florida is somewhat like a rainforest in the summer, but so little like a rainforest the rest of the year that the analogy breaks down.

Florida weather and watering needs are unique. They are very different from the rest of continental United States, and matching the watering to the weather is one of the secrets of successful growing here.

Understanding the Water Needs of Plants

Plant roots, especially the little root hairs, take up moisture from the soil. The plant then transports this moisture up through the stem or trunk to the leaves, from which it is transpired back into the air. That is one of the reasons why trees not only provide shade but are excellent air conditioners as well.

If, during transpiration, the plant loses more moisture from the top than it can take up from the roots, stress results and can lead to death. Transpiration varies with the kind and age of the plant, and the kind of soil. It increases with wind, light intensity, low humidity, and high temperature. The rate of evaporation from the soil and transpiration from the leaves of the plant may be charted as evapotranspiration or ET. This whole complex, amazing process is a high energy, anti-gravitational force that sucks the water out of the soil, into the roots, up through the stem, and out through the leaves.

Transpiration acts to cool the plant, and to move moisture to its cells. Water inflates the cells and keeps them turgid. When there isn't enough, the plant wilts.

Why Deep Watering is Important

Plant roots will seek water as far as they are able. This is why it is important to water deeply, so the roots will go down into the soil and find whatever moisture is there, often enough to see them through dry times. If you only water the top twelve inches of soil around permanent plants, roots will tend to develop only in that area, and they will be completely dependent upon your watering in dry times. On the other hand, many annual vegetables and flowers live out their lives without sending roots much deeper. So twelve inches is often deep enough to soak beds with only these plants.

Obviously, perennial plants and trees and shrubs will have much deeper root systems and therefore need less frequent irrigation than annuals.

Drought resistant plants in any classification will be more forgiving of watering mistakes than will oasis zone plants. This brings us to the next question:

3) Photosynthesis is performed by leaves in the crown. A cuticle on the upper side of each leaf controls evaporation; stomata on the under sides absorb carbon dioxide, emit water and oxygen.

2) Xylem tissue in the sapwood carries water against gravity toward the tree's crown.

1) Microscopic root hairs absorb moisture, which travels upward through lateral and taproots.

A large tree can transpire as much as 120 gallons of water every day. The aim of careful Xeriscaping is to provide enough water for the health of the plant without too much extra for unnecessary transpiration.

When to Water and How Much

Since water saving is as much a priority for us as garden success, no longer will we water just because it seems like a pleasant chore, or one we'd best not forget. Water misers must water only if there is a need.

Signs that a Plant Needs Water

I've heard of gardeners who can tell at a glance when a plant needs water and others who claim to feel it instinctively without even glancing. After gardening for almost half a century, I still do not have such talents. But I come closer to the latter, and call it guilt. I may suddenly remember in the middle of the night that I forgot to water something that by all rights should have been watered.

Of course, I can see when a plant wilts. Some can recover from the worst wilting, but others are stressed enough by then not to recover completely. If you find a container plant wilted and it is small enough to place pot and all in a bucket, do so until the leaves revive. But try to train yourself to see earlier signs like curling leaves, an off color, a lack of the usual shine to the foliage, edges that are brown or crisp. (See signs of lawn wilting in Chapter 2.)

In a water-conserving garden, you may not see such telltale signs as dry surface soil because of mulch and buried drip irrigation. Drought resistant plants are also less likely to show signs of stress and will give you more leeway for mistakes. So you must be more observant, take soil samples, or dig down far enough to check that your current irrigation schedule is not resulting in too much or too little water.

The Best Time of Day to Water

The general rule is that the best time to water is early in the morning. From 3 to 6 a.m. is prime time — watering then will prevent loss to wind or evaporation as well as other water uses sapping the pressure. If you water automatically, there is no reason not to choose this time. But anytime up until about 9 a.m. will do. Evening is second choice, early enough for any water on the foliage to dry before nightfall. Moisture on the leaves through the night is an invitation to mildew and diseases, though some experts think this danger is minor compared to water waste.

Keep high noon waterings for emergency measures only. As much as 50% of water from daytime sprinklings evaporates before it ever hits the ground.

With drip irrigation putting the water right into the root zone, neither evaporation nor wet foliage present any problems. So drip irrigation may be done at any time.

It was always thought that watering in the middle of the day was hard on plants. A very few plants like African violets and orchids can show spotted leaves from cold water hitting them while the sun is warm upon them. But for most plants that are seriously wilting, midday watering — even an emergency sprinkle — is better than midday stress. If your impatiens, newly-set plants, or potted plants are seriously wilting in the noonday sun, grab a hose or a watering can and give them a cooling shower. This is another case of anything worth doing is better done badly than not at all. Be aware that some midday wilting is normal with plants like squash in hot weather. For these you can wait until the next morning, by which time they will probably be revived by the dew. If not, water then.

How Much to Water

Every yard needs a simple rain gauge placed where wind, foliage, or runoff will not give a false reading. Rain gauges are inexpensive to buy, and two or more in different places are a good idea. Mine start out in the open, but too often something grows over them. Putting one on a fence post sometimes works. A plain tin can will serve as well. It is just not as easy to read.

This will tell you much more accurately than the evening news what Mother Nature has or has not provided and give you a better idea of whether you can take time off or not. As a general rule, one inch of water a week will be enough for most plants.

Usually, if the water reaches 60 percent of the plant's root zone, that is sufficient. So the more you know about a plant's root expectancy the better. Nut trees and other trees with tap roots often go as deep into the ground or deeper than they are tall. Trees with more spreading root growth often have roots extending much farther from the trunk than the branches do. Drought tolerant plants are often so because they are extremely deep rooted. Many annuals and vegetables, on the other hand, have most of their roots in the top 12 inches of the soil. So you have to be selective in how much as well as how often.

Checking Sprinklers

For any sprinkling or irrigation system, there are other ways to measure. Set six flat, straight-sided dishes (tuna cans work well) at intervals throughout each sprinkler's range and check these after 15 minutes of watering at the usual time and rate. Water pressure may vary from maximum to minimum use times. Then measure the depth of water in each dish; it should not vary more than $1/4$ to $1/2$ inch. If it does, you need to clean or change sprinkler heads. Add all six measures and divide the sum by six to find the average, then multiply by four for the hourly amount of water released. Use this to determine the amount of time you need to irrigate per week. If your system puts out one inch of water an hour and your fruit trees need $1\frac{1}{2}$ inches, then plan to water for 90 minutes. Divide this into two waterings (see sidebar).

Apply no more than one inch of water at one time or it will move down through sandy soils past the plants' root zones. Apply no less than $1/2$ inch at once or it will encourage shallow root growth.

Another way to gauge watering time is to dig down to see how far the water has penetrated into the soil. Soil sampling tubes show the moisture level clearly. They are T-shaped, with a probe that goes 10 to 21 inches into the ground and a cutaway portion on the side. Moisture sensor gauges and tensiometers may also be used in more sophisticated systems (see Chapter 13).

You can also use a metal rod, $1/2$ inch in diameter, or the rod of a sprinkler. The rod will push through damp soil fairly easily, then come to a stop where the percolation does. I find that my asparagus cutter, stuck into newly watered ground gives a pretty good indication. If it doesn't go down far enough, I know to water longer. A light-colored wooden stake may also be used: sharpen it at one end, push it into the soil, and leave it for a few minutes so that the moisture darkens it.

How Much Difference Can Xeriscaping Make?
One gardener says, "Since replacing most of a 45- by 60-foot lawn with drought tolerant plants and converting sprinklers to drip irrigation, our two-month water bill fell from $135 to $45." Another allowed his lawn to go to ruin during dry times, then replaced it with drought-tolerant plants. Even during the year-long establishment period when they were irrigated, they required less water than the grass.

Air in the Soil

As important as water is to plant growth, air must also be present in the soil. Filling soil so full of water that all the air is expelled can lead to stress as well as plant diseases. On rare occasions it rains so hard that even the worms are driven up out of the soil. If this condition lasts long enough, the plant roots will die. Organic matter and soil conditioners like vermiculite work to hold air as well as water in the soil and maintain the needed balance.

Water Slowly

It is much better to water trees slowly than quickly. Set the hose for barely flowing and move it from tree to tree while you do other outdoor work. To avoid over or underwatering, use a five-gallon bucket with a few small holes in the bottom. Put it beside your tree and fill it. Let the water sink slowly into the root zone. Then move the bucket to the next tree and repeat. A young tree (from 4 to 14 feet) can take five gallons of water at a time. This should percolate deep into the soil and encourage deep roots.

Special Water Needs

Some plants will need water more at some times than at others. All plants will need less during the short days of winter when they are growing more slowly than during the long days of spring or summer when they are growing by leaps and bounds. Many people have killed fine plants by not making seasonal changes in their watering amounts.

Some plants you want to grow vigorously (fruits and vegetables, roses) while others you only want to grow slowly but with robust health (lawns and clipped hedges).

Fruit trees need much more water during the period from bloom until harvest than they do the rest of the year. Once, in Iowa, where we relied mostly on rainfall, I had two plum trees. Every year they bloomed, but any fruit they set soon fell off. I thought I had a pollination problem because the two did not bloom at the same time. Finally I cut one down, even

Primitive Drip Irrigation
It is an old practice to sink juice cans, with a hole in the bottom and the top removed, at the base of tomato plants and then fill them with every hose watering. This allows the water to sink in deeply and slowly. So does a milk jug with a hole in the bottom set at the base of a plant.

though I assumed that would ruin any future chance for fruit. I warned the other, "You have one more year to bloom because you do that so beautifully. But then you must go."

That winter we visited California and I began to understand about watering. Our hostess, only mildly interested in growing, remarked as we passed one walnut grove, "Those trees never bear fruit because they don't get the water when they need it." And a light flashed on in my head.

The next spring I was acutely aware of the importance of water. I did not think there was a chance of plums, but there were some ornamental ones in the neighborhood that might serve as pollinators. I watched carefully and watered only a few times when the rains were insufficient. And I had wonderful plum crops from that tree from then on.

The same is true of flowers. Daylilies can increase in size by almost an inch after a single shower. But they also need much less water from the time they finish blooming until buds show again in the spring.

Corn in tassel is extremely vulnerable. Half a day of dryness can damage the anthers and almost stop pollen production, thus resulting in poorly filled out ears. But once corn ears are set, the plants are very drought tolerant. Greens and cabbage cousins need water consistently. Grapes and berries can do with only a few thorough waterings as the fruit is maturing.

Citrus trees don't like to be too wet, and watering well once every two weeks is sufficient. They will let you know they are thirsty by wilting, yellowing, or curling leaves.

Shrub and species roses that bloom only in the spring need much less water after that.

With keen observation you can soon learn to recognize your own garden's wilt cycle. Like a new mother with her baby, no one knows its needs as you do. In hot weather and sandy soil, the time between wilt and permanent burn can be very short, and may vary with different crops. Pumpkin and squash vines can wilt severely and bounce back with complete forgiveness. Papayas, on the other hand, can change their flavor from sweet to strong over one case of neglect. Watch carefully, dig down to check soil moisture, make notes about crops, weather and watering and the results, and soon you will have an instinctive feel for your own landscape that is better than any advice anyone can give.

The Importance of Water During Germination

Seeds contain the embryo of life within them, and this can sometimes stay viable for decades if they are kept in a dry place. Because Florida heat and humidity play havoc with that viability, I always advise people to do what it took me three years to learn: keep seeds in the freezer in a plastic bag or moisture-proof container until planting.

Once moisture, even humidity, softens the seedcoat that protects the embryo, the miraculous process of germination starts. Germination time can vary widely. It may take as little as twenty-four hours for cabbage. I knew a man in Iowa who had tree seeds (with very hard seedcoats) that stayed in the ground for seven years before germinating. For most seeds, once the process begins, the tiny seedling is very vulnerable to drying out and can die in a few hours without proper moisture.

So a seedbed, or container with germinating seeds, is the only instance where light watering is recommended, since it only has to moisten the soil deeply enough to surround the seed. Because this soil is often close to the surface, it can dry out in a few hours and you will soon need to sprinkle again. Depending on the weather, soil, and seed type, you may need to sprinkle germinating seeds lightly several times a day. Once the seedlings are up and visible, watch them carefully and begin to water less frequently and more deeply for the next week or two. After that, for annuals, normal irrigation should suffice.

You should not cover tiny seeds with heavy mulch during germination or they will not have the strength to push through and may well smother. However, you can cover seeds as big as beans or sunflowers with a light sprinkling of dry grass clippings, shredded leaves, or pine needles. This will shade the soil somewhat, cut down moisture loss, and allow less frequent watering. The seedlings will grow up through the mulch, which you can then thicken between plants or rows.

You can also cover slow germinating seeds like carrots with a board or a burlap bag. Check often once germination is expected — most seed packets and catalogs tell how many days — and remove this cover as soon as the first seedling is spotted.

The Importance of Water During Settling-In

For years I told readers to always leave a dish-like depression around the base of a newly set plant to catch rainwater or irrigation water. Then I moved to Florida and learned about citrus and other plants susceptible to root rot. So now I recommend a donut instead, around the dripline of the plant. This keeps water from running off in the wrong direction but also prevents it from settling around the trunk. It also helps the roots reach out, instead of staying in a tight ball or encircling the trunk. As the plant grows, move the donut farther and farther from the crown. Donuts are easily made with a trowel at transplanting time for small plants. Make them around trees and shrubs with a hoe by digging in around the desired perimeter and pulling up the soil to the outside to provide a double barrier against water runoff. It is easy to renew them every time you weed or stir the mulch under the tree.

With rows of seedlings, you can make a trench between donuts so that the overflow from one plant will run to the next.

Cutting Down on Transpiration

Plants often wilt after transplanting; the more the roots are disturbed, the more they will wilt, because they have lost the tiny root hairs that take up the moisture from the soil. The transpiring topgrowth remains. In some cases, the plant will look so wilted that for several

⟨ How Long Does Establishment Take? ⟨

All new plants need a period of time to become established and send out enough root growth to sustain the top growth. This is true as well of drought resistant plants. Water them as needed, even in your natural rainfall zones, until they are well established. Annuals may take only a few weeks. Most perennials, ground-covers, and shrubs will become well established in a matter of months. Some trees took up to three years to establish a good root system in the north and I watched them grow slowly for that length of time and then show a great burst of growth thereafter. Everything grows more quickly and steadily in Florida, especially trees, so I would expect that time to be closer to two years. Watch for signs to indicate a need for water.

The old saying about vines is a good measure of root establishment: "The first year they sleep, the second they creep, and the third they leap." When your plants start leaping with vigorous new topgrowth, you can consider them settled.

days to over a week, you'll be sure it is going to die. Even watering will not help, because the plant is simply unable to take up the moisture. You can cut down on transpiration by:

1. Misting the leaves, especially the undersides where the stomata are, with a fine spray of water over the foliage several times a day, or
2. Shading the plant to cut down on wind and sun, or
3. Spraying all surfaces of the leaves with an anti-transpirant product like Wilt-Pruf. (See details in Chapter 13.)
4. Pruning away some of the top to balance what was lost in the root system. This was done more in the past. Current practice is to keep what topgrowth you really want unless wilting threatens to become death. But pruning away any growth that you don't need is always a good practice.

As your new plant settles in and forms new roots and new root hairs on old roots, water less often and more deeply. This will encourage roots to go down into safely moist soil, rather than up near the surface where the soil will first dry out. Begin this deeper watering as soon as the wilting stops. Water new plants in the drought resistant and natural zones less and less often, always watching for signs of stress. When you judge them settled, you can cease watering in the natural zones.

Weekly Watering Guidelines
∽ During the Establishment Period ∽

WARM MONTHS: APRIL–OCTOBER				
	WEEK 1	WEEKS 2–3	WEEKS 4–6	WEEKS 7–12
Ground covers, mass plantings	0.5" daily	0.5" every two days	0.75" twice a week	
Trees and shrubs from containers	fill basin twice per application, daily	fill basin twice per application, every 2 days	fill basin twice per application, twice a week	
Trees and shrubs– ball & burlap	fill basin twice per application, daily	fill basin twice per application, every 2 days	fill basin twice per application, every 2 days	fill basin twice per application, twice a week

COOL MONTHS: NOVEMBER–MARCH				
	WEEK 1	WEEKS 2–3	WEEKS 4–6	WEEKS 7–12
Ground covers, mass plantings	0.25" daily	0.5" twice a week	0.5" once a week	
Trees and shrubs from containers	fill basin once daily	fill basin once every 2 days	fill basin once, twice a week	
Trees and shrubs– ball & burlap	fill basin once daily	fill basin once every 2 days	fill basin once every 2 days	fill basin once, twice a week

Source: Southwest Florida Water Management District,
"Water Requirements for Newly Planted Landscape Plants"

Chapter Nine
Reusing Water — A Natural Solution

All water is reused. Mother Nature is set up to recycle it in three ways: 1) Through the soil into lakes and rivers, or 2) Through the ground into the aquifer, or 3) Through evaporation from plants back into the atmosphere.

For centuries this system worked fine. It is only in recent decades with increased population, pollution, and lack of the normal time such natural purification takes, that we've run into trouble.

People also recycled water naturally before it was so easy to get. In light of present and future needs, we will be wise to go back to some ancient methods of water reuse, to improve them with modern technology, and to adjust our thinking to appreciate them. From state of mind, to homeowner use and demand, to market feasibility is the usual route. Eventually, as water becomes more and more scarce, laws will make such common sense solutions mandatory. That will be a mixed blessing. But we water misers will be ahead of the times.

Collect Rain for Your Garden

It was in the summertime that I went to the Xeriscape Demonstration Workshop. They are offered monthly and free by several Water Management Districts. You may be asked to pre-register, but will be welcome anyway unless the room is overcrowded. Most workshops include a tour of a Xeriscape planting that will be sure to give you new ideas, motivation, and knowledge of local plant material. I recommend this tour for every interested homeowner.

As usual, I learned from talking to the other people there as well as from the instructor, Lou Kavouras. One couple told me about the large garbage cans they've put under their downspouts. "Those 14-gallon cans fill up in 15 minutes in a rain. Then we put a hose into them and water the garden by suction."

Now this sounds very simple, but there are complications. Like how to get garbage cans under downspouts that run all the way to the ground. And what kind of garbage cans to get. But I've found that if I wait for all the answers, nothing gets done. If I start on a project, I usually find the answers along the way.

How Much Rain Runs Off Your Roof?
The area of your roof is larger than the floor area of one story of your house. We have 2070 square feet of living space, plus the slant and overhang of the roof, plus the area over the storage room, carport, and screened-in porch — roughly 2500 square feet. If we get one inch of rain on our roof and catch and save it all, it will provide one-half inch of water for irrigation for 5000 square feet of garden a few days later.

So I started. I went to the home supply store where my friends had bought their containers and shopped very carefully among the garbage cans. I found some nice brown ones that would compliment our house in color. They were tall and thin, had wheels, and held 17 gallons. I put two in the cart, no mean feat. Later I

Place your water collection container among foliage where it will be less conspicuous.

began to question the strength of the thin-looking plastic, so I put one back and chose a black, circular one that was half the price and looked twice as strong.

I took them home and set them near the downspouts until I could figure out the next step. But it was summer then, and soon the rains came. I ran about with great excitement, placing my reservoirs under the prime spouting leaks or overflows. In a short while, though a bit more than 15 minutes, both were full.

I found out that, indeed, the thin plastic was prone to bulge and fall over under such a load, while the thicker plastic held up well. The brown can has come into the garage to be our prime trash container, trading places with a stronger one.

So went the first step in my plan, and I admit I stalled out there for quite a spell. But even so, I saved at least 100 gallons of prime rainwater. And because it was free and handy and best used before the next rain, I watered plants that would not have been watered otherwise.

By happy accident I set each container near a fragrant plant, one near a butterfly ginger and the other near a white four o'clock. So the dipping out of free water was an extra pleasant chore.

I got the suction to work very well in the back garden, just by putting one hose end in the container and sucking on the other end like a straw until the water got started. (Be sure not to swallow the water, as it may not be pure after sitting.) The water, all 15 gallons or so, ran out slowly once started. I just moved the hose as needed from place to place. But for some reason, the flow from the front container kept stopping and I ended up dipping that water out by the bucketful.

Now that rains are fewer, farther between, and less intense, there is less overflow, so I am finally forced to take the next step. But in the meantime, I've again found it better to do something badly than not at all. Spouse did not want me to "destroy" the permanent downspouting on the house for fear we may someday wish to sell it to someone less water conscious. He wanted me to remove it intact and save it, but when that proved to be a formidable job, I convinced him to cut the downspout off with a hacksaw just above the level of the container. After that, I had no qualms about "destroying" the lid with my pruning snips to cut out a small hole for the inlet. Some of the cut-away plastic now serves as a funnel between the wall and the opening. Now we get water from the gentlest, lightest rain, and I no longer have to remember to open and close the lid.

When we visited Tom Carey's Sundew Gardens in Oviedo, we found an even simpler water-collecting first step. Carey's new house has yet to get its spouting. Eventually, Carey plans to channel the runoff from the roof into a small lake. But in the meantime, dozens of five-gallon buckets stand side by side to save the rain that runs off the roof for the gardens.

Another rain collection idea is presented by John M. O'Keefe in his excellent book, *Water-Conserving Gardens and Landscapes*. To each downspout, attach a length of 18-inch-wide, PVC pipe and paint this to blend with the house. Put a cap on the lower end to hold in the water (about $30 each) and install an outlet at the bottom that can

spouting

18" diam. PVC pipe

outlet

cap

to drip system

be connected to a drip irrigation system. Each 10-foot length of this pipe, which costs about $7 per foot, would hold 132 gallons of water. O'Keefe also suggests using old, above-ground pools as reservoirs.

Rainwater is excellent for washing hair. It smells wonderful and has all God's conditioners built in. We once had a cistern and collected rainwater for washing clothes as well. It was a luxury that few people enjoy these days. Start thinking about how you can collect rainwater for your garden or household. It is well worth the effort.

The Rainwater Room

Once upon a time, in Ohio, we traded a hail-damaged greenhouse and an unprofitable flower shop with a nice apartment above for an old farmhouse with 2.3 acres. Both my husband and our banker were leery of the trade and spent almost a year trying to sell before they consented to the trade. I loved that old house from the beginning, dreamed about it, and prayed that we'd get it.

The trade went through at last. But we did not ask many questions for fear the other party might do likewise. So when we moved in, we had some surprises.

"Do be sure," said Mrs. White, the former owner, "that none of the children gets into that trough. They could drown in there."

"What trough?" My eyes bugged out.

"Why, the one in the rainwater room above the bathroom." Up until then the door had only opened part way, onto a dark and unfinished room that we "could turn into a second bath someday."

"Show me," I said now. Mrs. White took me up to the room. There in the dark stood a cattle watering tank, about 3' x 2' x 8'. The downspout on that side of the house came into the room above the tank and filled it when it rained. The tank never overflowed because another section of downspout just below the top rim ran back outside and continued down to the lawn below.

The tank filled fast in any rain. There was a ¾-inch pipe welded to the bottom of the tank that led through pipes in the wall to a valve in the basement marked "gravity feed." When we turned that on, it fed the rainwater into the regular system that led to everything but the drinking water faucet in the kitchen sink. That was permanently connected to the well.

Is There a Downside to Collecting Rainwater?

It is important to remember to cover the water between rains, so that mosquitoes will not use it for a nursery. Darkness is usually enough of a control, so you don't have to worry about a mosquito-tight cover. Remember to open the cover before the next rain to refill the supply. There are some mosquito repellents that can float on such water to kill larvae (see Chapter 13). It was surprising how dry many parts of the garden got between summer rains, so the water saved was well used.

A roof should not be painted with a lead-based paint or be rusty or otherwise corroded. Ideally, one could have a T-junction to determine whether the water would go to the storage container or onto the ground. Or just let the first rainfall wash the roof and eaves before opening the storage to collect it. As a rule, if rainwater isn't killing the vegetation where the spout has been emptying, it won't do any damage if stored and used in less concentrated amounts throughout the yard.

A filter on the downspouts will keep out leaves and other debris that could make the water sour should it sit too long.

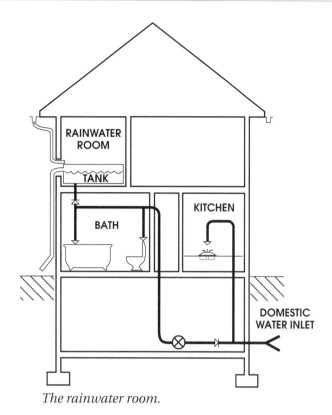

The rainwater room.

We had an underground cistern as well, and it got the water from the other side of the house. But that took a pump and electricity to go into the system, so we always used the free, gravity-feed water first.

There were some minor drawbacks. There was not much pressure and it took forever to fill the washing machine. Also the water supply only lasted for about two dry days.

There was one major drawback. We figured the tank held about 360 gallons and weighed about 3000 pounds when full. It sat above the bathtub and the floor began to sink. We envisioned a more powerful shower than anyone wanted and eventually sealed it off. But that was before we appreciated the water crisis.

Such tanks were not uncommon a few decades ago. When I was in college in Pennsylvania, we once had a snow and ice storm that shut off electricity for a full week. For the first several days we existed on water from a tank in the attic that was meant for fire protection.

My rainwater room was one of fourteen home-built systems for saving and using rainwater and greywater featured in a fascinating book by Murray Milne called *Residential Water Re-Use* and published by California Water Resources Center, University of California/Davis, in September of 1979. Other systems included one which used an old water bed for a storage tank in the crawl space under a house, one with a garbage can on a heavy-duty dolly that then transported the water to the garden, another that used a stock tank outdoors, and another with a cistern under the patio. A septic tank may also be adapted for water collection if a house hooks up to the sewer and no longer needs it.

At that time, there were already at least seven systems on the market for sale as complete package units; more have been developed since.

It is time to open our minds to water reuse and to do so in any way we can. Methods may vary from catching rainwater in a bucket to installing an intricate saving system in the building of a new home. The costs of such building-in or even retrofitting will be absorbed in savings on water, energy, and sewer bills, in more beautiful and productive landscapes with less water wasted, and ultimately in lower taxes or at least in fewer tax increases, as a result of reductions in city water and sewer problems.

Greywater Use in the Garden

Greywater — water used in shower, tub or washing machine — is not a popular subject. But I have been fascinated by it since the first time we had land of our own in Ohio. We had a well and I was terrified for the first several years that it would go dry. It never did, and I gained confidence in it over the years, but in the meantime I learned to use greywater on my garden in the simplest way.

I already had tubs beside my washing machine to catch the sudsy water and reuse it at least once. When the first summer drought hit the garden, I brought a hose into the kitchen and attached it to the tub holding the rinse water. This the hose carried out through the screen door and onto the garden. Since our kitchen was up about three steps above the yard, gravity gave us a nice, slow flow, and I moved the watering end of the hose from bed to bed as

∽ Greywater Guidelines ∽

Seedlings are more sensitive, so use it on mature plants.

Use greywater sparingly on container plants and alternate with plenty of fresh water, since their roots are in a restricted soil zone.

Soap makes greywater alkaline, so avoid using it on acid-loving plants. Check soil pH more often and use sulfur (3 to 5 pounds per 100 feet) and plenty of organic matter to lower the pH.

Use greywater over a large area and dilute it with rainwater to avoid buildup of salts. The more water you conserve indoors, the more concentrated greywater pollutants tend to be.

Apply greywater directly to the root zone. Never use it to sprinkle or spray. Don't use it where it will puddle, or on play areas where children will be rolling around on the ground.

Use the mildest and most biodegradable soaps and cleaning products possible. Avoid using products with boron, as it can become toxic to plants if allowed to build up. Liquid detergent is often lower in sodium than powder.

Sodium can make clay soil sticky, hindering drainage. If this happens, dig agricultural gypsum into the top several inches of soil; use 5 to 10 lb. per 100 square feet.

Grasses are the most tolerant of water impurities as well as the thirstiest plants, so greywater works well for lawn irrigation. Ornamental trees and shrubs would be next in line, then most fruit trees (other than citrus, peaches and apricots).

When rains are insufficient to dilute the greywater and leach away harmful substances; alternate irrigations between greywater and fresh water. Twice a year, say in February and May, flush the soil with a heavy sprinkler irrigation of fresh water.

Though cantaloupe, broccoli and tomato are quite tolerant of greywater, avoid using it on vegetables you plan to eat raw.

Fruit crops, especially peaches and apricots, are sensitive to greywater, as are beans. Use less greywater or none at all on these. Flush beds of root crops with fresh water on a regular, rotating basis.

Desert and seashore plants, as well as many other Florida plants are charted for their salt tolerance, which also applies to the salts in greywater.

Use greywater in drip or trickle irrigation systems only after filtering it through layers of sand and gravel or through an air conditioning filter.

When hand watering, tie a cloth bag over the watering end of the hose to catch any sediment that could cause scum on the soil. Change and clean bags weekly.

Tap tub and shower first, washing machine second and only if not washing diapers or sickroom linens. Dishwashers and the kitchen sink are less desirable, for their water may contain grease and meat scraps or other harmful ingredients.

Short term storage of greywater is good; it lets rinse water mix with suds, lets hot water cool, and lets fresh or rainwater dilute greywater. But do not store it for more than one day, or odors may develop.

needed. It wasn't a very convenient solution, especially since I often forgot to switch the hose from the washing machine at the right time and mopped up many a flood. Eventually Spouse said he couldn't afford for me to save any more water at the cost of ruined floors. But my theory was sound.

My conviction that greywater is good for the garden has grown over the years. Backed now by research, here are some reasons why:

- Greywater is plenty good enough for flushing toilets and for much outdoor irrigation. Even a partial reuse system can result in a 25% reduction of water consumption and a 52% reduction of sewer system needs. Septic tanks automatically leach extra "black water" into the landscape and water deep-rooted plants.

- Residential on-site water reuse systems are already available, are economically feasible, and are environmentally sound.

- Health officials consulted know of no documented cases of illness from using greywater. The dangers are far less than we will soon encounter if we continue to waste and pollute our fresh water systems.

- Greywater carries almost no harmful organisms.

- Rainwater is only available after a rain, when we need it the least. Greywater is available all the time, and we are able to use it year round, thanks to our mild Florida climate.

- An average household produces 40 gallons of greywater per person per day. Used on only 1000 square feet of landscape, it would be equivalent to 58 inches of rainfall a year, enough to change your yard or a section of your yard from a dry climate garden to almost a rainforest. Research done in California showed 20 gallons of water a day will support 100 square feet of intensively grown vegetables.

- Not only could we grow more plants with greywater, but many of them would grow better with fewer problems because of the nutrients in the water. Grandma's prize roses often grew best where she threw out her dishwater.

- Over time, we have discarded some methods of water reuse and adopted others. Once, sudsaver washers were in common use. But they've become obsolete, mostly because few households have the necessary tubs. When we were kids, the local swimming pool was drained every Wednesday and refilled with the runoff from the ice factory next door. And that pool was freezing until at least Sunday. City kids went every day nevertheless. Farm kids went on Sunday. When I was in college, that institution could have afforded the pool, but not the water, so we rented use of one at a nearby camp for certain hours in the summer. The filter systems in use today clean and recycle pool water, greatly reducing waste.

I am not going into the technicalities of greywater systems in this book, but I urge you to tuck the idea into your mind. The day will come when you will use it. If I were building a house, I would talk to as many plumbers as necessary to get a sensible greywater saving system built in. This could require conformance with building codes. To check with your county health department, look for Environmental Health Services or Health Services under county listings in your phone book.

Sources:
Milne, Murray, *Residential Water Re-Use*, California Water Resources Center, University of California/Davis, Report #46. September 1979.

Milne, Murray, *Residential Water Conservation*, California Water Resources Center, 1977.

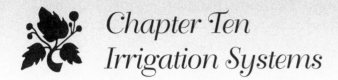

Chapter Ten
Irrigation Systems

This chapter deals with various methods of watering your landscape, from hose dragging to fully automatic systems. Hose dragging is not all bad. Many gardeners report that this is the time when they make the most important observations about their gardens, notice new buds and new bugs that they might not see otherwise. Hand watering also allows you to water some plants in a bed and not others, to sprinkle seed beds lightly until germination, or water deeply a newly planted tree or shrub.

Armando Mendez, who has fruit trees and shrubs growing in containers between and around most of his in-ground plantings, says that the need to water the containers every other day keeps him on the ball and forces him to water other plants as needed.

But sooner or later, most of us will want to move on to some other equipment. Going away on a trip or some indoor emergency may otherwise result in neglect of watering. Or we find we are just more likely to water, the easier it is to do. And drip and soaker hose irrigation take less water and allow less to evaporate than applications with a hose. So most of us eventually aim for some of each.

Dr. Celso Gomez-Sanchez has drip irrigation to many of his trees and shrubs. In his nursery bed his young plants are automatically watered with a water computer — available for about $30 from a builder's supply store — set to water for 10 minutes every morning when water use is most efficient. His also comes on for a one-minute misting three other times during the day, thus making propagation by cutting and grafting much more successful. These two measures allow the doctor to grow abundant fruit and have a beautiful, edible landscape while sometimes being away or busy elsewhere for as much as two weeks at a time.

Joe and Betty DaPonte have a half-acre yard from which they ship a ton of fruit to their children in New England every year. In 1994 they had well over 100 pineapples ripening at once. Joe had installed a sprinkler system, but later reverted to hand watering. In dry times, he waters every other day, for one hour at 5 a.m. and again at 8 p.m. "That way I can put the water exactly where I want it," he says. His water bill? Between $22 and $27 per month.

Do You Need Irrigation?

Certainly plants need water and some form of watering is necessary, especially during the dry months in Florida. True, we have more rainfall during every summer than some western states average in four years. But having most of our average 46 to 62 inches come in just three months makes watering necessary for oasis and occasionally for drought resistant areas the rest of the year.

It is possible to get along with hoses and sprinklers if your yard and/or your oasis zone are small. I have five or six hoses myself hooked up to three different outlets and with these can reach the entire yard. One Christmas my Florida sons Mike and Tom gave me three new hoses, six sprinklers, and three Y-connectors with shut-off valves so I can attach one hose with sprinkler and one drag-around hose to each faucet. It is a crude system and does waste some water, but it works for me for now. My drip system worked better while it worked, but it was disconnected in an early replanting and has been neglected for too long. The fact is, if I had to drag the hose from faucet to faucet each time to water, the watering would seldom get done when it should.

Wells vs. Municipal Water Supplies

Many people find it worthwhile to have their own well, either for irrigation alone or for total water use. This allows you to avoid the chlorine and chemicals used in city water, but you will still have soluble minerals from whatever rock the water comes through, most of which are beneficial to the plants. The great advantage of a well is that the water you use on the yard percolates back through the ground to the aquifer and returns in purified form again and again. The disadvantage is the cost of the drilling and maintenance of the pump.

Whether you need a shallow or deep well depends upon where you live. In coastal Florida a well may not be an option at all, because of high salt content in groundwater. If you can get by with a shallow well in your area you will save money, but you run a greater risk of the well going dry in times of drought. Water from shallow wells is suitable for irrigation, but not for household use. Consult irrigation contractors in your area for advice. You should also ask your city or county building department whether a permit is required and if so, its cost.

In much of Florida, a deep well — 50 to 200 feet — is a necessity. The current price is around $8.50 a foot for the drilling, casing, and drive shoe. The pump is a separate cost of $900 to $1000, so a deep well will cost between $2000 and $2600. If you go this route, you may also want a tank for other outside water uses like car washing, shower near the pool, etc.

Bob Baker, who grows some thirty different varieties of bananas in his yard, has a 300-foot-deep well and gets excellent quality water for both home and garden use. A neighbor only two doors away from him has a well that produces water high in sulfur content — fine for irrigation, but not exactly tasty for drinking. Baker recommends using galvanized casing rather than PVC, on the outside chance of a lightning strike that would damage the latter. Both cost the same, he says.

A shallow well will cost much less than a deep one, for two reasons. First, less pipe and labor are required to reach water. Second, a smaller pump can be used, since the water does not have to travel as far against the force of gravity. In most places a shallow well can be installed for $700 to $1000. The cost varies depending on how many well points are needed, how deep the well is, and how large a pump you select.

Moving Into the New Technology

Some people make the transition from hose to automatic watering all at once when they purchase a property with an irrigation system in place. This can be either an advantage, a disadvantage, or some of each. My friend Betty Mackey bought a Florida home with sprinklers in the front yard for

Sprinklers Don't Waste Water . . .
An enormous amount of water is wasted in Florida through automatic irrigation systems overwatering lawns, streets, driveways, rain-soaked soil and drought tolerant plantings. Leaks develop and go undetected. Spray patterns go wrong. Many of these operate in the dark of early morning when only the paperboy is apt to notice problems. Yet it is not the system that is at fault. It is the people behind it.

the lawn but nothing in the back where she wanted gardens. "I'd have done it just the opposite if I'd had the chance," she said.

So if you inherit an irrigation system, you may want to change it, especially if it results in wasting water. In any case you will need to learn how it works so you can keep it in repair.

Facts to Consider

For those of us who take more deliberate steps from hose-dragging to the help of our wonderful, water saving, modern-day irrigation technology, there are some points to ponder. Most people don't consider options other than sprinklers for their yards. But drip or low-flow irrigation, including microsprinklers and bubblers, has many advantages for the rest of your watering needs. These include:

- Up to 30% less water lost from runoff and evaporation
- About 45% less water needed to deeply water trees and shrubs
- Low cost, possibly less than those hoses and sprinklers, and easy assembly (even I can do it) and maintenance
- The ability to water various shapes, levels and kinds of gardens without erosion
- Less possibility of fungal disease from too much moisture on foliage
- Less time needed to water, less timing required as it can be done anytime, day or night, or while you are working in the garden
- More efficient use of irrigation water, a savings of as much as 70% as compared to sprinkler or hand/hose watering
- Having the option to put plants with different watering needs in close proximity to one another, while still giving each only what it needs
- Ability to use collected water with gravity feed systems or systems with low water intensity
- Water going only where needed, not on paths or hardscapes, so you have fewer weeds
- The ability to replace the water the plant uses every day prevents the stress to plants that is inevitable with the drought and drown cycle of even the most efficient hose or sprinkler system
- Ease of adding a fertilizer injector to both feed and water plants effectively
- Can also be used for container or hanging planters
- Avoids uneven coverage that can result when foliage or wind block or change sprinkler patterns
- Components can be buried under soil or mulch or left on top of the soil for pulling out of the way during cultivation or replanting

You can install a complete drip irrigation system to cover the oasis zones of an average-sized lot for $300 to $400 if you don't use a timer. Best of all, you can start small and add on as your needs, finances, and installation time and skills increase.

While it is only fair to mention a few disadvantages as well, these problems are not difficult to work around and it's well worth the effort:

- A permit, inspection, and/or backflow device may be required. The backflow device ensures that contaminated water, e.g. from puddles in the garden, does not reenter the tubing and get back into the in-house system. The need for this device is more clearly seen, but not limited to, cases where fertilizer is injected into the line.
- Drip systems require clean water, or the tiny holes will clog. Use filter systems where necessary. Phosphate fertilizers reacting with calcium in the water, or even rust in the water, can clog lines. Self-flushing emitters will eliminate most of the problems.

- Some soils may puddle. Drip works best in sandy soils, of which Florida abounds. But in can work even in heavy clay soils if enough organic matter is added. If puddling occurs, turn the water off for an hour or more and then resume watering.

- Irrigation must be frequent, every other day during peak growing seasons.

- A drip system may cost more initially than a single sprinkler in the middle of the bean patch. They also take more planning before making the investment.

- The tubing can be delicate and must be treated with care, especially when changing crops, as in vegetable or annual gardens. A trowel or hoe can break, chop, or disconnect tubing. For this reason you may want to invest in the more durable kinds.

- Animals like raccoons, dogs, and armadillos can cause holes in passing or digging or may even chew through lines to get a drink.

It's Easy to Start with a Kit

My first drip irrigation system came from two basic kits that cost about $20 each and provided everything needed to water a garden 10 by 25 feet. Most of the tubing looked like paper, but it worked, and it is supposed to last up to ten years if it is protected from the sun.

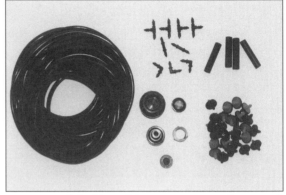

A starter drip kit: tubing, connectors, hose-end clamps, pressure regulator and filter, swivel adapter, reducing washer, and emitters.

Articles and ads about drip irrigation had been running around the outside edges of my vision for several years but I managed to ignore them. There was still something in me that said rain should fall on a garden and when it doesn't you just don't have such good production. I knew that was ridiculous and unnecessary. Why live with failure when you can have success? Still, it was not easy to overcome ingrained ideas. Our trip to California and our plum tree success (see Chapter 8), plus gardening in a new soil and climate sharpened my awareness of the fleeting nature of water in sand.

Then I read the excellent book *Complete Guide to Gardening* from Better Homes and Gardens on an assignment to help update it. I found that I was the one in need of updating, especially about drip and trickle irrigation and how it makes a little water do a large job.

What seemed even less likely at that time was the fact that anyone can put the system together in custom measurements for each garden. At least I let the advertising in a nursery catalog convince me of that. I ordered two kits and they arrived within the week. Once I saw them I was less convinced and decided to wait until Spouse had time to help me.

When I got tired of waiting and decided to try it myself, I found it was really not difficult even for someone absolutely unhandy. It took me about an hour to figure it all out, then perhaps half an hour more to put it all together and into position in my garden. It was a great moment when I turned the water on, just a quarter turn or less, and watched the white tubing swell and then begin to ooze out little drops. Recommended watering times vary from 45 minutes to several hours and the best way to decide for each situation is to dig around and see just how wide and deep the water is reaching in your soil (see Chapter 8). But I'd swear the beans perked up within two days.

The possibility for getting difficult seeds like carrots or petunias to sprout was certainly a relief. Seeds are cheap, but I expect I soon saved enough on seeds alone to pay for the system. The possibilities for maximum production are even better.

You can leave the tubing exposed for the first week or so until you are sure you have it in the right place. I moved it around some. Then I picked up a bag of grass clippings and leaves and lightly covered the tubing, even in the middle of just sprouting wide rows of peas and beans. No problem. An easy job. A fascinating, useful toy for anyone with anything to grow. I recommend it.

Irrigation Systems Can Be Easy to Assemble

The most important lesson of my first irrigation system was that even a klutzy person can put something simple together to make watering easier. And once you realize this, you open your eyes to what other people are doing and open your mind to the possibilities, and soon your garden is soaking up just the water it needs and producing better and better as you learn more.

This opening of the mind is not an easy or a one-step process for me. Little things set me back. That first layout required change as my trees grew, shade patterns forced me to move my beds, and crops varied with the time of the year. You have to hoe very carefully around such a system and it doesn't pay to forget what is buried where.

So for a time I went to a series of soaker hoses. These work almost as well, if a person connects them as needed. That last can be a serious problem, as it proved for me.

My visit to Tom Carey's Sundew Gardens in Oviedo showed me something else that has been around for a while but was new to me: instant hose connectors that allow you to click the hose onto another hose or irrigation system without all that twisting and leaking.

Are you getting the idea? Now go to your stack of nursery catalogs, open to the index, and check out the page under watering devices or irrigation. Most garden catalogs have some pages of irrigation equipment. I especially recommend and suggest you send for and study the material from Mellinger's, The Urban Farmer Store, Raindrip Inc., and Rain Bird. Their addresses are given in Appendix B.

You can now find a great deal of irrigation equipment locally, more and more so all the time here in Florida where irrigation systems are considered essential by many people. Look in your phone book under Irrigation or Sprinklers for special places. Or check what is in both the plumbing and the garden section the next time you are in a builder's supply store. You'll be amazed at the easy-to-install, inexpensive, effective equipment available. There will probably be a free brochure showing a complete line of irrigation equipment and sometimes giving helpful charts. Take one of these with you and study it carefully when you have time.

You may also feel like I did the day we bought our first computer — completely overwhelmed. But we managed to learn how to use that, with a little help, and drip systems are

---

∽ Make Your Own Soaker Hose ∽

Tom Carey also made some soaker or trickle hoses himself, by making small holes every 12 inches along a piece of hose. In some cases he also cut cap-like pieces from another hose and put them over these holes to direct the water into the ground instead of into the air. Any leaky hose can be recycled into a soaker. If the plug comes out of the end and gets lost, just fold the end over for a few inches and tape or wire it closed.

not nearly as complicated or as expensive. Start small if you want. Try out various kinds of emitters, fittings, tubing, and filters. Soon you will feel comfortable with the whole idea.

If you can stay with one brand name or supplier, you can be sure that the parts will all fit together. So far one of the problems is that not all drip irrigation fittings are standardized.

Planning is Important

It is even more important to have a paper plan for an irrigation system than it is for design. I did this in my head when I laid out my first kit because I planned to go only as far as the kits permitted. Using a kit will give you enough hands-on experience to make good decisions about expansion from there. Just like measuring a room to decide how much wallpaper to buy, you must measure your planting to decide how many feet of which type of tubing, how many of the various kinds of emitters, etc. you will need.

If you have your landscape plan already drawn and your oasis plants grouped in their zone, that will be the place to start. You may want to do a larger drawing of this section only.

You now need more detail: which plants are now in place or soon will be, which vegetable beds can be watered with paper tubing and which trees or shrubs will need microsprinklers. Sketch your desired system in place, then connect it, on paper, to the water source and check to be sure your system will use no more than 75% of the outside tap capacity. This is a safety measure so pressure fluctuations won't cause problems. You don't want an irrigation system that works only when no one indoors is taking a shower or vice versa.

You Can Hire It Done

If you don't want to bother with installing or even planning an irrigation system yourself, you can call in professionals. There are many to choose from here in Florida, so you need some knowledge. All that you have learned in this book about saving water will be a big first step. You want to find a contractor who is equally knowledgeable and committed to water conservation. The fact that he advertises drip irrigation as well as sprinklers is a good sign. Some installers will help you plan your system, sell you the equipment and let you install it yourself. Most advertise free estimates.

When you call, do not hesitate to ask:
— for references,
— how much they know about Xeriscaping,
— how long they have been in business,
— if they are insured against damage to your property, and
— if they will service your system after installation.

So far, people in the irrigation business are required only to take the basic test for contractor proficiency. Special licensing and certification is not yet required.

When You Hire a Professional

- Be sure to get a printed plan of your system. That way you will know where all the lines, zones, sprinkler heads, and valves are located for maintenance and protection during other construction. Also, if your original contractor should pass on, another could take over.

- Be sure that there is a rain detector. This is now required by law as well as common sense and is not much more expensive. There are also detectors that can sense high winds or low temperatures.

- Be sure that there are at least three separate watering zones. Some people want five to serve the needs of individual plant groups.

- Be sure all the valves are accessible. Have them enclose each valve in a box with the lid at ground level.

- Be sure to have a backflow valve. This is required in many places, and is very important if you are planning to use any fertilizer injections. It will keep water from the system from siphoning back into your indoor water supply.

- Plastic or brass are both fine for sprinkler heads, but the nozzles should be of brass. They will cost more but last longer, maintain a set spray arc more accurately, and provide more even coverage.

- For the automatic controller, gear-driven controls that look like a revolving clock can wear out and slow down, thus throwing off the timing. Solid-state controls have no moving parts and work better longer.

- Prices vary with the complexity of each system, but average between $2000 and $3000 to set up and install irrigation for 5,000 square feet. Obviously, grouping or limiting the thirsty plants into a smaller area will save first on installation costs, then on maintenance and water use.

Converting a Sprinkler System to Drip

It is possible, inexpensive, and not too complicated to convert parts of a sprinkler system to drip irrigation as you let other plantings replace excess turf. There are kits for this, too. Just be sure to install a regulator and filter. Put it at the main water valve if you have more than one line. If you have only one, the regulator and filter can go either at the main valve or the sprinkler riser that feeds that line. Drip lines can extend up to 100 feet from this riser.

A pressure regulator may be optional with a completely drip system. If you don't have one, be sure to explain the system to your children or your roommates so they won't go out and turn on the tap full force to wash their car without disconnecting the hose from the drip system. Should this happen, they could blow all the emitters out.

With a combination sprinkler and drip system, the regulator is necessary, for much more pressure must go to the sprinklers than into the drip lines.

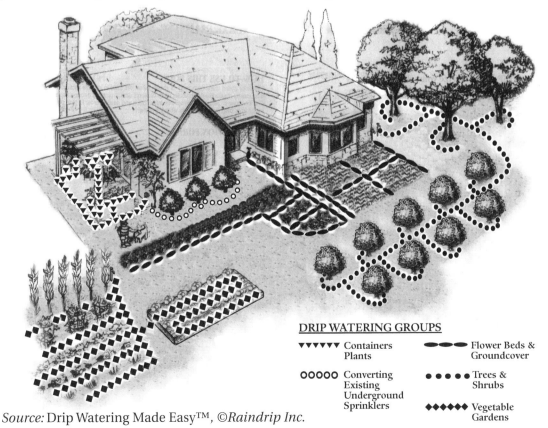

DRIP WATERING GROUPS

▼▼▼▼▼▼ Containers Plants

OOOOO Converting Existing Underground Sprinklers

●●●● Flower Beds & Groundcover

●●●●● Trees & Shrubs

◆◆◆◆◆ Vegetable Gardens

Source: Drip Watering Made Easy™, *©Raindrip Inc.*

Questions About Drip Irrigation

What about all those dry areas between lines or emitters? Soaker hoses are easy enough to understand. Laser soaker tubing has laser-drilled holes every nine inches along its length and is ideal for closely-spaced plants. But what about the plants between the lines of tubing? This seemed a problem to me. If I can't see the soil getting wet, how do I know that it is?

There are three ways: 1) Follow the directions and assume the experts know what they are talking about; 2) Watch and see if all the plants are thriving. If they are, assume all roots are getting enough water. 3) Dig down and check at a few places as described in Chapter 8.

How close do the lines or emitters need to be to cover an entire area? I like to garden in swathes rather than in single plant rows. No one seems to know how far the water spreads laterally for sure. It depends upon the soil structure, of course. Some estimate that water will spread about 18 inches in sandy soil. If you will feel better, use microsprinklers so you can see what is happening. Or let your tubing go all around the tree so you are sure that the roots will develop on all sides.

Setting the Timer

As convenient as a timer can be, it puts upon the homeowner the responsibility to use it wisely. Setting it and forgetting it is a prime way to waste gallons of water, money, and plants as well, for overwatering is as hard on them as underwatering. If you read Chapter 8, you now have a sound idea of what plants need, when and why, and how the Florida climate puts much of this burden upon you.

It is now the law that all automatic irrigation systems *must* be fitted with a rain sensor device or switch which will override the irrigation cycle of the sprinkler system when adequate rainfall has occurred. If your system predates that law or your rain sensor stops working, either buy and install a new one or call an irrigation professional. He can retrofit yours at a reasonable cost.

There are also sensors that will shut off the system in heavy winds when the wetting pattern would be too spotty to be of use. The best sensors are those that react to soil moisture. They are slightly more expensive, but not excessively so, considering what they can save in water, plants, and decision-making frustrations. You may need more than one to serve the different microclimates and zones of your landscape.

Ideally, you should be aware of all weather conditions and plan to reset your timer at least every month and sometimes more often. Even in the heat of summer, cloudy skies can reduce water use by half compared to clear days. We seldom have more than one cloudy day at a time in Florida, but on rare occasiosn it does happen. At such times, adjust your system accordingly.

Watering Guidelines for Drip Systems*

Weather	Duration & Frequency of Watering	Vegetables & Flowers	Vines & Shrubs 2'–3'	Shrubs & Trees 4'–5'	Shrubs & Trees 5'–10'	Trees 10'–20'	Container Plants
Cool	Time (hrs.)	2	2	4	6	6	10 min.
Cool	Days/week	1–2	1–2	1–2	1–2	1–2	1–2
Warm	Time (hrs.)	3	3	5	7	8	20 min.
Warm	Days/week	2	2	2	2	2	2
Hot	Time (hrs.)	4	4	6	8	10	30 min.
Hot	Days/week	3	3	3	3	3	3

*Source: *Drip Watering Made Easy*™, ©Raindrip Inc.

I joke that the temperature changes in Florida are so subtle that the weatherman could record his message and repeat it for weeks at a time. But you will find that the short days of winter use less water, even when warm, than the long days of spring. You will need much less water in December, a great deal of water in May.

Maintaining the System

The best planned, most expensive irrigation system in the world can soon become worthless without routine maintenance.

In Any Household: It is important to practice monthly checkups on any water system and do any needed repair at this time. Keep washers on hand to replace them as needed on hoses and faucets. Expect to replace outdoor faucets perhaps every ten years or less. Hoses will last longer if rolled up out of the sun and brought in before any freeze. I personally prefer to have the hose handy and absorb the cost. If a single leak develops, duct or electrician's tape will seal it. If many develop, turn the hose into a soaker (see page 87). Even I can replace worn couplings with inexpensive repair parts from the discount store. The old adage of a leak adding up to a river of waste still holds. If you get a water bill that is higher than usual for that particular month, check for leaks. Don't just read the cost on your water bill. Read the gallons used and keep track. Use the water meter test (see page 129), call in a plumber or an irrigation specialist with a leak detector.

Drip Irrigation Maintenance: Three or four times a year, perhaps at the change of seasons in September, February, and June, remove the end closures and flush each circuit until the water runs clear. There are several products that will help break up all sources of emitter clogging (Royal Flush™, Eject™). These are used by nurseries and citrus growers, optional for homeowners.

Clean the filter and check for leaks. Replace any damaged tubing by cutting out that section and using a compression coupling or barbed connector. Raise up and set aside any soft tubing during cultivation or replanting of beds.

During winter, even in northern Florida where freezes are frequent, you can still leave the system in place. But remove end closures to allow excess water in the tubing to drain before any freeze.

Filters in any system: These can be system savers, but only if they are cleaned at regular intervals and replaced as needed. Unscrew the cover and remove the strainer for weekly cleaning. Elements should last about one year. Strainers may last for three. If the system clogs up in spite of cleaning, replace the screen with one of smaller mesh.

Sprinkler system maintenance: Adjust at installation for alignment and move accordingly so only plants get watered, not paved areas, fences, or structures. Impact sprinklers have moveable clips that can restrict the degree of rotation. Some also allow adjustment of the length of the water stream. For gear sprinklers, you may need to call in an irrigation specialist to make the adjustments.

Turn on each zone separately and check for proper pop-up and reseating and spray throw. Trim grass often and carefully around each head or remove any obstruction. If the spray is too misty (easily windblown), reduce water pressure. If the spray throw is too short, increase it.

Adjustment is Crucial

The average homeowner never touches the controls of his automatic sprinkler system. Lawn grasses are among the few plants that are hard to kill with overwatering, so lawns that get twice the amount of water they need often manage not to show the stress.

If you adjust the controls of your system only twice a year, you can cut water use (from the waste, not from what is needed) by 40 to 45 percent.

If you adjust it eight times a year, monthly except in the summer, you can cut that water use (still from the waste) by up to 75 percent.

To repair broken or damaged parts in PVC pipe, first remove the soil around the malfunction to get to the break. Then cut the pipe clean with a hacksaw and replace the damaged section by gluing on a fitting of the appropriate size and screwing the head into the fitting. Clean out clogged heads or replace if needed.

Also, if your sprinkler heads are at tripping height and you are expecting company who will be wandering around the yard without you, it is a good idea to turn a brightly colored pot over each one as a warning.

Putting All These Ideas to Work:
Bill Adrian's Irrigation Set-Up

The fame of Bill Adrian's water system brought me to his door. And before I saw the process, I was surrounded by the beauty of the product: blooming hibiscus and birds-of-paradise, including a rare white-and-blue one, Dutchman's pipes vining with the rich, dark blue of butterfly peas on the porch, avocados and citrus hanging heavy from the trees that frame and shade his house.

Around the back corner, where the downspout comes off the roof, Adrian has erected a platform about 54" tall. On this sit four 50-gallon barrels. They once came from a pickle factory and cost $5 each.

The downspout drops the water perhaps a foot into one of the barrels. But underneath they are all connected with $1^1/4$"

Gravity moves rainwater to Bill Adrian's plants, thanks to the high platform on which these collection barrels sit.

PVC pipe, so the water rises in all barrels at the same level. A fifth barrel is stationed on the ground in case of overflow, so in a normal summer rain, he collects 250 gallons of rainwater. There are cutoff valves to control the flow from the barrels to the garden.

"One problem with collecting rainwater is that the plants don't need it for a few days after a good rain," says Adrian. "But even in the summer, neither rainfall nor collected water is always enough for overall growth in my yard."

So another of the barrels is connected by pipeline to the well. When rainwater is not enough, Adrian turns on that faucet and the well pump fills all barrels in ten minutes' time. Then the electric power stops. But hoses connect the barrels to a drip irrigation system, most of which is shallowly buried. The barrels empty very slowly over the next hour, directly to the

root zone of the plants. Three lines lead into raised beds in the back yard and have cutoff valves to adjust the amounts. Another line leads to in-ground beds on that side of the house.

Adrian designed, constructed, and connected the entire system himself. He is a retired electronics technician and in spite of being legally blind, is amazingly more capable of such work than the average homeowner. But as he explains about using a hole saw to connect the pipes and eventually paper tubing to distribute the water through the beds, one realizes that such systems need not be difficult.

PVC pipe links the collection barrels to drip system water inlets. Manual valves allow selection of zone to be watered.

Chapter Eleven
Maintenance Makes a Difference

E ven if you haven't yet implemented any of the material you've read so far into your garden, you have programmed your mind, planted the seed for common sense Xeriscaping. You have made, or will soon make, much maintenance obsolete. If your landscape is largely of natural zone plants, it will require very minimum upkeep. The time saved is time to use for what you enjoy, and those of us who consider gardening time our play time may well call it living happily ever after.

The Garden Walk

One of the best things you can do for your garden is also one of the most enjoyable: the garden walk. It is my daily treat and often involves absolutely no work at all. I just mosey around and look over everything.

Important fact: *The more water a landscape uses, the more maintenance it will require.*

I celebrate when I find a bud pouch on an orchid plant that summers on the branch of a young oak tree. I stand under the carambola and search among the flowers, counting the first tiny, long-awaited fruits. I check to see if the last seeds I planted, sugar pod peas and mustard greens and radishes above carrots, are peeping through the soil and note how much they've grown since the day before.

I also notice, whether I want to or not, what needs watering and if the gardenia has yellowing leaves that cry out for some acid fertilizer or the bean leaves are too pale a green and need more nitrogen. I note that a sprinkler head is not working correctly or a part of the drip system has sprung a leak. I unconsciously check for insect or disease damage and often catch a hornworm or a webworm colony in the earliest stages when I can quickly pick and squash it, preventing a full-scale infestation.

I finally found a little clipper that fits easily in my pocket, and as I walk, I often use it to do some minor pruning, to cut off deadheads, or to pick a few flowers for a bouquet or a few stems of something to make cuttings.

The Garden Notebook

Another excellent practice to make any homeowner an expert gardener is keeping a notebook. Even a few scribblings on a calendar will serve to remind you when you planted what. I have not yet developed this habit well and have often regretted that I let information slip away. I am always sure I'll remember what varieties I planted, and when. I make notes on seed packets, but these often get lost. Now and then I interview a gardener like Samm Philmore (see Chapter 12) who brings out a notebook and refers back to accurate information and I am filled with admiration.

There are several fine books on the market just for this purpose. Get one of these, or just a simple spiral notebook. But make yourself use it. And like a diet, if you miss a few days, don't quit. Pick it up again. Whatever you write down will help later. Use a pocket notebook if that

Samm Philmore's garden notebook helps him remember which plants and techniques succeeded for him — and which didn't.

will work for you. Make a computer file if that is your style. I find that I am much more apt to write anything on the computer where I can so easily erase, revise, append, save, and not misplace it.

There is nothing worse — and I've done it more than once — than having a wonderful crop of beans or coreopsis and then realizing that you aren't even sure what variety you planted. How can you repeat success that way? And when you do have a failure, you need to know what you did and what you planted so you can avoid making the same mistake again.

A garden notebook will help you to save water because you can use it to record when you last watered what. This is especially important with citrus and other trees that need a good soaking only every two weeks; you need to know when the two weeks are up.

A garden notebook will help you to use less fertilizer, especially in Florida where feeding is an ongoing chore. Overfeeding can lead to extra growth, extra pruning, extra work, and *extra water.* Who needs it? Don't do it. Underfeeding can lead to poor growth, few or no blooms, excessive fruit drop, and poor production. We don't want to do that either. The only sure way to avoid one or the other is to know when you fed last.

A garden notebook will save you other trouble. Over- or under- watering or feeding lead to stress, which is the "open sesame" to insects and diseases. A thriving garden doesn't appeal to the smaller pests. (It will still draw raccoons to eat the corn and squirrels to eat the nuts, though!)

A garden notebook will tell you where your original landscape plan needs a bit of revision, and between your walk and your perusal of your notebook, you may find you have many improvements taking form in your mind.

If you can't make yourself do a bang-up job on notebook entries, do whatever you can. I have lately leaned toward a list of garden chores. Rather than depress me, this guides me in my priorities later in the day. Whenever I get a few minutes, I can duck out and accomplish something meaningful — like planting a row of beans, picking a bunch of bananas, or pruning and training the grapevines over the arbor. I can also select long-time chores, short-time chores, clean clothes chores, or dirty clothes chores from such a list.

Weeding

Once I thought this might be my number one garden problem, but over the decades weeds have dwindled to nuisance status. There are always some pestering, but they no longer take over my garden as they did every August when I was a child. Nor do they even surround it with a tall curtain as they did on the Iowa farm. I didn't mind that too much, but it made Spouse feel guilty and he was glad when we moved to town. After that, he could mow what I did not pull, sit on the porch and enjoy, and feel more in control.

By now, weeding is part of my life like breathing or laundry — no big deal but definitely necessary. Mulching and watering only when and where needed have reduced the problem even more in my Florida landscape. I also find that Florida weeds are invasive in a different manner from weeds elsewhere. The grasses are the worst offenders, but instead of creeping underground, many Florida "weed grasses" crawl over the top of the soil. At the end of every summer I have a few areas that I almost roll up with a hoe, cutting away the roots as I roll. Using more cover crops in my empty spaces would eliminate much of this problem.

Mulch kills unwanted plants (even turf — see Chapter 7 on mulching instead of tilling) by smothering them, cutting off their air and light.

Make Weeding Easier and Waste Less Water

Whether help comes from your family, your friends, or someone you've hired, gardening in general and weeding in particular are more fun, and more likely to be done right if you work together.

Think of weeding as great group exercise — kneeling, lifting, stretching, pulling. It also helps the environment when you carefully remove weeds by hand, then prevent them from returning by mulching. This also cuts water needs and stress to desirable plants and insures success for your landscape.

Weeds in the Lawn

Weeds can move in and take over any home lawn, especially if insects or diseases kill off part of the grass, as often happens with St. Augustine. Fortunately, the weeds are easy to pull out by hand or by hoe, and nearly any child can handle the task if an adult demonstrates how to do it correctly. It is also easy to tell the difference between the weeds and the wanted grass.

The best time to pull weeds is after a rain, when the earth is loose or soft. Because a weed's roots can grow much longer below ground than its above-ground height, it is important to pull straight up to remove as much of the root as possible. It's also important to grasp the weed at the crown, the thick-stemmed area just above the soil surface, in order to pull out the entire plant whenever possible.

One place, however, where you do not have to worry about the weeds that are there, is between plugs of runner-spreading grasses (i.e., anything except bahia). In this case, just mow both grass and weeds. If the weeds are kept low enough to prevent their going to seed, the grass runners will eventually crowd out and kill them. This is especially true in a healthy lawn; it is in the bare patches of pest-damaged grasses that weeds take over.

If a lawn has an abundance of broadleaf weeds, a weed-killing spray can be applied, but only as a last resort. Too many unnecessary pesticides are one of our main water pollution problems already. On the rare occasions when you must spray weeds, read and follow directions carefully, wear shoes, socks, and washable clothing: long pants and a long-sleeved shirt.

Weeding Aid:

A little tool called an "asparagus cutter" in other climates is a great help in digging weeds in Florida. I bought one at a local nursery and the man said mine was the only one he'd sold. This tool has a flat blade with a notch in the end that you put around the base of the weed. Then the tool is lifted to remove the weed. It gives you fulcrum force, saves strain, and gets more roots out of the ground without harming surrounding plants. But paint the handle or tie on a brightly-colored piece of cloth, because this is one of the easiest tools to lose in the garden.

I use the same tool to test how deep water has gone, by just pushing it straight down into the soil. In my sandy soil, the tool stops where the water does.

Weeds in the Landscape

This is one place where any mulching material can help and putting an underlayer of plastic, landscape fabric, even newspapers, can make all the difference in the world. Even this is not a complete answer, for I have used old carpets for mulch and had them disappear completely, obscured by grasses that grow in from the sides.

On his first visit to Florida, our grown son Mike laid out a path to the pool with paving blocks set in a bed of sand. Within a year, the path was entirely lost in encroaching grass. We dug out the blocks, removed the weeds and grass from the area, put black mulching cloth underneath the sand and plastic edging along the sides, and reset the paving stones. We still have to dig out a few weeds or douse them with Round-Up™ occasionally, but the path has been clear and clean for several years now. Now that I've learned about BioBarrier™ (see Chapter 14), I will try it the next time we do such a landscaping project.

The previous owners of our house put in a sandbox/play area larger than the living room and surrounded it with railroad ties. We wish they had used mulching cloth under the sand, because grass and weeds grow right through, and we can never keep it clear. I hate to waste time weeding a sandbox when gardens need it more. I am pretty sure that planting ground-covers there will be easier than digging up the whole thing, since our youngest daughter Teresa is getting too old to use it. A few stepping stones will allow the grandchildren to still use the slides and swings.

Maintenance Means . . .	Xeriscape Solutions
Weeding	*Mulch*
Feeding	*Soil improvement*
Watering	*Grouping plants*
	Installing an irrigation system
Plant replacement and renewal	*Adequate space between woody plants*
	Removal of herbaceous ones as needed
Pruning and mowing	*Wise planning and plant placement*
Pest control	*Reducing plant stress*

Neighbors have a similar problem in a bark-mulched area beside their driveway and in front of their house. It looks nice and is an excellent idea as a parking area for extra cars when needed and to cut down on lawn area. But weeds are constantly creeping through. Mulching cloth would prevent most of those weeds.

Weeds in Flower and Vegetable Gardens

Here again, weeds are easier to remove if two or more people work together. It is also more important for you to be on hand to show your helpers which are the desirable plants and which are the weeds — and you must also learn to forgive yourself or them for whacking out a treasure now and then. Tell yourself it wouldn't have thrived among all those weeds anyway, and its loss doesn't hold much weight in balance with the good you are doing. Ranting about such losses is the surest way to scare everyone else out of your garden forever. I know from sad experience and wish I'd learned sooner to be silent.

You can often make such mistakes work for good, however. Take the piece that you cut off to your cutting box and make cuttings. The last time I accidentally chopped a section off a marigold it became six more plants, and the original is now blooming better for the pruning.

Landscape Fabric Instead of Chemicals

One of the best ways to cut required weeding, avoid using potentially dangerous chemicals, and help plants thrive by saving moisture is to cover the entire bed with a landscape fabric such as WeedBlock™. These fabrics permit air and water to travel through to the soil, but block sunlight from weed seeds, thus keeping the area weed-free.

If a bed is empty, it is easy to spread the fabric to cover the entire area, then cut holes or X's into the fabric with scissors everywhere you intend to put a plant or a row of seeds. Cut the holes large enough to insert the plant directly, cover the roots with soil, then pull the fabric back up around the base of the plant. Or use the mulch instead of tilling method described in Chapter 7.

Important fact: *To make your bending and pulling seem more important, remember that one-half of all the water and nutrients you and Mother Nature together apply can be used by weeds in a weedy planting.*

If flowers or shrubs have already been planted, putting down landscape cloth is much harder, but it's still not impossible. Cut holes or X's into the fabric, slightly larger than the plants. Gently pull the fabric over the plants so that the fabric lays flat on the soil surface.

Weeds Around Shrubs and Trees

Though most grasses won't grow in the shade around the bases of shrubs and trees, some weeds seem not to mind. Any family member can remove the weeds by pulling them out by hand or by hoe, then use a spade to dig up any weed roots remaining below the soil surface. But try not to go too deep, or you will damage tree roots.

The next step may require two or more people, depending on the size or shape of the shrub or tree. Place a strip of landscape fabric on the soil in a ring around the trunk, securing it with Fabric Pegs. The inside edge of the fabric should come up to the trunk. Once the fabric is in place, cover it with gravel or wood chips.

Disadvantages of Landscape Fabric

The more holes you make in your landscape fabric, the more weeds can sneak through.

Fabric that extends even a tiny end into mowed areas can catch in the lawnmower and cause mechanical problems. (We also have little blooms of black cloth in strange places.)

When the organic mulch covering the fabric inevitably breaks down, it will sustain growth of weed seeds already there or blown in on the wind. If this occurs, either rake the organic mulch gently to disturb the germinating weeds or pull them by hand.

Rocks hold the edges of this plastic mulch cloth in place. The next step is to carefully spread mulch around and in between the plants.

Fabric can prevent groundcovers or perennials from spreading as you wish, so you may have to extend the holes or cut new ones periodically, and peg down runners.

Obviously such fabric is best used where there will be wide areas between plants or no plants at all (as beneath a shrub or tree) in softscape areas. But used wisely, it has great potential for preventing weed takeover in Florida landscapes.

❧ Signs of Nutrient Deficiency ❧

Boron	*Upper leaves light green, then veins turn purple or streaks turn yellow, then orange; growth stops; buds fall off.*
Calcium	*Upper leaves distorted or curled, ragged edges, thin yellow bands.*
Iron	*Severe yellowing of new leaves, more often visible in woody plants.*
Magnesium	*Leaves turn yellow between veins, sometimes in spots or streaks, then brown, then die starting at bottom of plant; poor fruit production.*
Manganese	*Similar to magnesium, but starts at top of plant.*
Molybdenum	*Similar to nitrogen; yellowing appears first on mature leaves; newer leaves may be severely twisted and die.*
Nitrogen	*Slow growth, pale green to yellow leaves in young growth, orange to purple in mature leaves, delayed bud opening, low production.*
Phosphorus	*Similar to nitrogen, but leaves either turn bluish green with tints of purple or bronze with brown leaf spots or edges.*
Potassium	*Thin stems to stunted or dead; leaves dull bluish-green, often streaked with yellow, browning tips and edges, rolled edges; poor development.*
Sulfur	*Slow growth, leaves curl at tips, similar to nitrogen deficiency.*
Zinc	*Mottled spots on leaves, yellowish to purple-red in late summer, early leaf drop, leaves small and crinkled.*

Feeding Your Plants

There are as many different notions about feeding plants as there are about feeding people. While organic gardeners consider chemical fertilizers dangerous to the environment, those who use them consider them perfectly safe. Using either organic or chemical fertilizer is better than starvation. I use several different products, but I find Osmocote™ the easiest to use because it is slow-release and concentrated. I buy a 50-pound bag every year or so and that does the basic feeding of everything on my half acre for just under $50. But I do sometimes notice signs of hunger in my plants in spite of feeding that should still be in effect. I suspect this is due either to leaching out by heavy rains, or limitations in the soil where I still haven't worked in enough organic matter.

Foliar Feeding

One of the quickest and most efficient ways to satisfy plant hunger is with foliar feeding: spraying the leaves with a fine mist of fertilizer solution. If you do this correctly, you should notice improvement within 48 hours. Research at Michigan State University showed that it was eight to ten times better for correcting deficiencies and increasing production and quality than if the fertilizer were put in the soil. This conclusion was based on the amount of nutrients actually taken up by the plant.

The stomata, small openings on the underside of the leaves, can take up the nutrient solution directly, bypassing that trip through soil, roots, and stems. Some does, it seems, go down to the roots and back up throughout the plant.

The stomata close up in the sunlight or in high temperatures. So we Floridians need to spray before 7 a.m., if possible (no later than 10 a.m. in the winter, 8:30 in summer or on a cloudy day), or after dusk in the evening. The temperature should be below 80°, ideally at 72°. So, as I venture out in my nightgown with a flashlight and a watering can at 4 a.m. on a summer morning, I'll be doubly grateful for my privacy fence!

Since the stomata are so small, the finer the mist, the better. A pressure pump works well. But if you don't have one, don't wait. A fine mist from a hose-end sprayer is much better than nothing at all. Whatever runs off the leaves will go into the soil, be slowed down but not lost. Direct the spray to the underside of the leaves. It is also best to use a wetting agent, either a product made for that purpose like Basic-H from Shakley, or a tablespoon of cooking oil, dishwashing liquid, or castille soap. This will lower the surface tension of the solution and spread the droplets, so they are not large enough to act as prisms to let the sun burn the leaves. Samm Philmore (see Chapter 12) says he can see a fine mist rising from the tree when he sprays. If misting is done in sunshine, the sun sucks up the mist like a vacuum hose and you could lose up to 40% of your nutrients to evaporation.

You can also add a spoonful of baking soda to the solution to make it sweet for young plant growth, or a spoonful of vinegar to make it more acid when it is time to encourage flowers, fruit, grain, or vegetable production.

Also, use the "law of little bits" for foliar feeding: it is better to spray more often with smaller amounts.

Soil Feeding

The more conventional way to feed plants is to spread the fertilizer either on the soil around the plant, as a side dressing along the rows after the plants are up, or into the soil before planting. This nutrition doesn't even have a ticket for the trip until it gets wet enough to go into solution, so give recently fertilized plants more water. Also, you should never feed plants that are very dry, for that increases the possibility of burning and the plants' ability to take up the nutrients is decreased.

If you have plants close together — groundcovers, vegetables, or flowers, for example — you can only broadcast the feed over and alongside the edges of the planting. Most organic fertilizer and encapsulated fertilizers will not burn. Neither will aged manure. But fresh manure or dry chemical fertilizers can, so I usually brush them off the leaves with a broom or wash them off with a hose spray, just to be sure. Where there is room, cultivate the fertilizer into the soil or the mulch. You can see the advantage here of solutions applied through drip irrigation systems, directly to the root zone.

Feeding through Mulch

Fertilizer spread over mulch will eventually wash through and reach the roots. So unless plants are starving and time is of the essence, this is the easiest way to apply it. Raking back the mulch and putting the fertilizer in a band underneath will get it to the roots quicker. A water solution or foliar feeding will give even quicker results.

Sometimes the application of mulch and/or enzymes should be accompanied by an extra application of nitrogen fertilizer (see Chapter 6).

Feeding Trees

Trees benefit from foliar feeding, especially if they have deficiencies. They also benefit from fertilizer broadcast over the soil surface if it is not used up first by turf or groundcovers. For feeding deeper roots, drill holes one inch in diameter in the area between the trunk and dripline. Make them 6 to 18 inches deep, depending on the size and maturity of the tree, and put them 2 to 3 feet apart. Add the amount of fertilizer recommended on the bag, dividing it among the holes, or use about one pound of 6-6-6 per inch of tree diameter for young trees, two pounds for large trees. Cover the holes with organic material or soil and water well.

Watering and Irrigation Maintenance

This is covered in Chapters 8 and 10.

Plant Spacing

The tendency to place trees and shrubs too close together or too close to the house or the property line is a frequent mistake of both homeowners and landscaping contractors. I can understand how the bare, unfinished look of a new home might prompt people to overdo their early planting schemes. But such crowding is poor Xeriscaping practice and absolutely unnecessary in Florida where even oak trees can grow up to five feet a year. Many other trees grow even faster.

New plantings in Florida need bare space between plants — often a great deal of bare space — because they can spread so widely. A shrub like pentas can spread six to twelve feet in the first season. Until a plant does spread out, if the open space is covered with an attractive mulch, it can add to the color, texture, and neat appearance of the landscape. After the mulch disappears from view beneath a canopy of foliage, it will still contribute to the humus and water holding capacity of the soil.

Plant Renewal

Don't waste water on plantings, especially annual flowers and vegetables, that are past their prime. Annuals need to be replaced often. Places like Cypress Gardens keep most annuals on display for only five to six weeks. In the home garden, a few months is the outside limit. Beans grown in Florida very seldom yield a second flush of bloom and bearing as they do in northern states. Once the first crop passes, diseases and insect damage are prone to take over. Consider this a message from Mother Nature and start over.

Pruning

Pruning can be kept to a minimum by careful planning. The right shrub or tree in the right place won't constantly overgrow its space.

I have a personal aversion to clipped hedges because they take a great deal of time to maintain (up to a full day to clip a slightly overgrown, 100-foot-long privet) and this chore must be repeated as often as three or four times a year. But you may especially like to clip hedges, or be willing to hire the labor to do it. Such hedges do take less water than a naturally growing hedge, because there is less foliage and therefore less transpiration. They also take less space. Special forms, like bubble or Japanese pruning, have much the same benefit. But most of us still favor using smaller shrubs that will stay in place and letting them assume their natural forms.

Shaping any shrub, tree, or vine is important from the first planting. The shape to choose is dictated by the desired function: fruit production, shade, privacy screening, etc. I am currently training two grapevines, one allamanda, and some annual vines to cover a newly-built arbor over our front entrance. I want fruit, color, and shade that will cool the front room in summer, then a thinner cover after the grape leaves drop which lets in the warming winter sun.

❧ Basic Principles of Pruning ❧

- *Always use sharp, clean instruments.*

- *Prune ornamentals very little, mostly to establish proper shape.*

- *Do not top trees unless you want shrubby growth. If nature tops one accidentally, train a new "leader" to take over.*

- *Remove lower branches as ornamental trees get taller. Until then, shorten them if necessary to keep them from spreading too widely.*

- *Keep fruit within picking reach.*

- *Cut back to the branch collar of any branch you are removing. This is almost, but not quite flush with the branch of origin. Leave no stump, just a slight swelling so the bark can grow over the wound.*

- *Wound treatment is no longer used in most cases. If you do use it, watch that water doesn't get in under it.*

- *If you must remove a large branch, use three cuts to prevent tearing.*

- *The best time for most pruning is whenever you have the snippers, loppers, or saw in your hand. For extensive or severe pruning, there may be a preferred time. For roses that is December or January when they are closest to dormant. For grapes and other deciduous vines, trees, and shrubs, it's whenever the leaves are off, fruit trees when they are still small, etc. Break pine "candles" of new growth in half when they are young to promote thicker growth.*

- *Prune flowering plants after flowering, not before.*

- *Make constant light pruning a habit. Snip off those rose suckers and those grape stems that are growing out from the arbor whenever you notice them and have the snippers handy. Not only will your plantings look neater, but they will be using the available water to make the growth you want rather than growth you don't want.*

Keep your own personal goals in mind. Also keep the principles of pruning in mind. And most of all, use common sense. Those small clippers in my pocket are very handy to cut off unwanted growth when I first notice it, before it gets bigger and uses up more water. The end of Florida's rainy season is a good time to prune back vines and anything else that has become overgrown during the period when it was too hot to do so many chores. Allowing the overgrowth to remain during the dry season will contribute to water waste.

Mowing and Other Lawn "Pruning"

As stated in Chapter 2, mow grasses high: 3 inches for St. Augustine and bahia, $1\frac{1}{2}$ to 2 inches for Bermuda, zoysia, or centipede grasses. This means mowing a few days less frequently in the summer and adding a week or more between mowings through the winter in Florida. This allows the grass blades to mature and develop a more healthy defense against insects and diseases. It also allows the grass itself to shade its own roots and soil surface, thereby cutting down on evaporation and encouraging deeper root systems.

Sharp mower blades also reduce stress that can lead to water waste. Some experts say that blades should be sharpened as often as after every second mowing. If that sounds a bit extreme, let it at least prod you to sharpen as often as possible. Learn how to do it yourself or give the job to a mechanically-inclined son or neighborhood teenager, who may amaze you with his abilities and persistence, especially if a bit of spending money is involved.

Thatch Control

This is a problem unique to Florida in its severity. St. Augustine lawns can become so encrusted with thatch that they are largely nonporous surfaces. Neither rain nor irrigation water can penetrate and run right off.

To improve an existing lawn and increase its water absorbing and retaining abilities, aerate with a hand or power aerator. Fill in the holes made by the aerator with a mix of vermiculite and compost. For St. Augustine, one really should hire a lawn company or rent a verticutter every several years. The chunks that are cut out can go on the compost pile. If you have a trunk full, pile them behind the shrubs or out of view and add enough material and amendments to heat the pile sufficiently to kill the roots. Or turn or till it often enough to let the sun do the job. St. Augustine is not easy to kill when it is where you don't want it.

Pest Control

This subject looms larger in the mystic of gardening than is at all necessary. Companies with profit in mind work to keep it that way. You will also hear that bugs are much worse in Florida than anywhere else. That can be true, but isn't necessarily so.

What Is Eating My Garden?

When the bugs are eating more of your garden than usual, there is a reason: stress. Whatever the cause and whenever it happens, the insects are waiting.

I gardened for years before I realized bugs don't bother the healthy, thriving plant. But just let a plant show the slightest sign of weakness, and the insects are all over it.

This is part of a master plan. If it weren't for insects and smaller creatures that eat what we don't, we'd all be living on heaps of garbage. Thanks to earthworms, insects, and microorganisms, waste is constantly broken down. From something icky comes something valuable — humus.

But in our own gardens, we'd like to say when and where and if the process should begin. In other words, bugs, wait until we get our share of the tomatoes and beans.

There is a program of pest control called Integrated Pest Management (IPM). It incorporates all existing forms of pest management and guards against all pests: insects, diseases and weeds.

Prevention, early detection and combative action are the three keywords of IPM. Actually, the whole concept, for all its new name, is just a common sense combination of the techniques most of us have been using all along. In case you've missed them, here is a checklist:

- Use pest resistant varieties. Insects just don't care for the taste of some kinds of plants. Purple beans are the last ones the bugs will eat. Tomatoes with VFN behind their names (check your seed catalog) are less likely to come down with verticullum or fusarium wilts or to be bothered by nematodes.

- Suit the plant to the site. If it is getting more or less sun or more or less water than it likes, it will be stressed. The pests will pounce on any plant that isn't happy with its home.

- Mulch your plants. In all the many ways described in Chapter 7, mulch reduces stress and makes plants healthier.

- Keep your eyes peeled. Take that daily or frequent walk around your yard to see what is sprouting, growing and blooming. Watch also for harmful or beneficial organisms. Pick and destroy diseased leaves, weeds, and harmful insects. Don't be like Noah, who missed his chance to swat the flies when there were only two. Often this hand-picking will be enough to keep problems under control.

- Avoid both too much and too little fertilizer and water. Either one can encourage or aggravate problems with certain insects, diseases and weeds.

- When you must use a pesticide, first use the mildest and safest ones, like insecticidal soap, and resort to stronger ones only if needed. Then select one that will kill the cause of your problem without harming other organisms. Avoid spraying with broad-spectrum insecticides which kill both good and bad insects. For example, *Bacillus thuringiensis* will control cabbage worms and many other worms and caterpillars without doing any harm to humans, pets, birds, or good bugs. Apply pesticides strictly according to label directions. This is definitely another case of the littles — "If a little is good, a lot is NOT better." When using potentially poisonous chemicals, we repeat from the section on lawn weeds and herbicides: Never apply in the presence of children and pets. Always wear shoes, socks, long pants, and long sleeves, and wash those afterwards.

Wash Problems Away

Spraying with a forceful spray of plain or soapy water will dislodge many unwanted insects and disease spores before they get a chance to settle in. Make this a practice whenever you have your hose out at a suitable time — up until early evening, so the foliage will dry by nightfall.

Using the other practices of Xeriscaping and natural, common sense gardening will also eliminate plant stress and thereby stop most pest problems before they begin. Diversity of planting and soil improvement will go far to keep the bad guys from calling in all their friends and relatives for a major orgy in your garden.

If an insect infestation or disease does get out of control, it is often best to remove and burn the infected plant or parts. Many plants will start over from the roots. For grafted plants, be sure the new growth comes from above the graft point.

Not All Bugs Are Bad

Anyone who ever chased lightning bugs (fireflies) knows this. They are something I sorely miss in our section of Florida, but I am thrilled to know that there are lightning bugs in some parts of the state. There are also beautiful butterflies, fascinating caterpillars, some of which become the butterflies, harmless spiders that weave magical webs, ladybugs that eat aphids, and many more. Bees have a painful sting — I know all too well since I helped my son Mike with a 4-H beekeeping project — but they are amazing to watch in their honey production and essential to the pollination and production of many of our foods.

Soon after we moved to Florida, my spouse and I returned home to find our three daughters huddled on the doorstep in the dark because "There's a huge bug in the house." They have since learned to curb their screams and coexist with the occasional palmetto bug.

Try to develop a curiosity about insects. Many of them are beneficial and fascinating. Don't kill indiscriminately. Rather, observe carefully, then consult a good insect book or chart to understand what you have seen and predict what may happen next. Then you will be ready to take early action.

Fortunately, there are an ever-increasing number of natural and mechanical controls available that will control damaging pests without interrupting the chain of life that is part of a healthy ecology.

∽ A Better Environment Can Begin in Your Yard ∽

FY &N

There is a program of the Florida Cooperative Extension Service, available in many counties and quickly spreading to the rest of Florida, that is a surefire way for all of us to help improve our personal surroundings AND our environment.

Called **Florida Yards & Neighborhoods,** *or FY&N, this program runs on the concept that our yards are our first line of defense for protecting Florida's natural beauty and her waterways. It embodies all of the principles of water wise gardening or Xeriscaping and goes a few steps beyond. Our yards and neighborhoods are pathways to our waterways. "The decisions we make—from developing a homesite to improving and maintaining our property—will determine the future of our treasured water resources," says the* Florida Yards & Neighborhoods Handbook.

"Nature knows no property lines. A rainstorm can wash fertilizers or pesticides from one yard to another. A butterfly attracted to one person's wildflowers can flit across and be poisoned in another landscape.

"Landscapes don't just connect people to the outdoors. They also connect one person's property to another, forming neighborhoods that are ultimately connected to water resources. This final connection may be immediate in a waterfront community, or gradual, through the flow of stormdrains, ditches, streams, rivers or ground water."

This program can supply you with information and incentive to do even better.

The first step is visiting or calling your County Extension Office and asking if they have the Florida Yards and Neighborhoods program. If not, refer them to Pinellas, Hillsborough, or Manatee Counties as models. If they do, ask for the FY&N questionnaire. It is easy to fill out. Just check off the facts that apply to you and send it back. There is nothing to buy and no one will bother you. You pay for these services with your tax dollars.

In return you will receive a packet of booklets and will also be put on the mailing list for additional information about scheduled classes as they occur. You don't have to attend any of these, but you might want to if you can.

The packet includes the 56-page Guide to Environmentally Friendly Landscaping *and* The Florida Yardstick Workbook. *These will help you to waste even less water and fertilizer and to need and use fewer and safer pesticides. The workbook has spaces for you to check off the things you need and want most from your yard—including vegetable, herb, and fruit gardens, play area, wildlife habitat, area for entertaining, pet space, etc. But the really fun part comes when you check off the actions and add up your points or "inches". Of 97 possible points, it only takes 36 inches to have a "Certified Florida Yard". When you believe you have achieved this, you can fill in the checklist and return it to the Extension Office. Within 4 to 6 weeks, a master gardener will come, not for consultation, but to verify. If all checks out—and by then you will probably have made more improvements—you will be given a certificate.*

This program is slowly growing and spreading statewide. You can be a true pioneer and add yours to the list of Certified Florida Yards. [My yard is anything but perfect, but I scored nearly 50 inches without changing anything, and have improved some since I got the booklets.] Hopefully your neighbors will follow your good example. Common sense conservation can make a definite difference in your enjoyment of your yard. It can also make a difference in the future of our planet for our children and our children's children.

This is one of those win-win opportunities. Don't miss it.

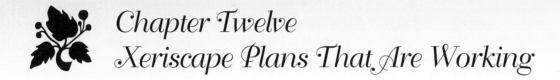

Chapter Twelve
Xeriscape Plans That Are Working

Samm Philmore's Five-Year Plan

Samm Philmore's back yard was a wonder of vegetable production when I first saw it in the fall of 1990. His front yard was then in the first stages of a five-year plan to change it to a low water-use, low maintenance, sure success landscape.

He had built raised beds that he could cover with shade cloth in the summer or with plastic during cold spells. So he was sure to produce something all year long in his just-east-of-Tampa location.

That fall his family was eating fresh collards, Chinese mustard, eggplant, cabbage, broccoli, green beans and lettuce. Better Boy tomatoes were ripening and a bed of watermelon was beginning to bloom. Cabbage, onions, and assorted herbs were coming along.

Before December was over he planted sugar pod peas, beets, carrots, Bibb, Iceberg, and Great Lakes lettuce, more cabbage, and turnips.

In the spring months he grows almost every kind of vegetable except corn and some of the vining crops that take too much space. Even during the summer he has some beds in okra and black-eyed peas. Collard greens do fairly well. Empty beds get cover crops of annual rye or cowpeas.

Whenever one sees such a thriving garden, one hopes to find some secret that will apply to his own. Samm Philmore's gardens offered several promising possibilities. The most unique and delightful of these is his working friendship with his grandson Eric and with another excellent gardener, Joe DaPonte.

Two Gardeners Are Better Than One

Philmore and DaPonte met when they both worked for Living Plant Nurseries. They were both supposedly retired by then. And even though retirement was taking better with Joe than with Samm, who keeps returning to new jobs, both found a special challenge and satisfaction in their gardening that was enhanced by their friendship. Ideas spark between them like electricity. "We do a lot of experimenting and it doesn't always work. But we keep trying," says Philmore.

The cooperation between these two men stimulates the enthusiasm and knowledge that both have in abundance. But they tend to disagree and debate to an extent that makes them both laugh.

"I don't have the book theory," says DaPonte, whose parents were from Portugal and whose family background includes professional nurserymen. But he has been growing plants all his life and he knows what works and what doesn't.

Samm Philmore grew up in Depression times. "We always had a garden," he says. "That was part of life. So whenever I've had a place, I've been growing something." But only in recent years have his knowledge and his gardening projects escalated, a result of twenty hours of classes in horticulture from Hillsborough Community College and the perusal of an extensive personal library of many of the latest books and garden magazines. Though Philmore has taken the necessary courses and become a Master Gardener, he doesn't always have time to volunteer.

No-Stress Vegetable Gardening

Samm Philmore's vegetable beds are separated from the rest of the back yard by a row of flower beds enclosed with border stones along front and sides and backed by a decorative post-and-rail fence. These are colorful with begonias, marigolds, papayas, pineapples, Mexican sage, shell ginger, fig, peppers, eggplant, variegated hibiscus. Many plants here are pampered volunteers. Behind the flowers and the open fence are 38 (last count) different beds of improved soil enclosed by untreated boards.

Loquat trees frame the scene on one side, but they shade only the mist propagating bed. A hedge of privet along the back fence is trimmed lower to let in more sun on the back beds in winter. Most of the beds get full sun.

Each bed is filled with a mixture of soil that Philmore is constantly improving with additions of professional potting soil and compost. He buys soil and mulch by the truckload from sources he finds at garden shows and in the news. Horse stable manure he gets free; he composts, sometimes shreds, and sifts it before use.

"I once used solarization in the summer to treat the beds for nematodes. Now I use Prosper Nema™ from Circle One International. It is nontoxic and quite effective. And it may soon change some things like the need for special, nematode-resistant rootstocks on roses."

He uses no poisonous sprays and follows the rules to qualify for organic certification, but thinks it is probably not feasible to pay the yearly cost for certification of a small garden like his. Many of his beds are interplanted with marigolds, which add color and deter certain insect pests.

Low-Flow Irrigation System

Each bed has its own soaker hose, which Philmore finds easier than drip watering tubes to remove when amending the soil and to replace after putting in new plants. "There are no restrictions on watering with these," he says, "because no water is wasted to evaporation or on the walking areas."

Raised vegetable beds have spigots for connecting low-flow soaker hoses. Some, like this one, also have short pieces of PVC pipe clamped to the inside of the wooden frame. These are used to anchor PVC supports for shade cloth.

Each bed has a separate turn-on valve and a water regulating gasket that allows only half a gallon through an hour. Philmore leaves these on as long as all night, depending on the wind, temperature, and daytime light intensity. He digs down with his trowel to check moisture penetration. Though he may not water again for as little as one day or as many as three or four, his plants are never stressed from lack of water. Nor does the foliage get wet, a factor that prevents the spread of many diseases.

The constant supply of water as needed is more important

∞ Hints from Samm Philmore ∞

❧ *For rooting, stick cuttings in a bed of vermiculite. "We have tried several things. But we like a mixture of vermiculite, sand and peat best. It forms like a sponge around the new forming roots."*

❧ *Although he uses straw, wood chips and other mulches, pine needles are Philmore's favorite. They are light and airy, weedless, easy to handle, and look nice around the plants.*

❧ *Philmore uses Safer's soap, thuricide, and crop rotation for pest control, but says careful watching and quick action are very important.*

❧ *One bed is largely compost. "Another Brandon gardener, Bob Dickey, taught me this. I still have some of the old tires like he uses [to hold compost]. Once I had over 100 tires, but they got to be impractical on my scale. I still like to use some of them for containing roots of plants like mint and sugar cane. But now the raised beds work better for me in most cases."*

❧ *Do not mulch petunias with cypress or pine bark. It causes a yellowing of the leaves (chlorosis) that is not due to nitrogen deficiency and cannot be corrected with fertilizer. Philmore credits Circular 59,* Annual Flowers for Florida, *published by the Florida Cooperative Extension Service, as the source of this advice.*

❧ *Save both water and electricity indoors by drying produce rather than freezing or canning it. Dried banana chips are great, and so are papaya slices coated with honey.*

❧ *Keep a close eye on your hoses. When he wasn't paying attention, a row of bananas completely ate up a soaker hose that got squeezed between new shoots.*

than feeding. "I don't do that enough," says Philmore, but his plants deny that. He once used Peters and Greenleaf, both liquids he applied with a hose attachment, and Osmocote, a slow-acting granular feed that he stirred into the soil. But because these are not organic, he has since switched to Fertrell granular, kelp or seaweed — liquid and dry forms can be used for foliar feeding or applied to the soil, respectively. Kelp is very nutritious as it contains 40 minor nutrients. Philmore also uses fish meal and fish liquid products. He applies liquids with a hose-end applicator or a watering can, and uses a pump-up backpack for foliar feeding. He finds that the pump sprayers do break down, but parts are available and he has found two shops that will repair them.

To one side of the beds are two sheds that keep tools and supplies handy but protected. One has sinks for washing vegetables, and by the time he gets pick-them-yourself customers, he plans to recycle water from the shed back to some of his beds.

Saving Greywater

Philmore's wife Peggy has one flower bed by the back door that gets its only water from rain and the washing machine. Her flowers thrive; red and blue salvias are as tall as the privacy fence. She uses only cold water and mild products like Amway's SAH, which is non-phosphoric, and one of the Shaklee products. In the rainy season, they drain the excess water elsewhere.

Composting

When I visited in 1990, two compost piles were in various stages of development. "That one under the plastic was made from 100 bags of bahia grass clippings. It is all ready to use now," Philmore explained. The other showed recent additions of grass clippings and garden waste at the top of a round circle of wire fencing, about ten feet across and five feet tall. The lower layers were already beginning to look like rich soil. Two tubes resembling dryer vents extended down through the material and helped aerate and aid the decomposition process.

Since then, Philmore has built a series of three bins made of wire and wood. He made the mistake of using non-pressure-treated wood and it composted right along with the bins' contents. And after a freeze last year, he filled the bins with ruined green papayas that grew into a papaya forest he chose to give away rather than cut down. He has a new Kemp composting drum which he uses to put the finishing touches on his product. "I use it more as a sterilizer, since I don't turn the other bins. I sift some of the nearly finished compost, add grass clippings , and turn it in the drum for about a month. If I use fresh manure on edible crops, it must be cured for a minimum of 90 days, and then used on crops that will not be harvested for 30 days more, for a total of 120 days aging." This cooks out most weed seed and disease spores and he uses the resulting "clean" compost in containers.

Two shredders ensure constant compost production. His Montgomery Ward 5-horsepower model worked great on leaves — until someone left a pair of pliers in one batch. Then it went to the repair shop. His Kemp 8-horsepower chips branches up to three inches in diameter.

On the other side of the garden is a small, pole-frame house with benches that hold potted plants. It is covered with shade cloth in the summer, with plastic in the winter to protect more tender plants.

Many of the vegetable beds also have frames of poly pipe or PVC curving above them for the addition of shade cloth in the summer, plastic in the winter. Most of these are made of 8-foot lengths for a maximum height of $2^1/2$ feet, but some arch as high as 6 feet for vertical crops like staked tomatoes.

Philmore's setup was adapted from directions in Jeff Ball's *60-Minute Garden* book from Rodale Press. He added a few refinements when he read *Square Foot Gardening* by Mel Bartholomew. He finds that the beds take much of the work and worry out of vegetable growing.

"But I don't have anything built in, just beds in the ground between strips of lawn," says his friend DaPonte. So what works for one is not necessarily the secret of success for another.

Both Samm Philmore and Joe DaPonte have vast stores of knowledge, energy, and enthusiasm, and they bring out all three in each other. In the end, it is their constant providing what the plant needs, when it needs it, that makes their gardens so beautiful, productive, and successful.

Samm Philmore tends lettuce in his garden. Behind him and to the left, his pole-frame shade/green house is visible.

Xeriscaping the Front Yard

Although the Philmore home was as well landscaped when I first saw it as any on their pleasant block in south Brandon, he was then beginning his five-year changeover to Xeriscaping. Large sections of what had until then been a St. Augustine lawn were already tilled and marked for mulched areas or shrubs and drought resistant plants. Eventually he tilled the rest of the lawn several times, going only two to three inches deep to avoid damaging the roots of his spreading oak trees.

He raked up the residue and put it into the compost piles. Then he added 40 yards of compost that he hauled home in his trailer and transported by the wheelbarrow load with the help of his grandson Eric. When it was all spread, he tilled again.

After tilling and before sowing, he rented a Ditch Witch to lay pipelines. He cut into the main water line connecting the well pump to the house, put in a $1^1/4$" cross and PVC pipe about halfway to the front yard, then reduced the diameter of the pipe to $3/4$" with another cross that ran in four directions for four faucets. To run pipe under the driveway, he used a piece of PVC on the end of the hose to wash a hole through beneath the pavement. He put double faucets on each outlet, mounting them on 4" x 4" pressure-treated timbers driven into the ground. He is now using vinyl hoses, but would prefer commercial-grade rubber ones (when he gets rich, he says) even though he knows they would be heavier to handle.

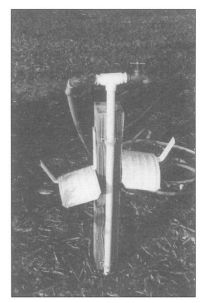

Double faucets and hose hangers in Samm Philmore's front yard. Relatively fragile PVC pipe is reinforced by attaching it to sturdy posts.

Once the water system was in, Philmore broadcast scarified bahia seed and took advantage of the thirty-day freedom from water restrictions to water his newly-planted lawn daily. The lawn is now thriving. But this year he sprayed with Deep Root and is over-planting rye grass in front to have things extra green for a January wedding for one of his children.

Xeriscaping Plan Works

"We conserve water wherever we can," says Philmore. From the earliest stages he had his landscaping plan sketched out on graph paper in his back porch-office. The design features a series of squares and rectangles that give a definite and unique formality that harmonizes with the house and the theme of using nature to its fullest advantage and then refining it to purpose with shade, sun, privacy and presentation.

"Most design experts talk about gracefully curving lines, but I liked the squares," says Philmore. A tall fence with attractive gates extends the line of the front of the house on either side and gives plenty of room for experimenting in the back.

The large squares of mulch beneath the oak trees he renews "not as often as I should. I will need 40 to 50 yards to cover it four inches deep now. But I've set a deadline to make myself get it done. It needs less if you do it more often — at least once a year." He stirs

A large arbor, built by Philmore and DaPonte and painted white, supports delicious grapes (I've tasted them) and shades beds of herbs and a long bench for rest and relaxation. It is such a peaceful place that it relaxes one just to look at it.

with a scruff hoe to remove any germinating weed seeds. The front bed along the driveway is colorful with such drought resistant plants as East Palatka and Burford hollies, star and confederate jasmine, giant liriope, variegated juniper, nandina (heavenly bamboo), and Indian hawthorn.

To the right of the drive stands a sign proclaiming "Organic Vegetables For Sale" in season, since his beds bear much more than the family alone can eat. He has become so convinced of the value of Circle One International products that he has become the area agent for their distribution.

Philmore is one of those rare people whose garden notebooks I so admire. Whatever you ask him, he can check there to verify dates, varieties, what succeeded, what failed, etc. (see Chapter 11).

What is left to do in the five-year plan? Philmore still wants to replace some big plants near the house with low growers like crotons and dwarf ilex. He may eventually convert some of his raised beds to recessed ones that will need less water. He will continue to experiment and improve because he so enjoys the challenge, but his Xeriscaped front yard will continue to need a minimum of both water and maintenance. 🌹

The Garianos' Nature Park

Sharon and Terence Gariano have the first Certified Wildlife Habitat in Pinellas Park. "There are others, but none of them are certified yet," says Sharon. Her detailed plans, drawings and plant lists were done partly for that certification.

"Terry and I have worked very hard to make our yard a wildlife habitat, not to keep animals within, but to feed them in their travels. We have many squirrels, a 'possum and a raccoon that visit us (when the dogs aren't out)." Many of the animals are not all that wild, but perch on her shoulder and eat from her hand. Birds and butterflies abound. She hasn't yet seen any hummingbirds, but trusts that if she plants for them, they will come.

Sharon and Terry got to know each other when she was working in the produce depart-

Sharon and Terry Gariano show off a beauty berry plant in their yard. The beauty berry has at least three points in its favor: it is drought-tolerant, a Florida native, and the attractive berries provide food for wildlife.

ment of a grocery. He took her some of his organically grown tomatoes and challenged her to match their flavor.

They were married in 1991 and joined their talents and goals for the 130 x 156-foot yard that surrounds their home. It is blessed by six slash pines that must be 75 years old and stand a good 50 feet tall. Towering above their two-story home, where they now live upstairs, is also a pecan tree, some young but lovely silk oaks, a red maple and live and laurel oaks.

"It is an off year for the grapefruit," says Sharon, of a tree that is still very fruitful. "In its on years, it layers the ground with fruit and I give it to anyone who asks. I've even had homeless people offer to buy it, but loaded them up for free. Whatever we have, we share."

Terry had already started that policy. Those tomatoes that brought them together grew on plants set along the outside of the chain link fence that surrounded the property "so anyone could pick them." Even so, he had ten pounds to take to Sharon that first time. "Talk about love apples," she says.

His vegetable garden outside the fence included lettuce, radishes, eggplant, beans, peas, broccoli, cauliflower, mustard that was as hot as horseradish, and snow peas. "I put tons of manure into that section. You can still tell the difference." Sharon had two horses in a stable that no one had cleaned to the ground in years. When she did, the horses were two feet shorter and their garden that much richer. Terry watered it with the hose as needed.

Terry had also nurtured as many trees as he could. He spends his nights printing the *St. Petersburg Times* and his days trying to grow enough trees to make up for what the newspaper uses. "I hate to even mow seedlings like these," he says, moving his foot from little oaks in the lawn. "I don't mind mowing them," says Sharon. "But he would be Johnny Treeseed, grow them all into healthy plants, and then give them to someone who needed them. He does that a lot."

Plans Preceded Changes

The Gariano yard, thanks to Terry's efforts for several years before, was already shaded and interesting. It has some major drawbacks. It is on the corner of two busy streets, and a short block away from the intersection with a major traffic artery. Their plantings have done a lot to add privacy to the yard and separate it from its urban surroundings. The chain-link fence that surrounds it is fast disappearing under a wide variety of flowering vines, ten different kinds at last count. On the east side and around the front corner it is already completely covered with Confederate jasmine. "When that is in bloom in March while the citrus blooms on the other side, the fragrance is wonderful," says Sharon.

The vegetables are mostly gone, except for a patch of herbs. They've been replaced by trees and flowering shrubs that will extend the privacy screen higher while they provide beauty for passersby and shelter and food for birds and butterflies. Sharon is now a veterinary technician. She is also a certified wildlife rehabilitator, which means that if someone cuts

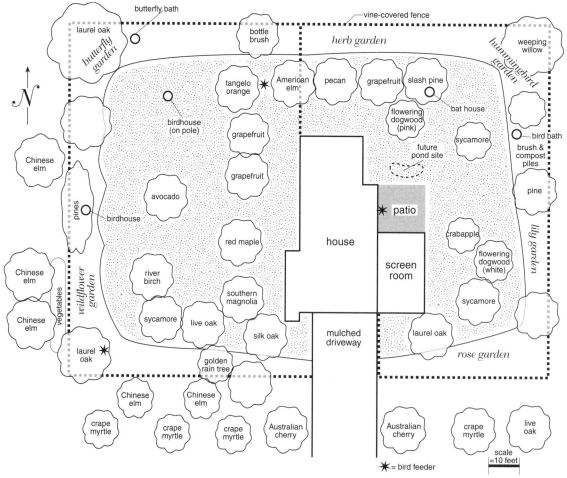

One look at the plan of the Garianos' yard shows Terry's love for trees. Plantings of azaleas, false heather, trumpet creeper vine grow underneath them, taking advantage of the shade they create. (Illustration based on plan drawn by Sharon Gariano.)

down a tree and then finds a nest of baby woodpeckers, they take them to her for nurturing care until the tiny birds grow big enough to be released into a suitable environment.

In the early stages of planning, Sharon went through her butterfly books and chose her plants from the lists of what those particular butterfly species needed for nectar, larvae, and shelter.

Her advice to others: "Before you start to put your yard on paper, decide what kind of wildlife you'd like to attract to your yard. Make a list right down to the variety of birds and butterflies you like best. Be sure that the creatures you choose actually do live in your area of Florida. You might also find out what species migrate through on their way north or south, and plant food that will ripen during this migration."

She then sketched out her landscape plan. It is amazingly unlike the impression of the yard. "You get a new perspective, especially about how much room each tree takes. I'm not real good about making the circles accurate." Several sections got separate, enlarged plans before planting.

Goals Directed the Progress

The Garianos' final goal is to have a low-maintenance yard with high privacy for avian and animal friends. It will be showy, for most of their trees and shrubs are highly colorful blooming and bearing kinds. And 90 percent of their planting will be beneficial to wildlife.

"It was a conscious choice," she says. "If you want butterflies to lay their eggs in your garden, you can't spray with anything, not even soap. And we count it a blessing when leaves of the Dutchman's Pipe are devastated by welcome larvae that go into their next stage before they do any permanent damage. The leaves grow back." The only chemical she uses is RoundUp™, as needed to clear grass and other rampant plants to make room for the selected ones.

"Wildlife gardening doesn't have to be dull,

Plants in the Butterfly Garden	
Beauty berry	*Callicarpa americana*
Bromeliads	*Aechmea* spp., *Billbergia* spp.
Butterfly Bush	*Buddleia officinalis*
Butterfly Milkweed	*Asclepias tuberosa*
Dutchman's Pipe (vine)	*Aristolochia durior*
Garden Canna	*Cannas* x *generalis*
Hibiscus	*Hibiscus* spp.
Kings' Mantle	*Thunbergia erecta*
Common Lantana	*Lantana camara*
Passion Flower (vine)	*Passiflora coccinea*
Pentas	*Pentas lanceolata*
Phillipine Violet	*Barleria cristata*
Porterweed	*Stachytarpheta jamaicensis*
Salvia	*Salvia* spp.
Sweet William	*Dianthus barbatus*

weedy or unappealing." Their yard is anything but. "We have to learn to settle for a little imperfection. Our yard is not manicured or artificial." But it is certainly neat in both senses of the word. Appropriate houses and feeders are set around the various trees. She is excited about getting a bat house. Bats are wonderful insect eaters.

What about wildlife that gets out of bounds? Sharon gladly lets squirrels eat the bird food. She likes them, too. She isn't fond of the fruit rats that often come to dinner, but says "Hey, they have to eat, too." She even finds them cute to watch outside, but draws the line when they come into the attic. The Garianos try to keep them out by blocking any entrance holes. If that fails, they put poison in the attic.

> ## Vines in the Nature Park
>
> *In addition to those listed as part of the hummingbird and butterfly gardens, the following vines grow on the Garianos' property:*
>
> | | |
> |---|---|
> | **Mandevilla** | *Mandevilla splendens* |
> | **Butterfly Pea Vine** | *Clitoria mariana* |
> | **Trumpet Creeper Vine** | *Campsis radicans* |
> | **Virginia Creeper** | *Parthenocissus quinquefolia* |
> | **Greenbriar** | *Smilax* spp. |
> | **Philodendron** | *Philodendron cultivar "Silver Queen"* |

Grouping for Lifestyles

The selection and grouping here have been chosen with wildlife in mind, rather than watering zones. The yard is divided by a lovely wooden fence and gate in the back. On the east side, their three dogs get to run. On the west, dogs are not allowed, so both wildlife and tender plants can go undisturbed. Their two cats stay indoors.

Fortunately, most of the plants needed for butterflies, hummingbirds, other birds, and wildlife in general are native plants that are drought tolerant. Most of the Gariano Nature Park is actually a natural zone. "We water when we first plant something. After that we water only if a planting is about to croak." But they are well aware that their new black tupelo, *Nyssa sylvatica*, is a swamp or oasis tree and have a hose ready to fill its donut-shaped depression as needed. Other oasis plants, like the white and red birds of paradise and the ficus tree, which must stay in its container so it won't become a pest, are placed to take advantage of the runoff from the roof.

Soil Improvement and Mulch

These are second nature to seasoned organic gardeners like Sharon and Terry. Sharon knows of a source of chicken manure so old it smells like cocoa beans. And Terry bags the grass clippings and carefully doles them out to the neediest spot. They get wood chips by the truckload from a free source and value fallen leaves and pine needles from the trees. When they prune severely they make a pile of branches and then rent a chipper to turn it into mulch.

Limiting the Wasteland

"Grass is a wasteland to wildlife," explains Sharon. "We plan to extend the beds well into the turf on all sides. We'll still need a little grass. Butterflies use it to sun themselves and some, like the hairstreaks, live in the turf."

Right now their lawn is St. Augustine in the shade, blending quite naturally into bahia in the sunny centers. Most of the St. Augustine will disappear as the shrubs' borders widen.

"We water once in a blue moon," Sharon says. The grass doesn't look perfect, but it looks quite adequate, even in the dry days of winter.

Watering

The Garianos water so little that they have put bird food in the birdbath. Sharon knows that her present schedule would not allow her to keep water always on hand, so she doesn't promise what she can't deliver. They use both soaker hoses and regular hoses. Though their house is on city water, they use a well for the yard.

"Whatever we put on percolates right back down to the source," says Terry. "It also brings up minerals that would stay deep in the ground otherwise. We can smell a bit of sulfur in it."

Their neighbor to the east is a landscape professional whose Xeriscaped yard includes nary a blade of grass. He doesn't water much either, but he does have a pipe running through the Confederate jasmine.

Happily Ever After

Both Garianos belong to Organic Matters gardening club. Terry is the treasurer and Sharon does such a good job as newsletter editor that the club voted to pay her a token fee rather than let her quit. "I'm the only paid member of the group." They find the meetings both informative and fun and a great source of new plants, as the members share with free seeds and a monthly plant raffle.

Both also work long and hard in the yard, but it is a labor of love. The "chore" they do most often, walking around to see who or what is budding or hatching or growing, is one of the most pleasant aspects of life in their wildlife habitat. It is also the time of early observation that leads to pruning, pinching, or pulling a weed while it is still just a threat and not a serious problem.

Neither mind hard work. Sharon is an old hand with a chain saw. "I'd have that chinaberry out of there by now, but it has electric lines running through the branches." They are busy remodeling the house and believe that eventually they'll have to sacrifice a section of yard for a garage and turnaround driveway, for backing out into the busy street is not safe. But whatever happens on their busy corner, there is a low water use, high wildlife population park growing lovelier and more interesting with every season. 🌸

Plants in the Hummingbird Garden

Aloe	*Aloe barbadensis*
Azalea	*Rhododendron* hybrid
Carolina Jasmine (vine)	*Gelsemium sempervirens*
Confederate Jasmine (vine)	*Trachelospermum jasminoides*
Daylilies	*Hemerocallis* spp.
Firespike	*Odontonema strictum*
Four O'Clocks	*Mirabilis jalapa*
Jacobinia	*Justicia carnea*
Snapdragon	*Antirrhinum majus*
Sweet Viburnum	*Viburnum odoratissimum*
Sweet William	*Dianthus barbatus*
Brown Turkey Fig	*Ficus carica*
Weeping Willow	*Salix babylonica*

Non-gardeners Don and Gayle Sloan in the front yard of their Brandon home.

Xeriscaping Works for People Who Hate Yard Work

Don and Gayle Sloan are non-gardeners. Their motto about yard work is MTRM ("Mow. Then Run to the Mall."). They pay only about $14 a month for water, but their home is attractive, comfortable, and inviting inside and out.

The publisher of this book asked me to find a home where the people do as little work as possible and still have a nice yard. We want this book to prove low-maintenance gardening is possible, and show how to make it work for you. When I saw this yard, I wondered if it might be a good example. But I was very much afraid the owners must really be gardeners, especially when I saw the table of plants in the sitting area. Finally, pushed to the deadline, I worked up the nerve to stop and ask.

"We hate yard work," Don Sloan assured me, to my great relief. "I don't know why we have such a big yard," said Gayle, "but our children and all their friends always used to play in it, and the grandchildren still do."

They apologized for not having the place spruced up, as if they expected I'd want them to. But I found it fine just the way it is, exactly the example I needed, and one I hope will appeal to other non-gardeners who want to save water and work and still have a successful landscape.

So the Sloans agreed to let me draw a plan of their yard. I hate drawing plans, but since several of the books and articles I've written (including this one) urge people to "get it all down on paper" in order to save work, failures, and frustration, I do draw them when backed against a wall — or a deadline.

Sloan Yard is Xeriscaping At Its Simplest

The Sloan house sits on the curve of a short street of similar houses, but it stands out from the crowd. I noticed it first because of an addition to the driveway, almost a second drive beside the first. But this one veers away from the garage and curves along the front foundation plantings and under the trees to make a play or sitting area, a space for two or three additional cars to park out of the way if need be, or a spot for one to pull right up to the front door.

"When we first moved here in 1971," says Gayle, "these oak trees were only about as tall as the house and the grass grew green right up to the door. But as the trees grew, the grass died. We tried everything, even resodding, but nothing worked."

There are no Florida grasses that do well in deep shade. Besides that, there always seemed to be at least three cars in the Sloan family while their children were growing up, and two of the cars had to be parked in the yard.

This second driveway was the perfect solution. It is made not of cement or asphalt, but of bark chips, a permeable material that lets the rainwater seep right back through the soil to the aquifer. It takes a little maintenance, but it is not only much less expensive originally than a hardscape drive (which would cost at least $2000), but it is easily reversible if they or a future owner should change plans.

"We put a good many of our leaves in that area," says Don, a teacher at nearby Horace Mann Junior High. "We wait until the last leaves are down in the spring, about March. Then we get a truckload of bark chips ($14 at a nearby nursery) and put that down and we're done with that for the year."

They found that the leaves alone tended to blow away, and while both leaves and bark continually decompose into the ground, the system works fine for them.

What looks like a fairly large yard from the front (200 feet along the road and 50–90 feet to the backyard fence) actually converges to form a pie-shaped wedge in the back. This small, cozy triangle measures 89 feet on the side abutting the house, 91 feet and 75 feet along the back two fences. Two large oak trees in the front and one on the west side tower above and shade the house. A willow laced with ropes gives grandchildren Christopher, 9, and Alissa, 2, a climbing tree on the west front corner.

"All of my children have climbed that tree in their time," says Gayle. "It was just about the same size when we moved here as it is now, always open like that and with branches touching the ground."

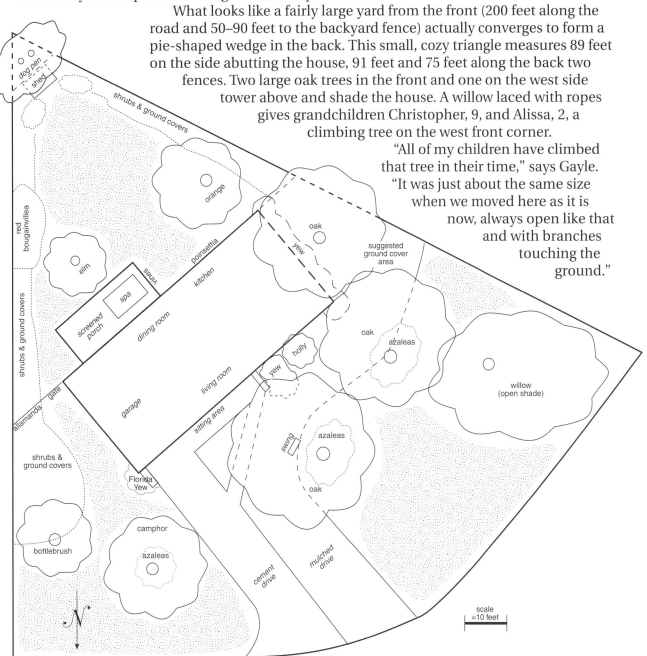

A bottlebrush tree on the east side gives color in the spring. Azaleas bloom in front under the trees and later each year caladiums come up and give summer color to the three beds around the tree trunks in front. Those beds also contain ground covers, an Easter lily, and other assorted herbaceous plants. Near the drive, a dracaena often known as corn plant makes an attractive accent.

A sitting area between garage and front door has chairs and blooming poinsettia plants. Hanging baskets and more plants decorate the back porch and hang from a tree in the back yard. "My favorite plant is the Christmas cactus and I have them in all colors," says Gayle. "I don't even water my potted plants outside except to put them out farther to catch the rains."

A triangular group of azaleas, boxwood, Moses-in-a-boat, and two tall elephant ears gives added privacy to the sitting area and added color to the yard. The subtle repeat of the triangle shape adds to the harmony of the landscape plan. Tall Florida yews and a holly under the bedroom window further frame the house. A camphor tree on the east side is fighting for its life in a battle with mistletoe.

A Low-Care, Unwatered Lawn

The lawn is bahia grass, the most drought tolerant of Florida's grasses and also the most maintenance free. You can see no definite change in green from the St. Augustine lawn on the east that is watered copiously. Part of that may be runoff. If you have neighbors who create an oasis zone that extends into your yard, you might as well make use of it. If the Sloans wanted to plant any thirsty shrubs or flowers, that would be the place to do it for now. But one must bear in mind that neighbors can move or change their watering habits. They may also cut down trees that give shade to your yard. The fact is, the Sloans don't want any oasis, high maintenance plants, and that is all right, too.

The lawn is slightly thin due to the shade, and it gets a bit dried out in dry times like Florida's typical April and May. But it always looks quite presentable, and greens up again when the rains come. Actually, even in dry times, the Sloans' lawn is considerably greener than most of the other bahia yards in the neighborhood. That is partly because most of it is shaded for part of the day.

"I don't hurry to rake all the leaves," says Gayle. "I find two benefits from leaving them there. If it freezes in the winter, they protect the grass [and often keep it green when other yards turn brown]. In the dry spring, a few leaves help protect it from dryness." They do indeed hold in the moisture, provide a little shade, and also rot down and add to the humus and nutrients the grass roots need. I have always been against excessive panic about leaf raking, but I've never met anyone before who could both say and demonstrate so well why not bothering can be better.

The Sloans do rake leaves when they get the time and inclination, and put them on the mulched driveway and on the groundcover plantings. They do not waste good mulch, trashmen's energy, or taxpayers' money by sending them to the landfill.

A Private, Pretty Back Yard

The Sloans' most-used outdoor living area is a screened-in back porch with a covered hot tub, a hanging swing, and a table of plants.

"We had to choose between a Jacuzzi and a pool, and we're very glad we chose this," says Gayle. "We use it every evening, winter and summer. It helps my arthritis." It also cost less and took less room to install, uses less water initially and loses almost none to evaporation since it is kept covered. It also takes much less maintenance.

The back yard is a lovely sight from kitchen window, dining room French doors, or back porch. A huge, blooming, red bougainvillea and a Chinese evergreen cover part of the privacy fence. Yellow allamanda is thriving on the chain-link fence between front and back yards, and an orange tree on the other side of the yard provides fragrance, color, and fruit. The family dog rules this area, but there is also a pen at the very point of the triangle and behind the garden shed where he can be confined if there is need.

A large clump of poinsettia, mixed reds and whites, was a beautiful blooming plant for much of the winter and is only now fading a bit in April. Clumps of amaryllis bloomed nicely, are wilting a bit in these dry times, but will also revive when the rains come. The Sloans know that and don't worry or run for the hose. In fact, I didn't see a hose.

Lesson to Learn

The Sloans just had a man come in and trim the oak trees to be sure no limbs would fall on the roof. Over the years someone has done additional and very wise trimming to remove some of the lower limbs of those trees to let in more light and air. As your trees grow tall, don't hesitate to take off the lower limbs as high as you want.

There has been great debate recently in St. Petersburg about a law forbidding people to have rock-mulched yards or areas for parking boats, extra cars and such. Some people seem to prefer grass in these areas, but from a water-use point of view, the rock or mulch makes much more sense. A law that forbids good sense and wise water use seems ridiculous. As long as a yard looks good and causes no one any problem, landscaping should certainly be a matter of personal choice. Mulched or rock areas can look quite neat, much better than abused grass.

The Sloans agreed to let me make suggestions for possible improvement, as long as they don't have to do them if they don't want. The first one I'm sure they don't want — but had they used mulch cloth under that bark and leaf driveway, it would take even less work. I'll admit I didn't use it under my own parking-on-chips area either, because I got the mulch unexpectedly before I had any mulch cloth on hand. It does, however, keep grass and weeds from coming up in thin spots, and slows down the decomposition rate of the mulch.

The Sloans' grandson Christopher in the "climbing tree."

More groundcovers and more shrubs would add more color, textures, and interest to the Sloan yard. They would add a little work at first and certainly aren't necessary. But they would use no more water than the grass, except when first planted. And if planting is done in the summer when the rains are usually ample, they'd take little watering even during their settling-in time. Within a year, they would make the yard work easier by cutting down on the area to be mowed. Don Sloan is planning to plant some Pampas grass along the west fence in the backyard, a good choice for low water use.

Other good choices would be aloe, beach sunflower, junipers, kalanchoe, lantana, liriope, sea oats, periwinkle, or golden creeper as ground covers. Shrubs like red Bauhinia, beauty berry, butterfly weed, crotons, firecracker plant, Indian hawthorn, Yaupon holly, oleander, palmettoes, yucca, ti plant (cordyline), and wax myrtle would also take little work or water. Drought resistant edibles like Barbados cherry, kumquat, natal plum, and sea grape, and herbs like rosemary would also be good. 🌿

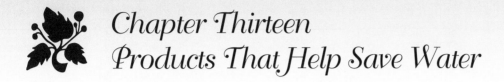

Chapter Thirteen
Products That Help Save Water

Xeriscaping, above all, is based on common sense and resulting efficiency. As this will take shape in different plans for different places, so will it require different products and equipment for each plan and the person who works it.

Some tools that are lifesavers for one person would be a complete waste for another. I've tried several hose nozzles, and find that for the most part, using my finger to regulate the water stream works best for me. I know a couple who invested in a trowel that cost $40 and found it a godsend. Wouldn't it be terrible to lose it, though? I work with the 79-cent kind myself, because I prefer to have a cheap tool handy wherever I look and replace them when needed. We can both have great gardens.

Our tools will also vary with time and circumstance. When we had an acreage and I had four sons at home to keep it running, I considered a heavy-duty tiller my liberation machine. Buying it was the largest expense of our lives except for homes and cars, and frightening at the time. True, such a tiller will last a lifetime. But not all the parts will, and if you are not mechanically inclined, there will also be labor costs for its upkeep.

My tiller is now in retirement. I have replaced it with the mulching instead of tilling method (see Chapter 7) and only rarely wish I could again till humus deep into the soil.

You must decide what you need at this time. Put the other information on a back burner for future use. Also, be aware that this is only a partial inventory of what is now available and that the concept of saving water while having a beautiful, productive yard will bring forth new products and tools to help us toward that end.

You needn't invest a lot of money in this endeavor. But you must open your mind and set achievable goals. Many useful items, like the leaking bucket and holey hose that were turned into low-flow irrigation tools (see Chapters 8 and 10), will be born of your own ingenuity. You may discover other items, like some of the irrigation equipment, which have been available to you all the time. I had no idea of the existence of many products and tools until I opened my eyes and looked around, asked questions of other gardeners, and made a few inexpensive experiments of my own.

Irrigation Equipment Should Come First

This can be as simple as enough feet of hose to reach all of your oasis zone for regular watering and drought tolerant zones for occasional watering. If you are young, strong, or determined, you can use buckets to water new plants in the natural zone until they are established, but hoses to reach everything make the job much easier. And I definitely find that easier jobs get done first and most often in my garden.

Irrigation systems can grow with your garden or be completely installed in the early stages of planning, before any planting is done. Check for details in Chapter 10, study some of the latest catalogs listed in Appendix B, and look over the products available at your local garden or builder's supply store. Consult with a professional if you feel that is the direction for you. In any case, be ready for welcome surprises. I'd been gardening for nearly 50 years, the last six in Florida, and still had my eyes opened and my gardening made easier and more successful by such simple additions as click-on hose connectors.

Your children or spouse may be thrilled to find something to give you for birthdays and Christmas. The category of "garden gadgets" has a wide price range for them. I get things this way I might never get around to buying for myself. It was my children who encouraged me to buy the microwave and the computer, and then showed me how to use them. They can bring us up to date on irrigation products, too, if we let them.

Soil Improvement

If you've done much growing in Florida, you've already started on soil improvement. For most gardeners this is a long-standing habit, but we can always increase our intensity and effectiveness with new discoveries like using legume inoculants and enzymes (see Chapter 6).

If you are a homeowner who wants to do the least work possible, soil improvement is the place to concentrate your effort. Add all the organic matter, compost, and humus that you can get.

As explained in Chapter 6, the bucket of kitchen waste collected by the sink becomes compost when you dump it right on top of the ground beneath the tree or shrub that needs it most. I can almost hear them calling, "My turn. Feed me," when I go out with humus in hand. And I notice that if I concentrate on one area for a while, it soon bursts into bloom or shows a spurt of growth.

Composting Aids

If having a series of bins or a compost drum will motivate you to make more compost faster and you want to invest, go for it. I have two plastic composters. One moved with us

Drum composter.

from Iowa after getting a good scrubbing. The movers were not pleased because they didn't know what to call the thing and seemed to feel it was beneath their dignity to move it when I told them. But it would have cost almost $100 to replace, and I've finally learned when to insist.

I did buy a drum composter second-hand and had to make two trips across the bay to bring it home. Be very careful when buying used composters. Mine has always been hard to turn, but is now becoming impossible as it begins to rust out along the turning grooves. The new ones I've tried turn much more easily than mine ever did. The Hillsborough County Cooperative Extension Service has an exhibit that shows all kinds of bins in use, and I've turned a few different kinds of drums there to check. Bear in mind also the difficulties in camouflage. Lower compost drums and piles can work away out of sight behind a single bush. My composter is something of an eyesore, irritating me all the more because I know it isn't doing its job. I wouldn't care so much if it were.

There are all sorts of compost activators available. You don't have to use any; you can't make bad compost, only make it more slowly. Less heat in a compost pile may also mean fewer weed seeds, insect eggs, and disease spores are killed, but any compost will do more good than harm. I've tried a few of the catalytic agents, but what I use most often is cotton-seed meal or rabbit manure. The first gives me an excuse to go to a feed store when I don't have anything but a compost pile to feed. A 50-pound bag lasts a long time. I learned to use cottonseed meal from Dick Raymond. In his book *Joy of Gardening* he also says that you can use a cheap dog food if you only get to the grocery store. Some of the people working on the Hillsborough County Cooperative Extension Service exhibit tell me they use compost ther-mometers. These help you to judge whether to add a catalyst and when to turn the pile, and might make composting more fun.

Soil Amendments

There are so many soil products, fertilizers, conditioners and amendments that you certainly don't need to use them all. Don't buy too much to keep track of and use. But do talk to other gardeners and find out what is working for them. Then make your own decisions and see what works for you.

Most of the things soil needs are close at hand and free, so recycle all the grass clippings, leaves, pine needles, potato skins, newspapers, cardboard boxes, and such that you can. We once bought a new mattress and tamed a large section of the yard for future groundcovers with the box until it rotted. This approach solves two problems, soil improvement and landfill overflow, at the same time.

Cardboard Funnel

Someone gave me one of these, but since the only things I bag in my garden are diseased branches that I want to eliminate to prevent the spread of spores, I did not use it. However, these funnels are a great idea for people who do bag and we might give them to the neighbors whose pine needles we most desire.

Water Retaining Gels

There are several gel products on the market — Soil Moist™ and Water Grabber™ are two — that absorb water and hold it in the root zone, where it can do the most good. Other similar products incorporate fertilizer also, but this reduces the amount of gel. Both kinds are slightly expensive, but in many cases a bargain nonetheless. I ordered a pound of Soil Moist from Mellinger's (see Appendix B) plus various other samples. I couldn't tell which helped my plants more — the products themselves or the increased enthusiasm they inspired and the improved garden care that resulted.

The gel has such astounding water-holding capacity that only a very minute amount should be dug in under a planting hole. Add too much and it will expand and push the plant right up and out of the ground, I found. If it is not buried deeply enough, the gel expands back to the surface of the soil, where it looks like lumps of clear gelatin. If this happens, dig it back into the soil right away, for it quickly becomes useless on the surface. In the soil it is good for several months to over a year, and by that time permanent plants are usually well enough established not to need it.

In containers, especially in hanging pots, the addition of gel can make the difference between having to water twice a day and every two days.

Other Moisture-Retaining Products

Another product that does much the same thing but in a different way is called Hydretain 75™, and is a liquid organic compound with hygroscopic properties. It forms a subsurface film that draws moisture through the soil, absorbing and storing it so that it is readily avail-able to plant root systems. The large, complex molecules of Hydretain cannot pass through the plant cells, but moisture can and does. Hydretain makes 50% to 100% more moisture available to the plant, whether that moisture comes from watering, rainfall, dew, or even just humidity.

Wholesale growers have been using Hydretain to cut labor costs and plant losses. Homeowners can use it in containers or in the ground to reduce regular watering, minimize stress, aid in transplant establishment, reduce fertilizer usage, and conserve water. It is said to help the moisture move laterally, so it should be especially helpful with drip irrigation. However, it should not be applied through the system. Its advantage over gels is that you can apply it in a water solution at any time before or after planting.

Another product that is similar, in application method and increased efficiency of water use, is Desert Bloom™. It has been used with great success in agriculture and in the seeding and plugging of lawns.

More such products will undoubtedly be developed in the future. Though we can live without them, they may become increasingly important if we let our water supply dwindle. We can't live without the water.

Mulch Cloth and Landscape Fabrics

These include plastics — which are useful — but more importantly, the newer porous fabrics, woven or nonwoven, that let air, water, and nutrients soak through. They also resist tearing and rotting. They are lightweight and effective at blocking weeds. Reemay makes a product called Typar™ that comes in circles of two sizes, designed to fit around trees. Easy Gardener has a white landscape fabric, as well as the usual black. The white is specifically designed for vegetable gardens and works well in Florida's cool season, reflecting light back onto the plant while blocking out 90% of the sunlight needed for weed germination and growth.

Reemay makes a fabric called The Germinator™ for covering grass seed. It slows soil drying and prevents seed loss through erosion, birds and wind, while speeding germination and allowing sunlight and rain to penetrate the fabric. It contributes to water conservation by eliminating the need to sprinkle germinating seeds several times a day to keep the surrounding soil moist.

Another product, Biobarrier™, will keep tree roots from coming up in paths and patios, but will also block any other roots from growing close to the surface in the area. For this reason, it should not be used under gardens or groundcovers.

Easy Gardener makes another white fabric they call Fast Start™ for use over seedlings, to create a greenhouse environment that collects and stores heat, releasing it slowly. This allows faster growth on short winter days. Reemay's floating row covers have much the same effect and can add 4° of frost protection. Both of these products let in enough light and air to stay on the plants for several days or even weeks during the winter. They could be invaluable for covering beds or plants when you go away for Christmas vacation, whether a frost comes or not, for they also cut down on evaporation, thereby decreasing water needs.

Moisture Sensor Gauges

Hand-held gauges are an efficient way to help you determine water needs. They are small meters you carry around and stick into containers, then compare the reading with a chart to determine when water is needed.

At the other extreme are tensiometers that can be permanently located in the garden and will tell you whether to water or not. These can be connected to the control box of your irrigation system to tell it when to skip preprogrammed watering cycles because the soil is moist enough. They require reprogramming your control box so that it checks with the sensor.

Many Florida farmers have completely automated watering to deal with specialized crops and conditions. Homeowners can save water without such systems, but their installation is worth considering.

There is also a biodegradable peat paper on the market. Because it will disintegrate, it can be dug right into the soil as an amendment. These mulch mats come in 10-inch squares with holes in the center to put around strawberries or newly-set annuals.

In summary, there are many materials that you can use with or without additional purchased or free mulches. I highly recommend these for use under porous hardscapes like mulched driveways, gravel paths and patios.

There are disadvantages to using these kinds of products. See Chapter 11 for a list of these.

Shade Cloth and Lath

These can be put up in summer to protect plants from Florida's relentless heat, then taken down in winter. They are especially useful for beds of rooting cuttings, newly-transplanted plants in containers, plants that grow best in shade in any climate, and plants that need full sun elsewhere but enjoy some shade, especially afternoon shade, in Florida summers. Water needs are greatly reduced in shaded soil and further reduced by shading foliage so that it transpires less.

The same effect can be produced, given a few months' to years' time, by deciduous shade trees or vines. They are less portable, but more attractive in the landscape as well as being productive. My peach and plum trees tend to have a light sprinkling of bloom on their bare branches for much of the winter, heavy bloom in early spring, and heavy fruiting in April to June.

Many people in Florida come to resent any woody plant that loses its leaves for the winter. I find it a poignant reminder, among all our lush tropical growth, of the bare branches the rest of the country has almost everywhere. And God didn't make leaves fall just on a whim. That added sunlight feels good in winter, even in Florida's mild climate.

Garden Shredder

This is a major investment that I am still contemplating. Bill Adrian is on his second shredder, one that throws the wood chips out to the side rather than directly below. He finds this a great improvement because it clogs less often.

A shredder would certainly make cleanup easier, quicker, and more rewarding to both the gardener and the trash collector. Right now I pile up woody branches behind some trees, but they take a long time to break down and aren't very attractive during the process. A shredder would make them into instant and attractive mulch. If you don't want to buy one, check to see if you can rent one for a day like the Garianos do (see Chapter 12). For many people it might be a more practical purchase than a trailer to haul mulch home from elsewhere.

Trucks and Trailers

My more serious organic gardening friends have trucks or trailers for hauling home horse manure from nearby stables, compost, etc. We had a trailer once and I used it well once I learned to turn it around in less than a seven-acre field. In Iowa, we had sons with pick-up trucks we could borrow. Tom Carey tells of one man who comes to the same stable he does and loads the used bedding right into the back of his new Cadillac. But Spouse frowns on that since we finally got a car made in this decade. Now I haul only bagged material. It's a limitation I can live with, since I produce so much of my own mulch and can grow cover crops for on-the-spot organic matter. See Chapter 7 for a comparison of wheelbarrows and garden carts.

Anti-Transpirant Sprays

Look in your garden store for any of these anti-transpirant or antidesiccant sprays: Wilt-pruf™, Safer's Forevergreen™, or Cloud Cover™. You may also find them labeled "Christmas Tree, Wreath, Indoor Green Plant Preservative" or "Christmas Tree Saver." These come in pints or quarts with a trigger sprayer ready to use. They cost from $5 to $9, will keep for years, and have many garden uses. ByoTron makes a product called Advantage Plant Shield™ with the added benefit of nutrients that can be absorbed by the plant as the shield breaks down.

Wilt-pruf invented their spray some thirty years ago. Other similar ones have appeared since then. Nurserymen have long used them to reduce needed watering, labor costs, moisture loss, transplant shock, frost injury, and stress from wind and drought. Wilt-pruf is a natural pine oil emulsion that is organic, biodegradable and nonhazardous. It now has a thinner formula that sprays more easily.

Some Christmas tree growers spray the trees before cutting. The spray coats the needles and twigs with an invisible film that slows down water loss or transpiration without stopping any of the natural processes. One grower sprayed his newly-transplanted trees and thus brought them through a serious summer drought. Christmas trees that have not been treated can be sprayed by the purchaser.

I like to have some of this spray on hand all the time. It works best if plants are well watered first. When we lived in Iowa, I used to spray all my treasured plants just before winter set in. Here in Florida, a spray prior to frost offers a few degrees of protection as well as keeping the plant turgid, thereby making it more resistant to damage. If you save one rosebush that would otherwise die, the spray pays for itself.

You can use the same spray when you transplant trees, shrubs, or vegetables to give them a better start. It is good for spraying on indoor plants, especially during that transition period when you put them out for the summer or bring them back in for the fall. It will also make your new plants adjust more quickly to your home. Try not to spray the flowers directly but only the foliage, and spray outdoors or against newspapers indoors. This spray can even save you a plant sitter when you go away, for tests show that it cuts the water loss from leaves by as much as 40% and lengthens time between waterings as much as 50%.

Mosquito Dunks

Most people know that mosquitoes lay their eggs in standing water. The eggs then hatch and grow into mosquito larvae. There is a struggle in my soul between always having a bucket of water handy and using it soon enough. I use it right away when I see the water full of swimming larvae or, worse, a cloud of young adult mosquitoes flying around the top of the rain barrel. This happened recently in just over a week, with cuttings left in a bucket outdoors.

I try to remember to keep the barrels covered, because mosquitoes will breed less rampantly in the dark, but lids come off during dipping or blow off in a storm. And even when they stay on, a few blood suckers get in the hole for the downspout.

So I was glad to find and try Mosquito Dunks™. These are little, tan, donut-shaped briquets that lie flat on standing water and control mosquitoes biologically for 30 days or longer. Each one is good for 100 square feet of water surface, regardless of depth. So I cut one into fourths for my rain barrels and they are working well. They weren't all that hard to cut. In fact, they were a bit crumbly, but I saved crumbs and all. Unused ones are best resealed and stored in a cool, dry, well-ventilated place.

The active ingredient in Mosquito Dunks is *Bacillus thuringiensis israelensis* (Bti), a natural biocontrol agent that is deadly to mosquito larvae but does not harm birds, dogs, cats, humans, other living things, or the environment. Bti has been used successfully by mosquito control agencies in the U.S. and in tropical countries where mosquitoes are a major carrier of infectious diseases. For years I've been using other strains of Bt to kill unfriendly bugs, with good results and a clear conscience, so this is most welcome news.

Besides rain barrels, you can put Dunks in wetland areas, unused swimming pools, ponds, ditches, woodland pools and tree holes. They are even recommended for birdbaths, but I find that the birds take care of the mosquitoes there.

126

Mosquito Dunks come in a package of six; I imagine one package will last me almost a year. If you can't find them in your local garden store, you can order them from the Smith & Hawken or Solutions catalogs.

Appendix B lists suppliers of the products mentioned in this chapter, as well as sources for seeds and garden tools.

Chapter Fourteen
Water Saving Suggestions

Start With Your Attitude

- When you get a leak, fix it or call the plumber right away. One drop a second wastes 200 gallons of water a month, or 2400 gallons a year. This also adds cost to your water and sewer bills and/or strains your septic system.

- Check for hidden leaks. Read your water meter before and after a two-hour period when no water is used. If it is not the same, you have some trouble somewhere that could get a lot worse the longer you don't find it.

- Get in the habit of listening for running water and satisfying your mind with the source. We once heard water running when it shouldn't have been and called in a plumber. He checked everything carefully, explained that we might have to dig under the foundation and spend $1600 replacing all our pipes. Then he found a hose that was slowly leaking — into the garden. We were overjoyed to replace that outdoor faucet and two other ones that were about to need replacing because of age.

- Teach your children the importance of saving water. Let them help you conserve. They may be the ones to hear the water running first.

- Support or initiate programs in the school system that encourage children to be aware of the problem and to conserve water.

- Avoid water toys that take a constant stream of water. If you already have them, use them on the lawn near your favorite tree or planting. The grass will make the play safer and the water will make the grass greener.

- Patronize businesses that are conserving water and let them know why you are doing so. Conversely, making your feelings known to water-wasting companies can help change their attitudes. One of my sons says, "I won't use those products precisely because their office looks too attractive. Why should we bear the cost of all that waste?"

- If you see flagrant violations of water restrictions — broken pipes, open hydrants, etc., report them to the property owner first, if possible. If he does not fix them or you cannot find him, call your local authorities or your Water Management District.

- Support government programs and vote for politicians who promote water conservation.

- Spread the word among your neighbors and friends and show them by example how well Xeriscaping and water saving can work.

- Learn to read your water meter and keep records of your progress in water saving.

- Save your water bills and try to shrink them. If they go up, find a good reason — like, the garden needs more water in May than in December, or the college daughter was home that month.

- If you are staying in a motel or hotel for several days, let the housekeeper know in writing that you do not want clean sheets every day. What a waste of wash water!

- Buy only products you really need. Besides the water we use directly, a great deal of water is needed for all aspects of manufacturing.

- Pass on products you don't use and really never will again. I am very bad about hoarding things myself. But giving surplus away will help someone else buy fewer products. We can adjust our economy to more service industries. We cannot adjust to lack of water.

- Eat less meat. It takes several times as much water to produce meat as it does to grow fruits and vegetables. I'll be the last one on earth to give up meat altogether, but I don't mind at all shifting the emphasis a bit, especially when Florida offers such a bounty of alternatives.

- Save any water from running down the drain when there may be another use for it, like watering plants or cleaning or carrying it outdoors to the birdbath or to your favorite tree.

- When you wash your car yourself, pull it onto the grass. Then the water will also water the grass and eventually filter back into the groundwater supply. Washing it on the driveway only overloads the sewer and makes twice the abuse out of what can be double use.

- When you go to a car wash, choose one that recycles the water. Many do these days. In more and more communities they are required to recycle water, so this choice may eventually disappear.

- Reject guilt feelings about using water. That is the tendency once we learn of the problems, but it does no good. Instead feel blessed above people of all eras up until this century. Then work however you can to make yourself a part of the solution instead of the problem.

- Rejoice if your children or your neighbors consider you weird for these efforts. My children did and said so, but I was proud to be so. Now that environmental sense is popular and they are older, they brag to their friends, "My mother was composting, mulching, and gardening organically decades ago." As for the neighbors, they either helped, joined in, or one of us moved away, so their opinions didn't matter.

- Thank God for giving us an abundance of water, the skill to pipe it into our homes, and the common sense to make it last.

Saving Water In the House

- "Take a shower with a tree" was a big theme at a San Francisco landscape show a few years ago. Buckets were on sale for the purpose, the idea being to put a bucket in every shower, kick it around a bit to catch the excess flow (being careful not to fall), then carry the water to a tree. That seemed a bit far out to this Floridian at the time, but we reinstall the bucket whenever rains are scarce.

- A more practical idea is to put a plastic pitcher under the washbowl spigot in each bathroom. Save the water you run before the tap is hot enough each time. Use this for watering the nearest tree or use it for a toilet flush. I was amazed to find that a friend had no idea how to flush a toilet with a bucket of water. We did it frequently when we lived on farms and the water went off with the electricity. Just pour $1\frac{1}{2}$ to 2 gallons of water right into the toilet bowl with as much speed as possible and it will wash down like a normal flush.

- Short showers take much less water, about half, than even moderately deep baths. My Aunt Joan told me this forty years ago and I didn't believe it until I plugged the tub and tried it. Try it yourself, and if the water comes over your ankles, you are standing too long or running the water too hard.

- Whether you are washing in tub or bowl, close the drain first before adjusting the temperature of the water flow. That first cold water warms up quickly in the volume, and you'll save a gallon or two right here.

- When changing water temperatures in tub or shower, turn the hot or cold — whichever is too much — *down*, rather than turning the other *up*.

- Always keep an eye on running water. Turn off spigots or hoses before answering the phone.

- Make it a contest, either personally or among family members, to try to get in and out of the shower without fogging up the mirror. Even a slow, luxurious shower can accomplish this if you turn the flow low for soaping and high for rinsing.

- Enjoy the water you are using to the fullest. I have been helping Grandma, who lives alone at 93, with her shampoos. She sits on an old chair in the tub and we use a hand-held, detachable shower head. We'd been doing this for a long time before we thought to plug up the tub and let the water accumulate so she could soak her feet, too.

- In cold weather, leave the bath or shower water to radiate heat into the room. Unplug the drain when the water has cooled.

- Try a low-flow shower head. Many people don't notice any difference, and some even prefer them. Your municipal water department may furnish them free. If your family complains too long and hard, make a compromise. Leave the low-flow on the shower in one bathroom and take it off the shower in the other. You'll still be saving a good bit of water.

- If you have a garbage disposal, use it as little as possible. Save that garbage for the compost pile or the shrubs. We find ours a wonderful luxury for the little debris that washes off almost-clean plates. Using a disposer this way or not at all can save up to 50% of your septic tank volume and cut down on maintenance and malfunctions. Flush the garbage disposal with *cold* water: this will solidify the greases and make them less likely to stick to pipes and form a blockage.

- If you have a septic tank, every month or so put some beneficial bacteria additive product like Rid-X down your toilets to activate the decomposition. We've been in our home for seven years and have never had to have our tank emptied, nor did it back up the September it rained for 15 days straight and flooded out Interstate 4.

- Consider water-saving plumbing. This includes faucets that you can easily turn down after you get the right water temperature, allowing you to soap up or shampoo in the shower under low or no water flow, then turn the water up for a final rinse. These are so convenient as well as sensible that you may want to replace other kinds of faucets right away.

- Flush the toilet only when necessary. Put that dead bug or piece of tissue in the trash can. Bury the goldfish out under the tree — he can be compost.

- Low-volume toilets take less water to flush. When you have to replace a toilet or any other major plumbing fixture, consider the water-saving alternatives first. A water-saving toilet takes about 1.6 gallons per flush, compared to 3.5 gallons for a standard toilet. These will eventually be required by law, but you'll be saving water and money while you are ahead of your time. One person I know got a new low-volume toilet and the water bill went down $10 a month with only two people in the family.

- Check toilets for leaks by putting a bit of food coloring in the tank. Check in half an hour to see if any has leaked into the bowl. Most replacement parts are easy to find and install, and are inexpensive. Flush away the food coloring after you check the toilet, or it could stain some plumbing.

- Put a milk jug filled with water, or a brick wrapped securely in a plastic bag, in your toilet tank to reduce the amount of water for each flush; check and replace as needed. When I used a half-gallon milk jug, it eventually floated and caused some trouble. The plastic bag will keep crumbs from the brick from blocking the plumbing.

- Run dishwasher and clothes washer only for full loads.

- Use a water softener only if you really need it. We once had a well so rusty we bought no white clothes and ate rusty spaghetti. The taste was great and we didn't need to take iron pills. The minerals in softened water can be beneficial to the garden in some cases, but move the hoses around so no area gets too big a concentration of salts.

- If you have your own well and pump, listen to see if the pump kicks on and off while the water is not running. If so, there is a leak somewhere.

- Instead of running water for ages while rinsing dishes, put a bucket or large pan in the sink and dip them. Then you can take that water out to the garden. If it has a few bits of garbage, all the better. I once read a story where the children had to wash the dishes without any soap so they could give that nutritious water to the family's pig. I miss my pigs, but I never did go that far. If rinsing under the faucet is a luxury you can't yet forgo, at least pile up the dishes first, and then rinse quickly at the lowest flow needed.

- If you must wash your hands often, because you have a baby in the house or for some other reason, keep a pan or jug of water on the sink. Room temperature is warm enough and this will save you running gallons of cold water down the drain to get warm. You might also use baby wipes. I don't know how much water goes into the manufacture of those, but I'm sure there were many times when it would have cut our water bill.

- Keep drinking water in the refrigerator rather than running the tap to cool it. This is justification for an in-the-door dispenser. One of my friends has a super hot water dispenser on her sink, and that also may be justified by water savings. If you don't have one of these, when you need a cup of hot water, heat it in the microwave.

- Instead of thawing meat under running water, get it out early and thaw it in the refrigerator, or defrost it in the microwave.

- Get some ice cube trays that flip out the cubes without your having to run water over them.

- Serve water with meals only to those who drink it and only as much as will be consumed. In restaurants, ask for water only if you will drink it. It isn't the water so much as the dishwashing that makes the big savings in restaurants.

- Clean with a broom or vacuum cleaner instead of soap and water whenever possible. Clean up small spills and mop the whole floor less often. At last, we have a good excuse!

Co-Exist with Teenagers

- Place a nicely printed sign in your bathroom saying "Water is a precious resource and this family tries to save it by limiting shower time and water intensity." Hopefully, this will do more good than your listening with increasing anxiety as the water runs full force for so long that finally you have to knock on the door and scream, "Aren't you almost finished? The water is running out!" In any case, it is less embarrassing for parent, teenager, and guest. (That bucket in the shower is also a good, no-nag reminder.)

- I found my 16-year-old daughter standing in the bathtub with the water running full force while she washed the Nair off her legs and talked on the phone at the same time. So I made a new house rule: No running water while talking on the phone.

Water Savings in the Garden

- Sunny areas will need more water than shady ones.

- Keep new washers on hand and replace them as needed on your garden hoses. Use them between spigots and hose and between hose connections. Check all spigots and hose connections regularly and fix leaks immediately.

- Find and use a good hose nozzle that will adjust from mist to force and turn off at the water end. The commonly-found ones only cause more leaks. Get a good one from a garden supply store or catalog.

- When using a hose nozzle, always turn the water off at the spigot end as soon as possible. The force can otherwise cause leaks and wear out your hose.

- Use a blower or a broom to remove leaves, acorns and grass clippings from driveway, deck or sidewalk to the mulch or compost pile. Using water force to clean hardscapes can take hundreds of gallons of water and sends everything into the sewer.

- If you've been watering, water less and see what happens. Chances are that many plants will do almost as well, some even better. This will also help you decide which of your established plants need to be in which Xeriscape zones, so you can move them accordingly.

- Give plants only as much water as they require. Overwatering makes for more diseases, stress on the plants from wet roots, and weak new growth.

- Set your irrigation system on automatic *only* after you have experimented extensively to see how long you can go between waterings and how short a time is needed to dampen the top several inches of soil when you do.

- In Florida, especially in summer, plants that are sun lovers elsewhere will thrive on less water in light shade.

- Cut back on watering during non-crucial times. This would be in the winter for plants that go almost dormant, after bloom and harvest for fruits, after flowering for ornamentals that flower only in certain seasons, like azaleas and dogwoods which bloom in the spring.

- Never overfertilize, for this leads to tender new growth with possible problems, and more water needs.

- If ornamental trees and shrubs are growing satisfactorily, feed them only once a year.

- Keep irrigation systems in good repair. Clean clogged sprinkler heads, tubing, or emitters. Replace broken parts.

- When water restrictions are stringent, first water the plants most likely to suffer. And if you have to choose between those, choose the ones most difficult or expensive to replace. The lawn is the last thing I'd water. If it should die, I'd replace it with something better. But my dogwood tree has several years of growth that are beyond price.

- Recycle kitchen wastes by keeping a decorative pan, with lid and handles, near the sink. Into this put potato peels, vegetable parings, egg shells, coffee grounds, the (unsalted) water you pour off when cooking vegetables, and anything else that will rot back into the soil. Dump it once a day into the worm box, compost pile, or under a bush. Cover it with soil or grass clippings if you want to be very neat. Bones and fat are the only items best disposed of elsewhere.

- Rinse vegetables first in a bucket in the garden and then pour both the water and the good soil back where it will do the most good. Then keep a bucket or large pan by the sink for further water-saving rinses and carry it to your oasis zone when it gets too full of soil, nutrients, and humus for more washing. All those things are great for the growing plants.

- If you both wash and cook vegetables with the least amount of water for the least amount of time, you save those very soluble nutrients as well as the water. After cooking, pour off the water. Save it in jars in the refrigerator if you will use it soon for soups, sauces, or gravy. If not, pour it into the garbage bucket for the compost pile.

- Use water from the fish bowl, the tooth cup, sprouting seeds, vases of spent flowers, etc., for watering indoor and patio plants. It contains valuable nutrients. What is yukky is not necessarily useless and what makes that fish water yukky will be treasure for growing plants.

Container Plants

- Group these together so they can shade each other.

- Put containers in the deepest shade the plants can tolerate — that will be more in the summer than in the winter.

- Put plants in the largest container that is practical. Large containers dry out much less quickly than small ones.

- For the same reason, put two or three smaller plants together in larger pots. Tom Carey of Sundew Gardens in Oviedo plants his vegetable, flower, and herb seedlings four to a four-inch pot, rather than in individual pots.

- Move rootbound plants to larger containers.

- Put a mulch on top of the pot surface. But dig down to the soil if you are using a finger to feel for water needs.

- Use a gauge to determine when a plant really needs water. One professional interior scaper, Ellen Skinner, inserts a moisture meter into each pot. A dial on the top registers water needs and she waters or not according to the reading, then pulls it out and probes the next pot. These meters sell at discount and home supply stores for around $10. They are supposed to last six months, but Skinner has used the same one all day three days a week for as long as two years.

- Use light-colored pots that don't absorb as much of the sun's heat.

- Add water-retaining products to the soil mix (see Chapter 13). These can cut watering from twice a day to every two days, and also cut down stress for the plants.

- Set small pots on the surface of larger pots. This way, you can water them all at once, and what drains from the small pots waters the larger one. But lift the pots often enough — once a month — to prevent the plants from rooting through the bottom hole into the larger pot. When this happens, it is usually time to repot.

- Use old pans or dishes under containers to catch the overflow. Learn to regulate your watering so any runoff is reabsorbed into the pot within 20 minutes. If it stays longer than half an hour, dump it into a bucket or suck it up with a baster and use it to water something else.

- Sink containers into the soil up to their rims and they will be insulated enough to dry out much less quickly.

- Set plants around trees or under shrubs, and the runoff from the containers will water the larger plants.

- Use hanging baskets sparingly, especially during the summer. They take the most water of all and need to be checked up to twice a day.

- If you use hanging planters, put thirsty plants beneath them to use up the overflow.

Fruit Trees

- Remove grass growing around fruit trees, especially citrus. This eliminates competition for water and nutrients and prevents damage from mowers and trimmers. Nicks they make in the bark can lead to diseases, pest infestation, and often to the death of the tree.

- Thin fruit to prevent fruit drop, branches breaking from overweight, and dinky fruits that are mostly peel and seeds. This allows the tree to produce better quality fruit with less water use.

- Water deciduous trees very little or not at all during the winter, depending on the tree and the weather.

Lawns

- Eliminate lawns where they are merely a cover-up. Use them only as design features or where needed for a safe play area.

- Use mulch for paths. It is easier to walk on since it never gets too high.

- Although experts agree that it is a necessity, the truth is that I have never watered a lawn in my life except where new grass was germinating or plugs were settling. And neither our St. Augustine nor our bahia has suffered any permanent damage.

- If you are determined to water your lawn, watch for signs that it is thirsty. Water only when the turf loses its resiliency and footprints show more, the grass takes on a bluish cast, and growth seems to slow considerably.

- When you turn on the sprinkler and go indoors, turn on an oven timer to remind you when to go back and turn off the water. A garden hose forgotten can pour out 600 gallons of water in a few hours.

Hot Tubs, Pools and Water Features

- Drain your pool if rainwater or a careless helper overfills it. Too much water is hard on the motor as well as wasteful. Explain this kindly to your helper.

- Fill your pool up to the recommended level. Too little water is also hard on the motor, but . . .

- Take a chance if a rainstorm looks likely, especially in summer. You'll only have to drain tomorrow if nature is too kind. If you must add a little water, do so, and if the rain doesn't come, add more when the sky clears.

- Drain, when you must, into sturdy growth of less-treasured plants, for the chemicals will do some damage. But the water filtering through the ground will also get back to the aquifer and be well filtered by the soil when it arrives.

- When draining the pool, for any reason, set a timer in the house that will keep ringing until you turn it off. I once remembered I'd left the pool draining when we were clear into Tampa to go out to dinner. We made a quick phone call — otherwise, the pool would have been empty before we got home. Shameful waste.

- If you do not already have a water-saving filter, consider getting one as soon as possible. A single backflushing with the older-style filters can use from 180 to 250 gallons or more of water.

- Cover the pool and spa when you don't expect to be using it for a time. In hot, breezy weather, more than an inch can evaporate in a week, and that can be more than 1000 gallons a month from a pool as small as 15 x 30 feet.

Mrs. Maryon Marsh of Brandon has a natural-looking pool with waterfall, aquatic plants and fish.

- When you remove a pool cover, be sure that no untreated rainwater or debris within the cover gets into the pool itself. Instead, put this on the garden where it will be beneficial. In the pool, it could upset the chemical balance. When we first moved to Florida we did not know any better and just pulled the cover away. It took a week, with the help of a professional pool man, to get the pool fit for swimming and longer to get it as clean as it should be.

- Feel free to put in a fish or lily pond, one or more. They use less water for the same amount of space than would be needed to grow grass.

- If you have a fountain or waterfall feature, be sure it is one that recycles the water. Place it where there will be a minimum of evaporation from wind and sun. Then use it when you are near, but turn it off when no one is around to enjoy it. Running the pump on a fountain or waterfall does increase water loss from evaporation.

Appendix A – Plant Selection Guide

The information in the following charts is excerpted from booklets compiled by the Northwest Florida, St. Johns River, South Florida and Southwest Florida Water Management Districts, augmented by information in Betrock's Reference Guide to Florida Landscape Plants, The Right Plants for Dry Places, *and* Florida Plants for Wildlife *(see bibliography). Plant selection guides, landscape design brochures, irrigation guides and other information can be obtained by Florida residents, usually free of charge, by contacting local Water Management District or Cooperative Extension Service offices.*

"Moderately Drought Tolerant" plants (✳*) are appropriate for the drought tolerant zone. "Very Drought Tolerant" plants (*✳ ✳*) are appropriate for the natural zone. Other plants should be placed in the oasis zone. See page 15 for definitions of these xeriscape zones.*

key to abbreviations

Drought tolerance
(Plant drought tolerance will vary depending on soil conditions and other environmental factors.)
  ✳ **Moderately Drought Tolerant**: Will require supplemental irrigation during extreme dry periods to maintain attractive appearance.
  ✳ ✳ **Very Drought Tolerant**: Will survive without supplemental irrigation after establishment.
Invasive
  Y – Yes, N – No
Growth Rate
  S – Slow, M – Medium, F – Fast
Native
  Y – Yes, N – No
Cold Hardiness Zone
  VH–Hardy throughout Florida
  H – Hardy to the Orlando, Tampa vicinity
  S – Subtropical, withstands light frost
  T – Tender
Salt Tolerance
  N – No, not salt tolerant
  M – Moderate salt tolerance
  Y – Yes, very salt tolerant
Wind Tolerance
  L – Low, M – Medium, H – High
Plant Type
  (For Shrubs and Trees)
  E – Evergreen, D – Deciduous, P – Palm
  (For Groundcovers)
  W – Woody, H – Herbaceous
  (For Vines)
  R – Rambling, T – Tendrils, TW – Twining, S – Spiny,
  E – Evergreen, D – Deciduous, AR – Aerial Roots
Foliage Color*
  G – Green, V – Variegated, PU – Purple, Y – Yellow,
  R – Red, W – White, S – Silver
Flower Color*
  G – Greenish, W – White, O – Orange, P – Pink,
  PU – Purple, R – Red, B – Blue, Y – Yellow,
  L – Lavender, BR – Brown
Flower Characteristics
  S – Showy, I – Insignificant, F – Fragrant

* *Two colors separated by "/" indicates a combination of colors. Two colors separated by "," indicates two separate flower colors.*

Flowering Season
  SP – Spring, S – Summer, F – Fall, W – Winter,
  Y – Year-round
Light Requirements
  L – Low, M – Medium, H – High
Nutritional Requirements
  L – Low, M – Medium, H – High
Soil pH
  W – Wide, A – Acid
Uses (Suggested)
  (Shrubs)
  SP – Specimen Plant, IH – Informal Hedge,
  FH – Formal Hedge, GC – Ground Cover
  (Trees)
  PK – Park, R – Residence, M – Medians, S – Shade,
  B – Boulevards, PL – Parking Lot, P – Perimeter,
  BU – Buffer, F – Fruit, SP – Specimen Plant
  (Ground Covers)
  T – Under Trees, B – Banks and Slopes,
  O – Open Areas, E – Edges, S – Seasides
  (Vines)
  T – Trees and Trellises, F – Fences,
  GC – Ground Cover, M – Masonry
Wildlife Value
  F – Food, N – Nest, U – None or undetermined
Protection Status
  P – Protected, E – Endangered, T – Threatened,
  N – Not Protected

TURFGRASS ABBREVIATIONS
Mowing Frequency
  Number of days between mowings.
Establishment
  Se – Seed, Sp – Sprigs, So – Sod, P – Plugs
Wear Tolerance
  E – Excellent, G – Good, F – Fair, P – Poor
Turf Density
  H – High, M – Medium, L – Low
Turf Texture
  C – Coarse, M – Medium, F – Fine
Maintenance Level
  H – High, M – Moderate, L – Low
Pest Problems
  H – High, M – Moderate, L – Low

Aloe
Aloe barbadensis

Blue-Eyed Grass
Sisrynchium spp.

turfgrasses

Drought Tolerance	Common Name	Scientific Name	Natural Height	Mowing Height	Mowing Frequency	Na
✳ ✳	Bahia grass	*Paspalum notatum*	20"	3–4"	7–14	
✳ ✳	Bermuda grass	*Cynodon dactylon*	16"	0.5–1"	3–7	
	Carpet grass	*Axonopus affinis*	14"	1–2"	10–14	
✳	Centipede grass	*Eremochloa ophriuoides*	4"	1.5–2"	10–14	
✳	Italian Ryegrass*	*Lolium multiflorum*	36"	1.5–2"	10–14	
✳	Perennial Ryegrass*	*Lolium perenne*	24"	1.5–4"	10–14	
✳	St. Augustine grass	*Stenotaphrum secundatum*	14"	2.5–3.5"	7–14	
✳ ✳	Zoysia grass	*Zoysia japonica*	9"	1–2"	10–14	

*Use for overseeding only — not suitable for lawns

ground covers

Drought Tolerance	Common Name	Scientific Name	Invasive Plant	Natural Height Range	Nominal Height	Growth Rate	Na
✳	African Iris	*Dietes vegeta*	N	24"	24	M	
✳ ✳	Allamanda, Wild	*Urechites lutea*	N	12–24"	15	M	
✳	Allamanda, Yellow	*Allamanda cathartica*	N	24–48"	36	F	
✳ ✳	Aloe	*Aloe* spp.	N	12"	12	M	
✳	Artillery Plant	*Pilea microphylla*	N	12"	12	M	
✳ ✳	Bauhinia, Red	*Bauhinia punctata*	N	48–96"	72	M	
✳ ✳	Beach Bean	*Canavalia maritima*	N	6–12"	10	F	
✳	Begonia, Star	*Begonia heracleifolia*	N	24–36"	20	M	
✳	Blanket Flower	*Gaillardia pulchella*	N	12–24"	18	M	
✳ ✳	Blazing Stars	*Liatris* spp.	N	12–48"	24	M	
✳	Blue Daze	*Evolvulus* spp.	N	10–12"	10	M	
	Blue-Eyed Grass	*Sisrynchium* spp.	N	12"	12	M	
✳ ✳	Bougainvillea	*Bougainvillea spectabilis*	N	72–96"	72	M	
✳	Bromeliads	*Bromeliaceae* fam.	N	6–18"	12	S	
	Bugleweed	*Ajuga reptans*	Y	8–10"	10	M	
	Caladium	*Caladium* X *hortulanum*	N	12–18"	18	M	
✳	Canna, Garden	*Canna* X *generalis*	N	36–60"	48	F	
	Canna, Golden	*Canna flaccida*	N	36–60"	48	F	
✳ ✳	Carissa, Dwarf	*Carissa macrocarpa*	N	12–18"	15	S	
✳	Cast Iron Plant	*Aspidistra elatior*	N	20–30"	25	S	
✳ ✳	Coontie	*Zamia floridana*	N	12–36"	24	S	
✳ ✳	Crown-of-Thorns	*Euphorbia milli*	N	9–36"	15	S	
✳ ✳	Daylily	*Hemerocallis* spp.	N	12–36"	24	M	
✳	Dichondra	*Dichondra micrantha*	Y	1–3"	2	M	
	Fern, Holly	*Cyrtomium falcatum*	N	12–24"	16	S	

Blue Daze
Evolvulus spp.

Cold Hardiness	Salt Tolerance	Light Requirements	Soil pH	Establishment	Wear Tolerance	Turf Density	Turf Texture	Maintenance	Pest Problems
VH-S	N	H	Wide	Se,So	G	L	M	L	L
H,S	Y	H	Wide	So,Sp	E	H	F	H	H
VH	N	M	A	Se,Sp	P	M	C	L	L
VH	N	H	A	Se,So,Sp	P	M	M	L	M
VH-S	?	M	A	Se	Varies	M	M	M	H
VH-S	M	L	A	Se	Varies	M	F	M	H
H,S	Y	M	Wide	So,Sp,P	F	M	C	M	M
H,S	M	H	Wide	So,Sp	E	H	F	M	M

Cold Hardiness	Salt Tolerance	Plant Type	Foliage Color	Flower Color	Flower Characteristics	Flowering Season	Light Requirements	Nutritional Requirements	Soil pH	Uses	Wildlife Value	Protected Species
	N	H	H	W/B/BR	S	Y	H	L	W	B,O,E	U	N
	Y	W	G	Y	S	Y	H	M	W	O,S	U	N
	N	E	G	Y	S,F	SP,S,F	H	M	W	B,O	U	N
	Y	H	G	R,P,Y	I	S	H,M	L	W	B,S,O	U	N
	N	H	G	G	I	Y	L,M,H	M	W	T,E,O	U	N
	N	W	G	R	S	SP,S,F	H	M	W	B,O	U	N
	Y	H	G	PU	S	Y	H	L	W	S	U	N
	M	H	G	P	S	SP	M	M	W	T	U	N
I	Y	H	G	R,Y,R/Y	S	Y	H	L	W	B,E,O	U	N
I	N	H	G	PU,P	S	F	H	L	W	B,E,O	U	N
	Y	H	S/G	B	S	Y	M,L	M	W	B,S,O	U	N
	N	H	G	B,W	S	Sp	M,H	L	W	O,B,E	U	N
	M	W	G,V	PU,O,R,W,P	S	Y	H	M	W	B,O	U	N
	N	H	G,R,PU,V	W,PU,R	S	S	L,M,H	L	A	T,E	U	N
	N	H	G,PU,V	W,PU	S	Y	L,M	M	W	T,B	U	N
	N	H	V	G/W	I	S	M,H	M	W	T,O,E	U	N
I	N	H	G,R,V	O,P,R,Y,Y/R	S	S,F	H	M	W	W,O	U	N
	N	H	G	Y	S	S	H	M	W	W,O	U	N
	Y	W	G	W	S,F	S,F	M,H	M	W	B,E,S,O	F	N
	M	H	G,V	PU	I	SP	L	L	W	T	U	N
	Y	W	G	N/A	N/A	N/A	M,H	L	W	T,E,B,S,O	U	T
	Y	W	G	P,R,Y	S	Y	H,M	M	W	B,E,S,O	U	N
	Y	H	G	Y,P,O	S	SP,S,F	H	M	W	B,S,O	U	N
I	M	H	G	?	I	?	L,M	M	W	T,E,O	U	N
	M	H	G	N/A	N/A	N/A	M,L	M	W	T,B,E	U	N

Beach Sunflower
Helianthus debilis

Daylily
Hemerocallis spp.

ground covers *(continued)*

Drought Tolerance	Common Name	Scientific Name	Invasive Plant	Natural Height Range	Nominal Height	Growth Rate	Na
❋ ❋	Fern, Bracken	*Pteridium aquilinum* var. *caudatum*	N	24–48"	36	F	
	Fern, Cinnamon	*Osmunda cinnamomea*	N	24–48"	36	F	
	Fern, Leather Leaf	*Rumohra adiantiformis*	N	18–30"	24	M	
	Fern, Maiden	*Thelypteris* spp.	N	18–30"	24	M	
	Fern, Royal	*Osmunda regalis* var. *spectabilis*	N	48–60"	48	M	
❋ ❋	Fig, Creeping	*Ficus pumila*	Y	10–12"	10	F	
❋ ❋	Fig, Oakleaf	*Ficus montana*	Y	24–36"	30	M	
❋ ❋	Fig, Trailing	*Ficus sagittata*	N	10–12"	10	F	
❋	Garlic, Society	*Tulbaghia violacea*	N	15–24"	15	M	
❋	Geranium	*Pelargonium* spp.	N	12–36"	24	M	
❋	Gerbera Daisy	*Gerbera jamesonii*	N	12–24"	18	M	
❋ ❋	Golden Creeper	*Ernodea littoralis*	N	12–36"	20	M	
❋ ❋	Gopher Apple	*Licania michauxii*	N	3–12"	6	M	
❋ ❋	Grape	*Vitis* spp.	Y	24–48"	36	F	
❋ ❋	Greeneyes	*Berlandiera subacaulis*	N	12–24"	20	M	
❋	Horsemint, Dotted	*Monarda punctata*	N	24–48"	36	M	
❋	Heather, False	*Cuphea hyssopifolia*	N	12–15"	12	M	
	Iris, Prairie	*Iris hexagona*	N	24–30"	30	M	
❋	Ivy, Algerian	*Hedera canariensis*	Y	8–12"	10	F	
❋	Jasmine	*Jasminum* spp.	N	24–72"	48	M	
❋	Jasmine, Small Leaf Confederate	*Trachelospermum asiaticum*	Y	6–12"	8	M	
❋ ❋	Juniper, Chinese	*Juniperus chinensis*	N	12–36"	24	M	
❋ ❋	Juniper, Shore	*Juniperus conferta*	N	12–24"	18	M	
❋ ❋	Kalanchoe	*Kalanchoe* spp.	Y	6–18"	12	M	
❋ ❋	Lantana, Dwarf	*Lantana depressa*	N	8"	8	M	
❋ ❋	Lantana, Trailing	*Lantana montevidensis*	N	18–24"	18	M	
❋	Lavender, English	*Lavandula angustifolia*	N	12–36"	24	M	
❋	Lily-of-the-Nile	*Agapanthus africanus*	N	18–48"	30	S	
❋ ❋	Lily Turf, Creeping	*Liriope spicata*	N	6–18"	12	M	
	Lily, Rain	*Zephryanthes* spp.	N	8–12"	10	S	
❋ ❋	Liriope	*Liriope muscari*	N	12"	12	M	
❋ ❋	Matchweed	*Lippia nodiflora*	Y	3"	3	F	
❋ ❋	Mexican Petunia	*Ruellia brittonia*	Y	18–24"	20	M	
❋	Mondo Grass	*Ophiopogon japonicus*	N	6–12"	9	M	
	Monkey Plant	*Ruellia makoyana*	Y	8–12"	10	M	
❋ ❋	Morning Glory	*Ipomoea* spp.	Y	6–12"	8	F	
❋ ❋	Muhlygrass, Pink	*Muhlenbergia capillaris*	N	36–48"	36	M	
❋ ❋	Oats, Sea	*Uniola paniculata*	N	36–72"	48	M	
❋ ❋	Palmetto, Saw	*Serenoa repens*	N	48–96"	72	S	

Coontie
Zamia pumila

	Salt Tolerance	Plant Type	Foliage Color	Flower Color	Flower Characteristics	Flowering Season	Light Requirements	Nutritional Requirements	Soil pH	Uses	Wildlife Value	Protected Species
	N	H	G	N/A	N/A	—	M,H	L	W	B,T,O,E	U	N
	N	H	G	N/A	N/A	—	M,H	L	W	B,T,O,E	U	N
	N	H	G	N/A	N/A	N/A	L,M	M	W	T,B	U	N
	N	H	G	N/A	N/A	N/A	L,M	M	W	T,B	U	N
	N	H	G	N/A	N/A	N/A	L,M	M	A	T,B	U	N
	Y	W	G	G	I	S	M,H	M	W	T,B,S	U	N
	N	W	G	G	I	S	L,M	M	W	T,B	U	N
	M	W	G	G	I	S	M,H	M	W	T,B	U	N
	M	H	G	PU	S	SP	M,H	M	W	O	U	N
	N	H	G	W,P,R,O	S	Y	H	M	W	T,E	U	N
	N	H	G	W,Y,P,O,R	S	W,SP	M,H	M	W	T,O,E	U	N
	Y	W	Y/G	P	I	Y	H	L	W	B,S,O	U	N
	Y	W	G	G	I	S	H	L	W	B,S,O	U	N
	H	H	G	G	I	SP	H	M	W	B,O	F	N
	N	H	G	G/Y	S	Y	H	M	W	B,O,E	U	N
	M	H	G	W/P/PU	S	SP,S	H	L	W	B,O,E,S	U	N
	N	W	G	W,P	S	Y	M,H	M	W	E,O	U	N
	L	H	G	W/PU	S	SP	H	M	A	E,O	U	N
	Y	W	V	W	I	SP,S	M,H	M	W	T,B,E,S,O	U	N
	N	W	G	W,Y	S,F	SP,S	H,M	M	W	T,B,E,O	U	N
	M	W	G,G/W	Y/W	I	S	H,M	M	W	T,B,O	U	N
	M	W	G	G	I	SP	H	L	W	B,E,O	U	N
	Y	W	G	G	I	SP	H	L	W	B,E,S,O	U	N
	M	H	B–G	P,Y	S	S	H	L	W	B,E,O	U	N
	M	H	G	Y	S	Y	H	L	W	B,O	U	N
	Y	W	G	L	S	Y	H	M	W	B,E,S,O	U	N
	N	H	S	PU	S,F	S	H	M	W	E,O	U	N
	N	H	G	B,W	S	SP	M	M	W	O,E	U	N
	Y	H	G	PU,W	S	S	M	M	W	T,B,O	U	N
	Y	H	G	P,PU,W	S	SP,S,F	M,H	M	W	E,S,O	U	N
	M	H	G,V	PU	S	SP	M	M	W	T,B,E,O	U	N
	Y	H	G	P	I	Y	H	L	W	T,B,E,S,O	U	N
	M	H	G	L,B	S	SP,S	H,M	M	W	O	U	N
	Y	H	G	L,I	I	SP	M,L	M	W	T,B,E,S,O	U	N
	N	H	PU-G	PU	S	Y	M	M	W	T,E,O	U	N
H	Y	H	G	PU,W	S	Y	H	L	W	S	U	N
	H	H	G	P	S	F	M,H	L	W	B,T,O,E,S	U	N
	Y	H	G	W	I	SP,S	H	L	W	S	U	P
	Y	P	G,B/G	W	I,F	S	M,H	L	W	T,O,B,S	F	N

Barberry (shown with honeysuckle)
Berberis spp.

ground covers *(continued)*

Drought Tolerance	Common Name	Scientific Name	Invasive Plant	Natural Height Range	Nominal Height	Growth Rate	Na
✳	Partridge Berry	*Mitchella repens*	N	4–6"	6	M	
✳ ✳	Peanut, Beach	*Okenia hypogaea*	N	6"	6	M	
✳ ✳	Pennyroyal	*Piloblephis rigida*	N	12–24"	18	M	
✳ ✳	Periwinkle	*Catharanthus roseus*	N	10–18"	14	M	
✳ ✳	Petunia, Wild	*Ruellia caroliniensis*	N	12–24"	24	M	
✳	Philodendron, Tree	*Philodendron selloum*	N	48–96"	60	F	
✳	Pittosporum, Dwarf	*Pittosporum tobira 'Wheeleri'*	N	12–24"	15	S	
✳	Plumbago	*Plumbago auriculata*	Y	24–48"	36	M	Na
✳	Porterweed, Creeping Blue	*Stachytarpheta jamaicensis*	N	10–12"	12	F	
✳	Pothos	*Epipremnum aureum*	Y	10–12"	12	F	
✳	Powderpuff	*Mimosa strigillosa*	N	6–10"	8	F	
✳ ✳	Puncture Vine	*Tribulus terrestris*	Y	12"	12	M	
✳ ✳	Purple Heart	*Setcreasea pallida*	Y	10–14"	12	F	
	Purpleleaf Wintercreeper	*Euonymus fortunei*	N	12–24"	24	M	
✳ ✳	Purslane, Sea	*Sesuvium portulacastrum*	N	12–18"	14	M	
✳ ✳	Railroad Vine	*Ipomoea pes-caprae*	Y	4–6"	5	F	
	Rosemallow, Scarlet	*Hibiscus coccineus*	N	48–72"	60	M	
	Rosemallow, Swamp	*Hibiscus grandiflorus*	N	48–72"	60	M	
✳ ✳	Scorpion-tail	*Heliotropium angiospermum*	N	24–36"	36	F	
✳ ✳	Sea Oxeye Daisy	*Borrichia frutescens*	N	24–48"	36	S	
	Selaginella, Blue	*Selaginella uncinata*	N	8–20"	15	F	
	Selaginella, Erect	*Selaginella involvens*	N	8–12"	10	S	
✳ ✳	Silkgrass, Narrowleaf	*Pityopsys graminifolia*	N	24–36"	30	F	
✳ ✳	Snowberry, Pineland	*Chiococca pinetorum*	N	24–36"	30	S	
	Spanish Shawl	*Dissotis rotundifolia*	N	5–6"	5	M	
✳	Spider Plant	*Chlorophytum comosum*	N	10–12"	10	F	
✳	Spiderwort	*Tradescantia ohiensis*	N	8–12"	10	F	
✳ ✳	Sunflower, Beach	*Helianthus debilis*	N	12–24"	18	F	
✳ ✳	Tickseed, Lanceleaf	*Coreopsis lanceolata*	N	12–36"	24	M	
✳ ✳	Tropical Sage	*Salvia coccinea*	N	24–48"	36	F	
✳ ✳	Verbena, Beach	*Glandularia maritima*	N	18–36"	24	M	
✳	Verbena, Tampa	*Glandularia tampensis*	N	18–24"	20	M	
✳	Wandering Jew	*Zebrina pendula*	Y	4–10"	8	F	

Dotted Horsemint
Monarda punctata

Gopher apple
Licania michauxii

	Salt Toler- ance	Plant Type	Foliage Color	Flower Color	Flower Charac- teristics	Flowering Season	Light Require- ments	Nutritional Require- ments	Soil pH	Uses	Wildlife Value	Protected Species
	N	W	G	W	I	SP	L	M	A	T,E,B	U	N
	Y	H	G	PU	N	S	H	L	W	S	U	E
	N	H	G	PU	S	W,SP	H	L	A	B,E,O	U	N
	Y	H	G	W,PU,P	S	Y	H,M	L	W	B,E,SO	U	N
	N	H	G	PU	S	SP,SU	M,H	L	W	B,T,O,E	U	N
	N	W	G	W	I	S	H,M	M	W	B,T,O	U	N
	Y	W	G	W	I	S	M,L	M	W	B,E,S,O	U	N
	N	W	F	B,W	S,F	S	H	M	W	B,E,O	U	N
	Y	H	G	PU	S	SP–F	L,M,H	L	W	T,B,E,S,O	U	N
	N	H	V	G	I	S	L,M	M	W	T,B	U	N
	N	H	G	P	S	SP,S	H	M	W	B,E,O	U	N
	Y	H	G	Y	S	SP,S,F	H	L	W	B,S,O	U	N
	Y	H	PU	P	I	Y	M,H	M	W	T,E,S,O	U	N
	M	E	G,PU	W	I	SP	M	M	W	T,B,E,S,O	U	N
	Y	H	G	P	S	Y	H	L	W	S	U	N
	Y	H	G	PU	S	S,F	H	L	W	B,S,O	U	N
	N	H	G	R	S	SP,SU	M	M	A	O,E	U	N
	N	H	G	P	S	SP,SU	M	M	A	O,E	U	N
	Y	H	G	W	S	Y	H	L	W	B,O,E,S	U	N
	Y	W	G	Y	S	Y	H	L	W	B,S,O	U	N
	N	H	B/G	N/A	N/A	N/A	L,M	M	W	T,B	U	N
	N	H	G	N/A	N/A	N/A	L,M	M	W	T,B,E	U	N
	N	H	G	Y	S	F	H	L	W	B,O,E	U	N
	N	W	G	W,PU/W	I	Y	H	L	W	B,O	U	N
	N	H	G	P	S	S,F	L	M	W	T	U	N
	N	H	G,V	W	I	Y	L,M,H	M	W	T,E,O	U	N
	N	H	G	B	S	Y	M,H	M	W	T,B,O,E	U	N
	Y	H	G	Y	S	Y	H	L	W	B,S,O	U	N
	N	H	G	Y	S	SP,S	H	M	W	B,E,O	U	N
	Y	H	G	R	S	Y	H	L	W	O,E,S	U	N
	Y	H	G	P	S	Y	H	L	W	B,O,E,S	U	N
	N	H	G	P	S	SP,S,F	H	M	W	B,O,E	U	N
	N	H	PU/G	PU	I	Y	M,L	M	W	T	U	N

Century Plant
Agave attenuata

shrubs

Drought Tolerance	Common Name	Scientific Name	Invasive Plant	Natural Height Range	Nominal Height	Growth Rate	Na
✳	Abelia	*Abelia* spp.	N	5'	5	M	
	Abutilon, Trailing	*Abutilon megapotamicum*	N	2–6'	4	F	
✳	Acacia, Sweet	*Acacia farnesiana*	N	8–10'	9	M	
✳✳	Adam's Needle	*Yucca filamentosa*	N	2'	2	M	
✳✳	African Milk-Bush	*Synadenium grantii*	N	6–8'	7	M	
✳✳	Alder, Yellow	*Turnera ulmifolia*	N	2–3'	3	F	
✳	Allamanda, Bush	*Allamanda neriifolia*	N	4–6'	5	M	
✳✳	Allamanda, Pineland	*Angadenia berterii*	N	2–4'	3	S	
	Angel's Trumpet	*Brugmansia X candida*	N	12–15'	14	F	
✳	Anise-Tree	*Illicium anisatum*	N	20'	20	M	
✳	Annatto	*Bixa orellana*	N	15–20'	15	M	
✳	Anthurium, Birdsnest	*Anthurium salviniae*	N	4–5'	5	S	
✳✳	Apple, Seven-Year	*Casasia clusifolia*	N	5–10'	8	S	
✳✳	Aralia	*Polyscias* spp.	N	3–10'	7	M	
	Aralia, Lacy-lady	*Evodia suaveolens* var. *ridleyi*	N	5–7'	6	F	
	Arrowwood, Southern	*Viburnum dentatum*	N	6–10'	8	M	
✳	Asian Butterfly-Bush	*Buddleia asiatica*	N	12'	12	M	
✳	Aucuba	*Aucuba japonica*	N	4–6'	5	M	
	Azalea	*Rhododendron* hybrids	N	2–6'	5	M	
	Azalea, Sweet Pinxter	*Rhododendron canescens*	N	10–15'	12	M	
✳	Barberry	*Berberis* spp.	N	4–6'	5	M	
✳✳	Bauhinia, Red	*Bauhinia punctata*	N	3–10'	7	M	
✳✳	Beauty-Berry	*Callicarpa americana*	N	4–8'	5	F	
✳✳	Bird-of-Paradise	*Strelitzia* spp.	N	3–20'	6	S–M	
✳✳	Black Bead	*Pithecellobium guadelupense*	N	15–20'	18	M	
✳✳	Blueberry, Darrow's	*Vaccinium darrowii*	N	2-3'	3	S	
✳✳	Blueberry, Highbush	*Vaccinium corymbosum*	N	10–15'	12	S	
✳✳	Blueberry, Shiny	*Vaccinium myrsinites*	N	1–2'	2	S	
✳✳	Bougainvillea	*Bougainvillea* spp.	N	6–12'	10	M	
✳✳	Boxthorn	*Severinia buxifolia*	N	3–4'	4	S	
✳	Boxwood, Japanese	*Buxus microphylla*	N	3–5'	4	S	
✳	Buckeye, Red	*Aesculus pavia*	N	10'	10	M	
✳✳	Butterfly Weed	*Asclepias tuberosa*	N	3–4'	3	M	
✳	Butterfly-Bush	*Buddleia officinalis*	N	10–20'	15	M	
	Buttonbush	*Cephalanthus occidentalis*	N	15'	15	M	
✳✳	Buttonwood, Silver	*Conocarpus erectus* var. *sericeus*	N	15–20'	18	S	
	Cafe Con Leche	*Pseuderanthemum atropurpureum*	N	4–6'	5	F	
✳	Calamondin Orange	*X Citrofortunella mitis*	N	8–10'	9	M	
✳	Camellia, Common	*Camellia japonica*	N	20'	12	S	

Bromeliads
Bromeliaceae

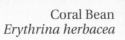

Coral Bean
Erythrina herbacea

©*Robin L. Cole/Colephoto*

	Salt Toler- ance	Plant Type	Foliage Color	Flower Color	Flower Charac- teristics	Flowering Season	Light Require- ments	Nutritional Require- ments	Soil pH	Uses	Wildlife Value	Protected Species
I	N	E	G	P,R	S	S	H	M	W	SP,IH	U	N
	N	E	G	R/Y	S	Y	M,H	M	W	SP	U	N
	M	E	G	Y	S,F	Y	H	M	W	SP,IH	U	N
◼	H	E	G	W	S	SP,S	H	L	W	SP	U	N
	Y	E	G,R	R	S	SP,S,F	H	L	W	SP	U	N
	Y	E	G	Y	S	Y	H,M	L	W	SP,GC	U	N
	M	E	G	Y	S	S,F	H	M	W	IH,SP	U	N
	N	E	G	Y	S	Y	H	L	W	SP,IH	U	N
	N	E	G	W,P,Y	S,F	S	M,H	M	W	SP	U	N
◼	N	E	G	Y/G	I	?	M,H	M	W	SP,IH	U	N
	Y	E	G	P	S	F	H	M	W	SP	U	N
	N	E	G	P	I	SP,S,F	L	M	W	SP	F	N
	Y	E	G	W	S,F	S	H	L	W	SP	F	N
	N	E	G,V	W	I	Y	L,M,H	M	W	SP,IH	F	N
	N	E	G	Y	I	S	H	M	W	SP,FH,IH	U	N
I	N	D	G	W	S	SP,S	M,H	M	W	SP,FH,IH	F	N
	N	E	G	W	S,F	W,SP	H	M	W	SP	U	N
I	N	E	Y/G	PU	I	S	L,M	M	W	IH,SP	U	N
I	N	E	G,R	W,P,R	S	SP	M,H	H	A	SP,IH	U	N
I	N	D	G	P	S, F	SP	L	M	A	SP, IH	U	Y
I	L–M	D	G	Y	S	SP	M,H	M	W	IH	F	N
I	M	E	G	R	S	SP,S,F	H	L	W	SP	U	N
I	N	E	G	L	I	SP	H	L	W	SP,IH	F	N
?H	L–M	E	G	W,O/B	S	S,F	M,H	M	W	SP	U	N
	Y	E	G	P	S	?	H	L	W	SP	U	N
I	N	E	G	W,P	I	SP	M,H	L	A	SP,IH	F	N
I	N	E	G	W,P	I	SP	M,H	L	A	SP,IH	F	N
I	N	E	G	W,P	I	SP	M,H	L	A	SP,IH	F	N
	Y	E	G,V	R,W,O,PU,P	S	SP,S,F	H	L	W	SP,IH	U	N
I	Y	E	G	W	I	S	H	L	W	IH	F	N
I	N	E	G	W	I	S	M,H	M	A	IH,FH,SP	U	N
I	N	D	G	R	S	SP	M,H	M	A	SP	U	N
I	N	E	G	O	S	S	H	L	W	SP	F	N
I	M	E	G	L	S,F	W	H	M	W	SP,IH	U	N
I	N	D	G	W	S	S	M,H	M	W	SP,IH	U	N
	Y	E	S	PU-G	I	S	H	L	W	SP,FH,IH	N	N
	M	E	PU	W/P	S	SP,S,F	L,M	M	W	SP,IH	U	N
	N	E	G	W	S,F	SP,S	H	M	W	SP	F	N
I	N	E	G	W,P,R	S,F	W	M,H	M	A	SP,IH,FH	U	N

Cocoplum
Chrysobalanus icaco

Firecracker Plant
Russelia equisetiformis

shrubs *(continued)*

Drought Tolerance	Common Name	Scientific Name	Invasive Plant	Natural Height Range	Nominal Height	Growth Rate	Nat
	Camellia, Sasanqua	*Camellia sasanqua*	N	10–20'	15	S	N
❋	Candle Bush	*Cassia alata*	N	6–10'	7	F	N
❋ ❋	Caper, Jamaican	*Capparis cynophallophora*	N	8–10'	9	S	Y
	Cardinal Flower	*Odontonema strictum 'Variegatum'*	N	3–6'	4	M	N
	Caricature Plant	*Graptophyllum pictum*	N	4–6'	5	F	N
❋	Carissa, Dwarf	*Carissa macrocarpa*	N	1–3'	2	S	N
❋	Cassia, Bahama	*Senna mexicana*	N	10–15'	10	F	N
❋	Cassia, Glaucus	*Senna surattensis*	N	5–15'	10	F	N
❋ ❋	Cats Claw	*Pithecellobium unguis-cati*	N	15–20'	18	M	Y
❋ ❋	Cedar, Bay	*Suriana maritima*	N	15–20'	18	S	Y
❋ ❋	Century Plant	*Agave attenuata*	N	2–5'	4	S	N
❋	Chaste-Tree	*Vitex agnus-castus*	N	10–15'	12	M	N
	Chenille Plant	*Acalypha hispida*	N	5–6'	5	F	N
❋ ❋	Cherry, Barbados	*Malpighia glabra*	N	6–10'	8	F	N
❋	Cherry, Brush	*Syzygium paniculatum*	N	12–15'	12	M	N
	Chinese Hat Plant	*Holmskioldia sanguina*	N	6–8'	7	M	N
	Chokeberry, Red	*Photinia pyrifolia*	N	6–9'	8	F	Y
❋ ❋	Christmas Berry	*Lycium carolinianum*	N	6–8'	7	M	Y
	Cleyera	*Cleyera japonica*	N	15–25'	20	M	N
	Clock Vine, Bush	*Thunbergia erecta*	N	4–6'	5	M	N
❋	Cocoplum	*Chrysobalanus icaco*	N	6–8'	7	S	Y
❋ ❋	Coffee Colubrina	*Colubrina arborescens*	N	15–20'	18	M	Y
❋	Coffee, Wild	*Psychotria nervosa*	N	4–6'	5	M	Y
❋ ❋	Coin Vine	*Dalbergia ecastophyllum*	N	6–9'	8	M	Y
❋ ❋	Conradina	*Conradina grandiflora*	N	3–4'	3	S	Y
	Copperleaf	*Acalypha wilkesiana*	N	5–8'	7	F	N
❋ ❋	Coral Bean	*Erythrina herbacea*	N	20–30'	25	M	Y
❋ ❋	Coral Plant	*Jatropha multifida*	N	12–15'	12	M	N
❋	Corn Plant	*Dracaena fragrans*	N	8–10'	9	M	N
	Crape-Jasmine	*Tabernaemontana divaricata*	N	6–8'	7	M	N
❋ ❋	Croton	*Codiaeum variegatum*	N	4–6'	5	M	N
❋ ❋	Cycad, Dioon	*Dioon* spp.	N	3–7'	5	S	N
❋	Daisy, African	*Gamolepis chrysanthemoides*	N	2–3'	3	M	N
❋ ❋	Devils'-Backbone	*Pedilanthus tithymaloides*	N	2–4'	3	M	N
❋	Dracaena	*Dracaena deremensis*	N	8–10'	9	M	N
❋	Dracaena, Gold-dust	*Dracaena surculosa*	N	3–6'	4	S	N
❋ ❋	Dracaena, Red-edged	*Dracaena marginata*	N	8–12'	10	M	N
❋ ❋	Dracaena, Reflexed	*Dracaena reflexa*	N	6–12'	8	S	Y

Crotons
Codiaeum varieagatum

	Salt Toler-ance	Plant Type	Foliage Color	Flower Color	Flower Charac-teristics	Flowering Season	Light Require-ments	Nutritional Require-ments	Soil pH	Uses	Wildlife Value	Protected Species
	N	E	G	W,P,R	S	F	H	M	A	SP,IH	U	N
	M	E	G	Y	S	F	H	M	W	SP	U	N
	Y	D	G	P-W	S	SP	H	L	W	SP	F	N
	N	E	V	R	S	S	L,M	M	W	SP	U	N
	N	E	V,PU	R	S	S	M,H	M	W	SP,IH	U	N
	Y	E	G	W	S,F	SP,S,F	M,H	L	W	FH,IH,SP	F	N
	N	E	G	Y	S	F,W	H	M	W	SP	U	N
	N	E	G	Y	S	F	H	M	W	SP	U	N
	Y	E	G	G/Y	I	S	H	L	W	SP	U	N
	Y	E	Y	Y	I	Y	H	L	W	SP	U	N
	M	E	G	Y	S	S	H	L	W	SP	U	N
	Y	D	G	B	S,F	S	H	M	W	SP	U	N
	N	E	G	R	S	S,F	H	M	W	IH,SP	U	N
	Y	E	G	P	I	Y	M,H	L	W	SP,IH	F	N
	M	E	G	W	S	SP,S,F	H	L	W	SP	F	N
	M	E	G	O,Y	S	Y	M,H	M	W	SP	U	N
	N	D	R,G	W,P	S	SP	M	M	W	SP,IH	F	N
	Y	E	G	B	I	S	M,H	L	W	SP	U	N
	N	E	G	W	F	SP	M,H	M	A	SP	F	N
	M	E	G	B,PU,W	S	Y	M,H	M	W	SP,IH	U	N
	Y	E	G	W	I	Y	H	L	W	FH,IH,SP	F	N
	Y	E	G	W	I	Y	M,H	L	W	SP	U	N
	N	E	G	W	I	SP,S	L,M	L	W	SP	F	N
	Y	E	G	W,P	I	?	H	L	W	SP	U	N
	N	E	G	B	S	Y	H	L	W	SP	U	N
	M	E	R,G,P	W	I	S,F	H	M	W	SP,IH	U	N
	M	D	G	R	S	S	H	M	W	SP	F	N
	M	E	G	R	S	SP,S,F	H	L	W	SP	U	N
	N	E	G,G-Y	Y	F	SP	L,M	M	W	SP	U	N
	M	E	G	W	S,F	SP,S,F	M,H	M	W	SP,IH	U	N
	M	E	R,Y,G,P	W	I	S	M,H	L	W	SP,IH	U	N
	M	E	G	N/A	CONE	S	H	M	W	SP	U	T
	N	E	G	Y	S	Y	H	M	W	SP	U	N
	Y	E	G,V	R	S	Y	H	L	W	SP	U	N
	N	E	G,V	W	I	S	L,M	M	W	SP	U	N
	N	E	G/Y	W	I	S	L,M	M	pH	SP	U	N
	M	E	G/R	W	I	S	M,H	M	W	SP	U	N
	N	E	V,G	W	I	S	H,M	M	W	SP	U	N

147

Prickly Pear Cactus
(shown with wildflowers)
Opuntia spp.

©Robin L. Cole/Colephoto

shrubs *(continued)*

Drought Tolerance	Common Name	Scientific Name	Invasive Plant	Natural Height Range	Nominal Height	Growth Rate	Nat
❄	Elder, Yellow	*Tecoma stans*	N	10–12'	10	F	Y
❄	False Aralia	*Dizygotheca elegantissima*	N	10–15'	10	M	N
❄	False Heather	*Cuphea hyssopifolia*	N	1–2'	1	M	N
❄	Fatsia	*Fatsia japonica*	N	3–4'	4	S	N
❄	Feijoa	*Feijoa sellowiana*	N	10–18'	14	M	N
❄	Fig, Edible	*Ficus carica*	N	10–12'	11	M	N
❄ ❄	Firebush	*Hamelia patens*	N	5–6'	5	M	N
❄ ❄	Firecracker Plant	*Russelia equisetiformis*	N	2–5'	4	M	N
❄	Firethorn, Red	*Pyracantha coccinea*	N	8–12'	10	M	N
	Flamingo Plant	*Justicia carnea*	N	4–6'	4	M	N
❄	Florida-Anise	*Illicium floridanum*	N	15'	15	M	Y
❄	Gallberry	*Ilex glabra*	N	6–10'	8	S	Y
❄ ❄	Garberia	*Garberia heterophylla*	N	4–6'	5	M	N
❄	Gardenia	*Gardenia jasminoides*	N	1–6'	4	S	N
	Glorybush	*Tibouchina urvilleana*	N	8–12'	10	M	N
	Golden Shrimp Plant	*Pachystachys lutea*	N	2–4'	3	F	N
❄	Golden-Dewdrop	*Duranta repens*	N	12–15'	14	M	Y
❄	Gooseberry, Ceylon	*Dovyalis hebecarpa*	N	10–12'	11	F	N
❄ ❄	Gout Plant	*Jatropha podagrica*	N	2–3'	3	S	N
❄	Grape-Hollies	*Mahonia* spp.	N	6–12'	8	S	N
❄	Green Island	*Ficus* 'Green Island'	N	3–6'	4	S	N
	Grumichama	*Eugenia brasiliensis*	N	10–12'	11	S	N
❄ ❄	Hawthorn, Indian	*Raphiolepis indica*	N	4–5'	4	M	N
❄	Henna	*Lawsonia inermis*	N	6–8'	7	M	N
❄	Hibiscus	*Hibiscus rosa-sinensis*	N	6–8'	7	F	N
❄	Hibiscus, Fringed	*Hibiscus schizopetalus*	N	8–12'	10	F	N
❄	Holly, Ambigua	*Ilex ambigua*	N	15–20'	15	M	N
❄	Holly, American	*Ilex opaca*	N	40–50'	20	S	N
❄	Holly, Burford	*Ilex cornuta*	N	5–6'	6	M	N
❄	Holly, Singapore	*Malpighia coccigera*	N	2–3'	2	S	N
	Holly, West Indian	*Leea coccinea*	N	4–6'	5	M	N
❄ ❄	Holly, Dwarf Yaupon	*Ilex vomitoria*	N	2–8'	6	M	Y
❄	Honeysuckle, Box	*Lonicera nitida*	N	5–8'	6	M	N
❄	Honeysuckle, Cape	*Tecomaria capensis*	N	6–8'	6	F	N
	Indigo, False	*Amorpha fruticosa*	N	8–12'	10	F	Y
❄ ❄	Inkberry	*Scaevola plumieri*	N	1–6'	4	S	N
❄	Ixora	*Ixora* spp.	N	3–8'	5	M	N
❄	Jasmine, Downy	*Jasminum multiflorum*	N	5–6'	5	M	N
❄	Jasmine, Orange	*Murraya paniculata*	Y	8–10'	8	M	N

Ixora
Ixora spp.

	Salt Toler-ance	Plant Type	Foliage Color	Flower Color	Flower Charac-teristics	Flowering Season	Light Require-ments	Nutritional Require-ments	Soil pH	Uses	Wildlife Value	Protected Species
	M	E	G	Y	S	S,F	H	M	W	SP	U	N
	N	E	G	W	I	S	M,H	M	W	SP	U	N
	N	E	G	L	S	Y	L,M,H	M	W	GC,IH	U	N
	M	E	G	W	I	S	M	M	W	SP	U	N
	M	E	G	W	S	SP	M,H	L	W	SP,IH	U	N
	N	D	G	G	I	Y	H	M	W	SP	F	N
	Y	E	G	R	S	S,F	H	M	W	SP	F	N
	Y	E	G	R	S	Y	H	M	W	IH,SP,GC	U	N
	M	E	G	W	I	SP,S	H	M	W	SP,IH,FH	F	N
	N	E	G	P	S	SP,S	L,M	M	W	SP	U	N
	N	E	G	R/PU	S	?	M,H	M	W	SP	U	N
	M	E	G	W	I	SP	M,H	L	A	SP	F	N
	N	E	G	PU	S	F	M,H	L	A	SP,IH	U	N
	N	E	G	W	S,F	SP	H	H	A	SP	U	N
	N	E	G	PU	S	SP,S,F	M,H	M	A	SP	U	N
	N	E	G	Y	S	S,F	H	M	W	SP,IH	U	N
	M	E	G	B,W	S	SP,S,F	H,M	L	W	SP,IH	F	N
	N	E	G,V	W	I	S	H	M	W	SP,IH	F	N
	M	E	G	R	S	S,F	H	L	W	SP	U	N
	M	E	G	Y	I	SP,S	M,H	M	W	SP,IH	U	N
	M	E	G	BR	I	S	M,H	M	W	FH,IH,SP	U	N
	M	E	G	W	I	SP	H	M	W	SP,IH	U	N
	Y	E	G	W	S,F	SP	H	M	W	FH,IH,SP	F	N
	M	E	G	W,P	F,I	Y	H	M	W	IH,SP	U	N
	M	E	G,V	R,Y,O,W	S	Y	H	H	W	SP,IH,FH	U	N
	M	E	G	R,P	S	SP,S,F	H	M	W	SP	U	N
	M	D	G	W	I	SP	H	L	W	SP	F	N
	N	E	G,V	W	I	S	M,H	M	W	SP,FH,IH	F	N
	N	E	G	W	I	SP	M,H	M	W	SP,IH	F	N
	M	E	G	P	I	S	M	M	W	IH,SP	U	N
	M	E	G	W	I	S	M	M	W	SP,IH	U	N
	Y	E	G	W	I	SP,S	H,M	M	W	FH,IH,SP	F	N
	Y	E	G	W	S,F	S	H	L	W	FH,IH	U	N
	M	E	G	O	S	S	H	M	W	IH	U	N
	N	D	G	PU	S	SP,S	H	M	W	SP,IH	U	N
	Y	E	G	W	I	S	H	L	W	SP	U	N
	M	E	G	Y,R,P	S	Y	H	H	W	FH,IH,SP	U	N
	N	E	G	W	S	S,F	M,H	M	W	SP,IH,FH	U	N
	N	E	G	W	S,F	SP,S	M,H	M	W	FH,IH,SP	U	N

Garberia
Garberia heterophylla

shrubs *(continued)*

Drought Tolerance	Common Name	Scientific Name	Invasive Plant	Natural Height Range	Nominal Height	Growth Rate	Na
❊	Jasmine, Primrose	*Jasminum mesnyi*	N	5–10'	8	M	
❊	Jasmine, Shining	*Jasminum nitidum*	N	5–6'	5	M	
❊	Jasmine, Wax	*Jasminum volubile*	N	2–3'	3	M	
❊	Jasmine, Yellow	*Jasminum humile*	N	15'	15	M	
❊	Java Glorybower	*Clerodendron speciosissimum*	Y	6–8'	7	F	
❊ ❊	Joewood	*Jacquinia keyensis*	N	15–20'	15	M	
❊ ❊	Juniper, Chinese	*Juniperus chinensis*	N	1–8'	6	M	
❊ ❊	Juniper, Shore	*Juniperus conferta*	N	1–2'	2	M	
❊ ❊	Kopsia	*Ochrosia parviflora*	Y	8–10'	10	S	
❊ ❊	Kumquat	*Fortunella japonica*	N	12–15'	14	M	
❊	Lady of the Night	*Brunfelsia americana*	N	4–6'	5	M	
❊ ❊	Lantana, Trailing	*Lantana montevidensis*	N	2'	2	M	
	Licuala, Spiny	*Licuala spinosa*	N	4–7'	5	S	
❊ ❊	Limeberry	*Triphasia trifolia*	N	2–15'	7	S	
❊ ❊	Lingaro	*Elaeagnus philippensis*	N	8–10'	9	M	
❊ ❊	Locustberry	*Byrsonima cuneata*	N	15–20'	18	S	
❊	Loropetalum	*Loropetalum chinense*	N	10–12'	10	M	
❊ ❊	Lyonia, Rusty	*Lyonia ferruginia*	N	10–20'	18	S	
❊ ❊	Lyonia, Shiny	*Lyonia lucidia*	N	5–7'	5	S	
	Magnolia, Star	*Magnolia stellata*	N	6–10'	8	S	
❊ ❊	Maidenbush	*Savia bahamensis*	N	8–10'	9	S	
❊	Marlberry	*Ardisia escallonioides*	N	12–15'	12	M	
❊	Mayten, Florida	*Maytenus phyllanthoides*	N	4–8'	6	S	
❊ ❊	Maytenus	*Maytenus undatus*	N	4–10'	6	M	
	Medinella	*Medinella magnifica*	N	4–8'	6	M	
	Miracle Fruit	*Synsepalum dulcificum*	N	6–8'	6	S	
	Mohintli	*Justicia spicegera*	N	4–6'	5	F	
	Myrtle, True	*Myrtus communis*	N	8–10'	8	M	
❊	Necklace Pod	*Sophora tomentosa*	N	6–10'	8	M	
❊ ❊	New Jersey Tea	*Ceanothus americanus*	N	2–3'	3	M	
❊	Night-Blooming Jessamine	*Cestrum nocturnum*	N	10–12'	10	M	
❊ ❊	Oak, Sand Live	*Quercus geminata*	N	6–10'	8	S	
❊ ❊	Oleander	*Nerium oleander*	N	12–15'	12	M	
❊	Oleander, Yellow	*Thevetia peruviana*	N	12–15'	12	M	
❊ ❊	Olive, Russian	*Elaeagnus angustifolia*	N	20'	20	F	
❊ ❊	Orange Wattle	*Acacia cyanophylla*	Y	14–18'	15	F	
❊	Pagoda Flower	*Clerodendron paniculatum*	Y	6'	6	F	
❊ ❊	Palay Rubber-Vine	*Cryptostegia grandiflora*	Y	6–8'	7	M	
❊	Palm, Areca	*Chrysalidocarpus lutescens*	N	15–25'	15	M	

Plumbago
Plumbago auriculata

	Salt Toler-ance	Plant Type	Foliage Color	Flower Color	Flower Charac-teristics	Flowering Season	Light Require-ments	Nutritional Require-ments	Soil pH	Uses	Wildlife Value	Protected Species
I	N	E	G	Y	S	W,SP	H	M	W	SP,IH,GC	U	N
	N	E	G	W	S	S,SP	M,H	M	W	FH,IH,SP	U	N
	M	E	G	W	I,F	Y	H	M	W	FH,IH	U	N
I	N	E	G	Y	S	SP,S	M,H	M	W	SP	U	N
	N	E	G	O,R	S	SP,F	M,H	L	W	SP	U	N
	Y	E	G	Y-W	S,F	Y	H	M	W	SP	F	N
I	M	E	G	?	CONE	SP	H	L	W	FH,IF,SP,GC	U	N
I	Y	E	B-G	?	CONE	SP	H	L	W	GC,SP	U	N
	Y	E	G	W	S,F	S	H	L	W	SP,IH,FH	U	N
	Y	E	G	W	S,F	W,SP	H	H	W	SP	F	N
	M	E	G	W	S,F	S,F	H	M	W	SP	U	N
	Y	E	G	L,P	S	S,F	H	L	W	GC	U	N
	N	P	G	W	I	S	L,M	M	W	SP	U	N
	M	E	G	W	I,F	S,F	H	M	W	FH,IH	F	N
	Y	E	S	BR	I,F	W	H	L	A	SP,IH,FH	U	N
	N	E	G	W,P	S	SP,S	H	L	W	SP	F	N
I	N	E	G	W	I	SP	H	M	A	SP,IH	U	N
I	N	E	G	W	I	?	H	L	A	SP	U	N
I	M	E	G	W,P	S	SP	H	M	W	SP	U	N
I	N	D	G	W,P	S,F	W,S	M,H	H	A	SP	U	N
	Y	E	G	G	I	SP	H	L	W	SP	U	N
	Y	E	G	W	F	F	L,M,H	L	W	SP	F	N
	M	E	G	W	I	S	H,M	L	W	SP	F	N
	Y	E	G	W	I	S	H,M	L	W	FH,IH,SP	U	N
	N	E	G	P	S	SP,S,F	M	M	W	SP	U	N
	N	E	G	W	I	SP,S,F	M,H	M	A	SP	F	N
	N	E	G	O	S	S	H	M	W	SP	U	N
I	N	E	G	W	S	SP	H	M	W	SP,IH	U	N
	Y	E	G	Y	S	Y	H	L	W	SP	U	N
I	N	D	G	W	S	SP,S	M,H	M	W	SP,IH,GC	U	N
	N	E	G	Y	S,F	SP,S	H	M	W	SP	U	N
I	N	E	G	G	I	SP	H	L	W	SP	F	N
I	Y	E	G,V	W,P,R,Y	S,F	SP,S,F	H	L	W	SP,IH,FH	U	N
	M	E	G	Y	S,F	SP,S,F	H	M	W	SP	U	N
I	Y	D	S	S	I,F	SP	H	L	W	SP	U	N
	M	E	B-G	Y	S,F	F,W,SP	H	L	W	SP	U	N
	N	E	G	Y,R	S	S,F	M,H	M	W	SP	U	N
	Y	E	G	PU	S	S,F	H	L	W	SP	U	N
	N	P	G	W	I	SP	M,H	H	W	SP,IH	U	T

Firebush
Hamelia patens

shrubs *(continued)*

Drought Tolerance	Common Name	Scientific Name	Invasive Plant	Natural Height Range	Nominal Height	Growth Rate	Na
✳	Palm, Bamboo	*Chamaedorea seifrizii*	N	6–8'	7	M	
✳ ✳	Palm, Cardboard	*Zamia* spp.	N	2–3'	3	S	
	Palm, Cat	*Chamaedorea cataractarum*	N	4–6'	5	M	
✳	Palm, European Fan	*Chamaerops humilis*	N	6–12'	10	S	
✳	Palm, Fishtail	*Caryota mitis*	N	15–20'	18	M	
✳	Palm, Lady	*Rhapis excelsa*	N	6–8'	7	S	
✳	Palm, Needle	*Rhapidophyllum hystrix*	N	3–5'	4	S	
✳	Palm, Parlor	*Chamaedorea elegans*	N	2–3'	3	S	
✳	Palm, Seashore	*Allagoptera arenaria*	N	5–6'	5	S	
✳ ✳	Palmetto, Dwarf	*Sabal minor*	N	5–7'	6	S	
✳ ✳	Palmetto, Saw	*Serenoa repens*	N	6–15'	8	S	
✳ ✳	Palmetto, Scrub	*Sabal etonia*	N	3–4'	3	S	
✳ ✳	Pampas Grass	*Cortaderia selloana*	N	5–8'	8	F	
✳	Pascuita	*Euphorbia leucocephala*	N	6–8'	7	F	
✳ ✳	Pawpaws	*Asimina* spp.	N	1–35'	4	M	
✳ ✳	Pencil-Tree	*Euphorbia tirucalli*	N	10–20'	12	M	
✳ ✳	Pentas	*Pentas lanceolata*	N	12–48"	36	F	
✳ ✳	Peregrina	*Jatropha integerrima*	N	5–7'	6	S	
✳	Philodendron	*Philodendron williamsii*	N	4–6'	5	S	
✳	Philodendron, Tree	*Philodendron selloum*	N	6–10'	8	F	
✳	Photinia, Red-Leaf	*Photinia glabra*	N	8–10'	8	M	
✳	Pittosporum, Japanese	*Pittosporum tobira*	Y	2–10'	8	S	
✳ ✳	Plum, Chickasaw	*Prunus angustifolia*	N	10–20'	15	M	
✳	Plum, Governor's	*Flacourtia indica*	Y	15–20'	18	M	
✳ ✳	Plum, Natal	*Carissa grandiflora*	N	5–8'	6	S	
✳	Plumbago	*Plumbago auriculata*	N	2–4'	3	M	
✳	Poinciana, Dwarf	*Caesalpinia pulcherrima*	N	8–10'	9	F	
	Poinsettia	*Euphorbia pulcherrima*	N	6–8'	7	F	
✳	Pomegranate	*Punica granatum*	N	10–15'	12	M	
✳	Red Powderpuff	*Calliandra haematocephala*	N	8–15'	12	M	
✳ ✳	Prickly Pear Cactus	*Opuntia* spp.	N	8'	8	M	
✳	Privet, Florida	*Forestiera segregata*	N	10–15'	10	S	
✳ ✳	Privet, Japanese	*Ligustrum japonicum*	Y	6–8'	7	M	
	Pseuderanthemum	*Pseuderanthemum reticulatum*	N	4–6'	5	F	
✳ ✳	Rapanea	*Myrsine guianensis*	N	15–20'	18	M	
✳	Reeve's Spirea	*Spiraea cantonensis*	N	4–6'	5	M	
	Rhododendron, Chapman's	*Rhododendron minus* var. *chapmanii*	N	4–6'	5	S	
✳ ✳	Ribbon Plant	*Dracaena sanderiana*	N	3–5'	4	S	
✳	Ribbon-Bush	*Homocladium platycladum*	N	3–4'	4	M	

Saw Palmetto
Serenoa repens

Walter's Viburnum
Viburnum obovatum

©*Robin L. Cole/Colephoto*

ld di-ss	Salt Toler-ance	Plant Type	Foliage Color	Flower Color	Flower Charac-teristics	Flowering Season	Light Require-ments	Nutritional Require-ments	Soil pH	Uses	Wildlife Value	Protected Species
	N	P	G	Y	I	S	M	M	W	IH,SP	U	N
H	Y	E	G	N	CONE	S	H	L	W	SP,GC,IH	U	T
	N	P	G	Y	I	S	L,M	M	W	SP,IH	U	N
	N	P	G	Y	I	SP	H	M	W	SP	U	N
	N	P	G	W	I	SP	M,H	M	W	SP,IH	U	N
	M	P	G	W	I	S	L,M	M	W	SP,IH	U	N
H	N	P	G	W	I	SP	L,M,H	L	W	SP	F	T
	N	P	G	Y	I	S	L	L	W	SP,GC	U	N
	Y	P	G	W	I	SP	M,H	M	W	SP	U	N
H	Y	P	G	W	I	S	H	L	W	SP	F	N
H	Y	P	G,S	W	I,F	S	M,H	L	W	SP,GC	F	N
	M	P	G	W	I	SP	M,H	L	W	SP	F	N
H	Y	–	G,V	W,P	S	S,F	H	L	W	SP	U	N
	N	E	G	W	S	S	H	M	W	SP	U	N
H	N	D	G	W,P	I,S (var.)	SP	M,H	L	W	IH,SP	F	N
	Y	E	G	W	I	S	H	L	W	IH,SP	U	N
	N	W	G	P,W,R,PU	S	Y	H	M	W	IH,SP,GC	U	N
	M	E	G	R	S	Y	H	L	W	SP	U	N
	N	E	G	W	I	S	L,M	M	W	SP	U	N
	N	E	G	G	I	SP	L,M,H	M	W	SP,IH	U	N
H	N	E	G,R	W	I	SP	H	M	W	FH,IH	U	N
H	Y	E	G,V	W	I	S	H,M	M	W	IH,SP	U	N
H	N	D	G	W	S,F	SP	H	M	W	F,SP,IH	F	N
	N	E	G	Y	I	SP,S	H	M	W	SP,IH	F	N
	Y	E	G	W	S,F	SP,S	M,H	M	W	IH	F	N
	N	E	G	B,W	S	S,F	H	M	W	IH,SP,GC	U	N
	M	D	G	O,Y,P	S	SP,S,F	H,M	M	W	SP	U	N
	N	E	G	R,W,P	S	W	H	M	W	SP,IH	U	N
H	N	E	G	R	S	SP	H	M	W	SP,IH	F	N
	N	E	G	R,P,W	S	S	H	M	W	SP	U	N
H	Y	–	G	PU,R,W,Y	S	SP	H	L	W	F,SP	F	N
H	M	D	G	W	I	SP	H	L	W	SP	F	N
H	M	E	G	W	S,F	SP	M,H	M	W	SP,IH,FH	U	N
	N	E	G-Y	PU-W	S	SP	L,M	M	W	SP	U	N
	Y	E	G	?	I	Y	L,M	L	W	SP	F	N
H	N	D	G	W	I	SP	H	M	W	SP,IH	U	N
	N	E	G	P	S	SP	L,M	M	A	SP,IH	U	E
	N	E	V	W	I	S	L,M	M	W	SP	U	N
	N	E	G	?	I	?	H	M	W	SP,IH	U	N

Snowbush
Breynia disticha

shrubs *(continued)*

Drought Tolerance	Common Name	Scientific Name	Invasive Plant	Natural Height Range	Nominal Height	Growth Rate	Nat
❄	Rice-Paper Plant	*Tetrapanax papyriferus*	N	8–10'	8	M	N
❄	Rose	*Rosa* hybrids	N	4–6'	5	F	N
	Rose, Swamp	*Rosa palustris*	N	4–6'	5	F	N
❄ ❄	Rosemary	*Ceratiola ericoides*	N	4–5'	4	M	Y
❄ ❄	Rosemary, Victorian	*Westringia rosmariniformis*	N	4–6'	5	M	N
	Sage, Blue	*Eranthemum pulchellum*	N	4–6'	5	F	N
❄ ❄	Sage, Texas	*Leucophyllum frutescens*	N	5–6'	5	S	N
❄ ❄	Sage, Wild	*Lantana involucrata*	N	3–4'	3	F	N
❄ ❄	Sago, King	*Cycas revoluta*	N	5–8'	8	S	N
❄ ❄	Sago, Queen	*Cycas circinalis*	N	6–12'	9	S	N
❄	St. John's Wort	*Hypericum* X *moserianum*	N	2–4'	3	M	N
❄ ❄	Salt Bush	*Baccharis halamifolia*	Y	5–7'	6	M	Y
	Sanchezia	*Sanchezia speciosa*	N	5–6'	6	F	N
❄	Sassafras	*Sassafras albidum*	N	30–70'	45	M	Y
❄	Schefflera, Dwarf	*Schefflera arboricola*	N	6–8'	6	F	N
❄ ❄	Sea Lavender	*Mallotonia gnaphalodes*	N	4–6'	5	S	N
❄ ❄	Sea Oxeye Daisy	*Borrichia frutescens*	N	2–4'	3	S	N
❄	Serrisa	*Serissa foetida*	N	2–3'	3	M	N
❄ ❄	Shining Sumac	*Rhus copallina*	Y	8–10'	9	F	N
❄	Shower-of-Gold	*Galphimia glauca*	N	7–9'	8	M	N
❄ ❄	Silverthorn	*Elaeagnus pungens*	N	15–20'	18	M	N
❄	Slender Buckthorn	*Sideroxylon reclinatum*	N	20–30'	25	M	N
❄	Snail Seed	*Cocculus laurifolius*	N	12–15'	13	M	N
❄ ❄	Snowberry	*Chiococca alba*	N	6–9'	8	M	N
❄	Snowbush	*Breynia disticha*	Y	5–6'	6	M	N
❄ ❄	Spanish-Bayonet	*Yucca aloifolia*	N	12–15'	14	M	Y
❄ ❄	Spanish-Dagger	*Yucca gloriosa*	N	6–8'	7	S	Y
	Spurge, Red	*Euphorbia cotinifolia*	N	6–8'	7	F	N
❄ ❄	Stoppers	*Eugenia* spp.	N	8–10'	9	M	N
❄	Sweet Shrub	*Calycanthus floridus*	N	6–8'	8	M	N
❄ ❄	Tarflower	*Befaria racemosa*	N	5–6'	5	M	N
❄ ❄	Tetrazygia	*Tetrazygia bicolor*	N	12–15'	12	M	N
❄	Thryallis	*Galphimia gracilis*	N	4–6'	5	M	N
❄ ❄	Ti Plant	*Cordyline terminalis*	N	3–6'	5	S	N
	Tibouchina	*Tibouchina clavata*	N	4–6'	5	F	N
❄	Torchwood	*Amyris elemifera*	N	12–16'	14	M	N
	Tropical Snowball	*Dombeya* spp.	N	8–10'	9	F	N
❄ ❄	Turk's-Cap	*Malvaviscus arboreus*	N	6–8'	7	F	N
❄	Tropical Snowflake	*Trevesia palmata*	N	8–12'	10	M	N

Sea Oxeye Daisy
Borrichia frutescens

©Robin L. Cole/Colephoto

	Salt Toler- ance	Plant Type	Foliage Color	Flower Color	Flower Charac- teristics	Flowering Season	Light Require- ments	Nutritional Require- ments	Soil pH	Uses	Wildlife Value	Protected Species
	N	E	G	W	S	SP,S,F	M,H	M	W	SP	U	N
	N	D	G	W,P,Y,R	S,F	Y	H	H	W	SP	U	N
	N	E	G	P	S	SP	H	M	A	SP	F	N
	Y	E	G	R,Y	I	Y	H	L	A	SP	U	N
	M	E	G	W	S	SP,S	H	M	W	FH,IH,SP	U	N
	N	E	G	B	S	W	L,M	M	W	SP	U	N
	M	E	S	L	S	S	H	L	W	SP,IH	U	N
	M	E	G	W,B	S	Y	H	L	W	SP	F	N
	M	E	G	BR	CONE	SP	H,M	M	W	SP	U	N
	M	E	G	N	CONE	S	H	M	W	SP,IH	U	T
	N	E	G	Y	S	S,F	M,H	M	W	SP,IH	U	N
	Y	E	G	W	I	F	H	L	W	SP	U	N
	N	E	V	Y	S	SP,S,F	M,H	M	W	SP	U	N
	N	D	G	Y	I	SP	L,M	M	W	SP,IH	F	N
	M	E	G	W	I	S	L,M,H	M	W	FH,IH,SP,GC	U	N
	Y	E	S/G	W	I	Y	H	L	W	SP	U	N
	Y	E	G	Y	S	SP,S	H	L	W	SP,GC	U	N
	N	E	G,V	W	S	S	H	M	W	SP,IH	U	N
	N	D	G	G	I	S	H	L	W	SP	F	N
	M	E	G	Y	S	Y	H	M	W	SP,IH	U	N
	Y	E	S	BR	I,F	W	H	L	A	SP,FH,IH	U	N
	Y	E	G	W	I	F	H	L	W	SP	F	N
	N	E	G	Y	I	S	M,H	M	W	IH,SP	U	N
	Y	E	G	Y	I	Y	H	L	W	SP	F	N
	N	E	V,G,P,W	W	I	S	H	M	W	IH,SP	U	N
	Y	E	G	W	S	SP	H	L	W	SP	U	N
	M	E	G	W	S	S	H	L	W	SP	U	N
	N	E	R	W	I	S	H	M	W	SP	U	N
	Y	E	G	W	I	SP,S	M,H	L	W	SP,IH	F	N
	N	D	G/PU	R	S,F	SP	M,L	M	A	SP	U	N
	M	E	G	W	S	SP,S	H	L	W	SP	U	N
	M	E	G	W	S	S	H	L	W	SP	F	N
	M	E	G	Y	S	S,F	M,H	M	W	SP	U	N
	N	E	R,G,P,Y	W,P	I	F	M,H	M	W	SP	U	N
	N	E	S-G	PU	S	SP,S,F	H	M	W	SP	U	N
	Y	E	G	W	I	F	M,H	L	W	SP	F	N
	N	E	G	W,P,R	S	S	H	M	W	SP	U	N
	N	E	G	R,P	S	SP,S,F	H	M	W	SP	U	N
	N	E	G	W	I	S	M	M	W	SP	U	N

155

Tarflower
Befaria racemosa

shrubs *(continued)*

Drought Tolerance	Common Name	Scientific Name	Invasive Plant	Natural Height Range	Nominal Height	Growth Rate	Na
❋ ❋	Varnish Leaf	*Dodanaea viscosa*	N	5–7'	6	S	
❋ ❋	Veitch Screwpine	*Pandanus veitchii*	N	12–15'	12	S	
	Viburnum, Sandankwa	*Viburnum suspensum*	N	6–8'	6	M	
❋	Viburnum, Sweet	*Viburnum odoratissimum*	N	12–15'	8	M	
❋ ❋	Viburnum, Walter's	*Viburnum obovatum*	N	6–12'	6	M	
❋	Vitex	*Vitex trifolia*	N	10–12'	10	M	
❋	White Indigo Berry	*Randia aculeata*	N	6–10'	8	S	
❋	Witch Hazel	*Hamamelis virginiana*	N	15–20'	18	M	
❋	Yesterday Today and Tomorrow	*Brunfelsia australis*	N	6–8'	7	M	
❋ ❋	Yucca, Spineless	*Yucca elephantipes*	N	15–20'	18	M	

trees

Drought Tolerance	Common Name	Scientific Name	Invasive Plant	Natural Height Range	Nominal Height	Growth Rate	Na
❋ ❋	African Tulip Tree	*Spathodea campanulata*	N	40–60'	50	F	
❋ ❋	Allspice	*Pimenta dioica*	N	15–30'	20	S	
❋ ❋	Almond, Tropical	*Terminalia catappa*	N	20–45'	30	M	
❋	Annatto	*Bixa orellana*	N	10–30'	25	M	
❋	Apple, Custard	*Annona reticulata*	N	20–25'	25	M	
❋ ❋	Apple, Pitch	*Clusia rosea*	N	25–30'	25	S	
	Apple, Pond	*Annona glabra*	N	25–40'	35	M	
❋ ❋	Apple, Rose	*Syzygium jambos*	N	20–30'	25	F	
❋	Arborvitae, Oriental	*Platycladus orientalis*	N	15–20'	20	F	
❋	Ash, Green	*Fraxinus pennsylvanica*	N	40–60'	50	F	
	Ash, Water	*Fraxinus caroliniana*	N	40–60'	50	F	
❋	Avocado	*Persea americana*	N	40–50'	45	F	
❋	Bangar Nut	*Sterculia foetida*	N	50–80'	75	F	
	Birch, River	*Betula nigra*	N	45–65'	50	F	
❋ ❋	Blolly	*Guapira discolor*	N	35–50'	40	M	
❋	Bottlebrush	*Callistemon* spp.	N	10–25'	15	M	
❋	Box Elder	*Acer negundo*	N	40'	40	F	
❋	Bridalveil Tree	*Caesalpinea granadillo*	N	30–40'	35	M	
❋ ❋	Buckthorn, Silver	*Sideroxylon tenax*	N	20'	20	S	
❋	Bulnesia	*Bulnesia arborea*	N	30–40'	30	M	
❋	Bunya-Bunya Tree	*Araucaria bidwillii*	N	60–70'	65	M	
❋	Bustic, Willow-Leaved	*Dipholis salicifolia*	N	30–50'	40	M	
❋ ❋	Buttercup Tree	*Cochlospermum vitifolium*	N	30–40'	35	F	
❋ ❋	Buttonwood	*Conocarpus erectus*	N	30–50'	35	M	
❋ ❋	Calabash, Black	*Enallagma latifolia*	N	20–30'	20	M	

Thryallis
Galphimia gracilis

	Salt Toler-ance	Plant Type	Foliage Color	Flower Color	Flower Charac-teristics	Flowering Season	Light Require-ments	Nutritional Require-ments	Soil pH	Uses	Wildlife Value	Protected Species
	Y	E	G	W	I	S	H	L	W	SP	U	N
	Y	E	G,V	?	I	?	H	L	W	SP,IH	U	N
	N	E	G	W	I	S	M,H	M	W	SP,FH,IH	F	N
	N	E	G	W	I	SP	M,H	M	W	SP,FH,IH	F	N
	N	E	G	W	S	SP	M,H	L	W	SP,FH,IH	F	N
	M	D	G,V	B	S	S	H	M	W	SP,IH	U	N
	Y	E	G	W	I	Y	H	L	W	SP	F	N
	N	D	G	Y	I	W	M,H	L	W	SP	F,N	N
	N	E	G	B,W,P	S,F	S,F	H	M	W	SP	U	N
	M	E	G	W	S	S,F	H	L	W	SP	U	N

	Salt Toler-ance	Wind Toler-ance	Plant Type	Foliage Color	Flower Color	Flower Charac-teristics	Flowering Season	Light Require-ments	Nutritional Require-ments	Soil pH	Uses	Wildlife Value	Protected Species
	M	M	E	G	O,Y	S	W	H	M	W	PK,R,B,S	U	N
	N	H	E	G	W	I	SP,S	H	M	W	R,PK,B,M	U	N
	Y	H	D	G	G	I	SP	H	L	W	PK,R	U	N
	N	L	E	G	P	S	F	H	M	W	R	U	N
	N	H	D	G	G,Y	I	F,W	H	M	W	F,R	F	N
	Y	H	E	G	P,W	S	S	H	L	W	PK,R	U	N
	M	H	E	G	W/Y	I	Y	H	L	W	BU	F	N
	N	M	E	G	W	S	SP	H	M	W	R,PK,F	F	N
	N	H	E	G	B	CONE	SP	M,H	M	W	PK,R,P,B	U	N
	N	H	D	G	G	I	SP	H	M	W	R,PK,B,P,S,M,PL	F	N
	N	H	D	G	G	I	SP	H	L	W	S,R,PK	F	N
	N	M	E	G	G	I	SP,S	H	M	W	R,F,PK,S	F	N
	N	M	D	G	R/Y	S	W,SP	H	M	W	PK	U	N
	N	M	D	G	BR	I	SP	H	M	W	S,R,BU	U	N
	M	H	E	G	G/Y	I	SP,F	H	L	W	R,S,B,PK	F	N
	M	M	E	G	R	S	SP,S,F	H	M	W	S,P,PL,M,B,R	U	N
	N	L	D	G	Y	I	S	M,H	M	W	R,PK,P	F	N
	N	H	E	G	Y	S	S	H	M	W	S,PL,M,R	U	N
	Y	H	E	G	W	I	Y	H	L	W	R,PK,B	F	N
	N	L	E	G	Y	S	SP,S,F	H	M	W	R,B,M,PK	U	N
	M	M	E	G	G	I	SP	H	M	W	PK,B,R	N	N
	M	M	E	G	W	I	Y	H	L	W	R,PK	F	N
	M	L	D	G	Y	S	W,SP	H	M	W	PK,P,R	U	N
	Y	H	E	G,S	PU/G	I	S	H	L	W	R,PK,B,M,PL	N	N
	Y	L	E	G	Y,P	I	SP	H	L	W	PK,R	U	N

Queen's Crape Myrtle
Lagerstroemia speciosa

trees *(continued)*

Drought Tolerance	Common Name	Scientific Name	Invasive Plant	Natural Height Range	Nominal Height	Growth Rate	Na
❋ ❋	Calabash, Mexican	*Crescentia alata*	N	30–45'	35	F	
❋	Capulin	*Muntingia calabura*	N	20–30'	25	F	
❋	Carambola	*Averrhoa carambola*	N	15–30'	20	M	
❋	Catalpa	*Catalpa bignonioides*	N	50'	50	F	
❋	Cedar, Atlas	*Cedrus atlanticus*	N	30	30	M	
❋	Cedar, Deodar	*Cedrus deodara*	N	60	60	M	
❋ ❋	Cedar, Southern Red	*Juniperus silicicola*	N	20–30'	25	M	
❋	Cherry, Black	*Prunus serotina*	N	60–90'	75	M	
❋	Cherry Laurel	*Prunus caroliniana*	Y	30–40'	35	M	
❋ ❋	Chestnut, Guiana	*Pachira aquatica*	N	25–30'	30	M	
❋ ❋	Chinese Pistache	*Pistacia chinensis*	N	35–45'	40	M	
❋ ❋	Citrus	*Citrus* spp.	N	10–30'	15	M	
❋ ❋	Cockspur Coral Tree	*Erythrina crista-galli*	N	15–25'	20	M	
❋	Colville's Glory	*Colvillea racemosa*	N	40–50'	45	M	
❋ ❋	Copperpod	*Peltophorum pterocarpum*	N	40–50'	45	F	
❋ ❋	Crabwood	*Gymnanthes lucida*	N	15–30'	20	S	
❋ ❋	Crape Myrtle	*Lagerstroemia indica*	N	15–25'	20	M	
❋ ❋	Crape Myrtle, Queen's	*Lagerstroemia speciosa*	N	30–45'	35	M	
❋ ❋	Cypress, Bald	*Taxodium distichum*	N	60–100'	70	M	
❋	Cypress, Italian	*Cupressus sempervirens* var. *stricta*	N	20–40'	25	F	
❋ ❋	Cypress, Pond	*Taxodium ascendens*	N	60–100'	70	M	
❋ ❋	Devilwood	*Osmanthus americanus*	N	30–45'	30	M	
❋ ❋	Dogwood, Flowering	*Cornus florida*	N	20–30'	25	S	
❋ ❋	Dogwood, Jamaican	*Piscidia piscipula*	N	35–50'	40	F	
❋ ❋	Dragon Tree	*Dracaena draco*	N	40–60'	45	S	
❋	Ear Tree	*Enterlobium cyclocarpum*	N	80–100'	90	F	
❋	Eggfruit	*Pouteria campechiana*	N	20–25'	20	F	
❋ ❋	Elder, Yellow	*Tecoma stans*	N	10–20'	15	F	
❋	Elm, American	*Ulmus americana*	N	· 80–100'	85	F	
❋ ❋	Elm, Chinese	*Ulmus parvifolia*	N	40–60'	50	M	
❋ ❋	Elm, Winged	*Ulmus alata*	N	20–25'	25	M	
	Fern, Australian Tree	*Sphaeropteris cooperi*	N	15–30'	20	S	
❋ ❋	Fiddlewood	*Citharexylum fruticosum*	N	25–30'	25	S	
❋ ❋	Fig, Fiddleleaf	*Ficus lyrata*	N	40–50'	45	M	
❋	Fig, Rusty	*Ficus rubiginosa*	N	15–20'	15	S	
❋ ❋	Fig, Shortleaf	*Ficus citrifolia*	N	40–50'	45	F	
❋ ❋	Fig, Strangler	*Ficus aurea*	Y	40–50'	45	F	
❋ ❋	Fig, Sacred	*Ficus religiosa*	Y	50–80'	60	F	
❋	Firewheel Tree	*Stenocarpus sinuatus*	N	35–45'	40	M	

Coconut Palm
Cocos nucifera

Cold Hardiness	Salt Tolerance	Wind Tolerance	Plant Type	Foliage Color	Flower Color	Flower Characteristics	Flowering Season	Light Requirements	Nutritional Requirements	Soil pH	Uses	Wildlife Value	Protected Species
T	M	L	E	G	G/Y	I	S	H	M	W	R,PK	U	N
S	N	L	E	G	W	I	SP,S,F	H	M	W	R,F,PK	F	N
S	N	M	E	G	P	S	Y	H	M	W	F,S,R	F	N
H	N	L	D	G	W	S	SP	H	M	W	S,R,PK	U	N
H	N	M	E	B/G	BR	CONE	SP	H	M	W	PK,R,P,BU	U	N
H	N	M	E	B/G,G,Y	BR	CONE	SP	H	M	W	PK,R,P,BU	U	N
H	Y	H	E	G	BR	CONE	SP	H	L	W	PK,R,P,B	F,N	N
H	N	M	D	G	W	S	SP	H	M	W	R,PK,F	F	N
H	N	H	E	G	W	I,F	SP	M,H	M	W	R,PK	F	N
S	M	M	D	G	W/R	S,F	SP,S	H	M	W	R,PK,B	U	N
H	N	M	D	G	W	I	SP	M	M	W	R,S	U	N
H	N	H	E	G	W	I,F	SP	H	H	W	F,R	F	N
H	N	M	E	G	R	S	SU,F	H	M	W	PK,R,B	F	N
H	N	M	D	G	O	S	F	H	M	W	R,PK,B	U	N
H	Y	M	D	G	Y	S,F	SP,S	H	M	W	R,PK,B,S	U	N
S	M	H	E	G	R	I	SP	H	L	W	R,PK	U	N
H	M	H	D	G	R,P,W	S	S	H	M	W	R,P,B,PK	F	N
S	N	H	D	G	PU	S	S	H	M	W	M,R,PK,B	F	N
H	M	H	D	G	G	CONE	SP	H	L	W	PK,S,R,B	F	N
H	?	H	E	G	BR	I	S	H	M	W	R,PK,P	U	N
H	M	H	D	G	G	CONE	SP	H	L	W	PK,S,R,B	F	N
H	N	M	E	G	W	F	SP	H	L	W	SP	F	N
H	N	H	D	G	W,P	S	SP	H	M	W	PK,R,M,B,BU	F,N	N
T	Y	M	E	G	W/L	S	SP	H	L	W	PK,R,M	U	N
H	Y	H	E	G	G	I	S	H	M	W	R,PK,B	U	N
S	N	H	D	G	W	I	SP	H	L	W	PK	U	N
S	M	M	E	G	W	I	S,F	H	M	W	R,F,PK	F	N
S	N	L	E	G	Y	S	SP	H	M	W	R,PK,B	U	N
H	N	H	D	G	G	I	SP	H	M	W	PK,R,S,B	F,N	N
H	N	M	E	G	G	I	SP	H	M	W	R,PK,S,B	F,N	N
H	N	H	D	G	G	I	SP	H	M	W	R,PK,M,B	F,N	N
H	N	M	E	G	N/A	N/A	N/A	M	M	W	R,PK	U	N
H	M	H	E	G	W	I,F	Y	H	L	W	PK,B,R	U	N
S	M	M	E	G	G	I	Y	H	M	W	PK,B,R	U	N
S	M	M	E	G	G	I	Y	H	M	W	R,PK,BU	U	N
S	M	M	E	G	Y	I	Y	H	L	W	R,PK,B	F	N
T	M	M	E	G	O	I	S	H	L	W	PK,S	F	N
S	M	M	E	G	G	I	Y	H	L	W	PK,S,B	U	N
H	N	H	E	G	R	S	SP,S	H	M	W	R,PK,B,M	U	N

Flowering Dogwood
Cornus florida

trees *(continued)*

Drought Tolerance	Common Name	Scientific Name	Invasive Plant	Natural Height Range	Nominal Height	Growth Rate	Nati
✻	Flame-of-the-Forest	*Butea frondosa*	N	35–40'	35	S	N
✻ ✻	Floss-Silk Tree	*Chorisia speciosa*	N	35–50'	45	M	N
✻ ✻	Frangipani	*Plumeria rubra*	N	15–25'	20	S	N
✻	Fringe Tree	*Chionanthus virginicus*	N	15–20'	20	S	Y
✻ ✻	Geiger Tree	*Cordia sebestena*	N	20–25'	25	M	Y
✻ ✻	Golden Rain Tree	*Cassia fistula*	N	30–40'	35	F	N
✻	Golden Shower Tree	*Koelreuteria bipinnata*	N	45'	45	M	N
✻	Golden Shower Tree	*Koelreuteria elegans*	Y	30–50'	40	M	N
✻ ✻	Grevillea, Bank's	*Grevillea banksii*	N	15–20'	20	M	N
✻ ✻	Gum Trees	*Eucalyptus* spp.	Y	30–100'	50	F	N
✻ ✻	Gumbo Limbo	*Bursera simaruba*	N	40–60'	50	M	Y
✻ ✻	Hawthorns	*Crataegus* spp.	N	15–25'	20	S	Y
✻ ✻	Hercules' Club	*Zanthoxylum clava-herculis*	N	25'	25	M	Y
✻ ✻	Hickory, Pignut	*Carya glabra*	N	80–120'	100	F	Y
✻ ✻	Hickory, Scrub	*Carya floridana*	N	20–70'	50	M	Y
	Hickory, Water	*Carya aquatica*	N	60–100'	60	S	Y
✻ ✻	Holly, American	*Ilex opaca*	N	30–45'	35	M	Y
✻	Holly, Dahoon	*Ilex cassine*	N	25–40'	30	M	Y
✻	Holly, East Palatka	*Ilex X attenuata*	N	25–40'	30	M	Y
✻ ✻	Holly, Yaupon	*Ilex vomitoria*	N	20–25'	20	M	Y
✻	Hondapara	*Dillenia indica*	N	30–45'	40	S	N
✻ ✻	Honey Locust, Thornless	*Gleditsia triacanthos*	N	50	50	F	Y
✻ ✻	Hoptree	*Ptelea trifoliata*	N	20	20	S	Y
	Hornbeam, American	*Carpinus caroliniana*	N	25–35'	25	S	Y
✻ ✻	Horseradish Tree	*Moringa oleifera*	N	20–25'	25	F	N
✻	Indian Jujube Tree	*Zizyphus mauritiana*	N	30–40'	35	M	N
✻	Indian Rosewood	*Dalbergia sissoo*	N	35–60'	40	F	N
✻ ✻	Ironwood, Black	*Krugiodendron ferreum*	N	20–30'	25	S	Y
✻ ✻	Ironwood, White	*Hypelate trifoliata*	N	30–40'	30	S	Y
✻	Jaboticoba	*Myrciaria cauliflora*	N	10–25'	15	S	N
✻ ✻	Jacaranda	*Jacaranda mimosaefolia*	N	40–50'	45	M	N
✻ ✻	Jerusalem Thorn	*Parkinsonia aculeata*	N	20–30'	25	F	N
✻ ✻	Juniper, Southern	*Juniperus sIlicicola*	N	25–30'	25	M	Y
✻	Kassod Tree	*Cassia siamea*	N	35–40'	35	F	N
✻	Lancewood	*Nectandra coriacea*	N	30–40'	35	M	Y
✻ ✻	Lignum Vitae	*Guaiacum sanctum*	N	10–30'	15	S	Y
	Loblolly Bay	*Gordonia lasianthus*	N	30–40'	35	M	Y
✻	Longan	*Euphoria langans*	N	30–40'	35	M	N
✻ ✻	Loquat	*Eriobotrya japonica*	N	15–20'	15	F	N

Pindo palm
Butia capitata

Salt Toler-ance	Wind Toler-ance	Plant Type	Foliage Color	Flower Color	Flower Charac-teristics	Flowering Season	Light Require-ments	Nutritional Require-ments	Soil pH	Uses	Wildlife Value	Protected Species
Y	M	D	G	O	S	W	H	M	W	R	U	N
Y	M	D	G	P	S	F	H	M	W	R,PK,B	U	N
M	M	D	G	W,Y,P	S,F	SP,S	H	M	W	R,P,M,B	U	N
N	H	D	G	W	S,F	SP	M	M	A	PK,R,P,BU,SP	F	N
Y	M	E	G	O	S	Y	H	L	W	R,PK,B	F	N
M	M	D	G	Y	S	S	H	M	W	R,S,M,B	U	N
N	M	D	G	Y	S	S,F	H	M	W	R,S,B,PK,P	U	N
N	M	D	G	Y	S	S,F	H	M	W	R,S,B,PK,P	U	N
N	M	E	G	R,W	S	SP	H	M	W	P,SP,R	U	N
N	L	E	G,S	W,G,R	S,I	Y	H	L	W	PK	U	N
M	M	D	G	G	I	W,SP	H	L	W	S,P,PL,B,R	F	N
N	H	D	G	W	S	SP	H	M	W	R,PK,B	F,N	N
M	M	D	G	W	I	SP	M	M	W	R,PK,M,B	F	N
N	H	D	G	G	I	SP	H	L	W	S,R	F	N
N	H	D	G	G	I	SP	H	L	W	P,R	F,N	N
N	M	D	G	G	I	SP	H	L	W	R,B	F	N
M	H	E	G	W	I	SP	M,H	M	A	R,PK	F,N	N
M	H	E	G	W	I	SP	H	L	A	PK,P,R	F	N
M	H	E	G	W	I	SP	H	L	A	PK,P,R	F	N
Y	H	E	G	W	I	SP	M,H	L	W	BU,R,PK	F,N	N
N	H	D	G	W	S,F	?	H	M	W	PK,R	U	N
M	M	D	G	O	I	SP	H	M	W	R,S	F,N	N
N	H	D	G	G	I	SP	M	M	W	BU,P,R	U	N
N	H	D	G	G	I	SP	M,H	L	W	R	F	N
N	M	E	G	W	S,F	Y	H	M	W	R,PK	U	N
N	M	E	G	W	I,F	S	H	M	W	PK,R	U	N
M	L	D	G	Y,W	I,F	SP,S	H	M	W	R,PK,S	U	N
M	H	E	G	Y/G	I	SP	H	L	W	R,PK,B	F	N
Y	H	E	G	W	I	SP,S	H	L	W	R,PK	U	N
N	H	E	G	W	I	Y	M,H	M	W	R,PK,F	F	N
N	M	D	G	B	S	SP,S	H	M	W	PK,B,R,S	U	N
Y	H	D	G	Y	S,F	SP,S	H	L	W	R,PK,BU,M	U	N
Y	H	E	G	BR	CONE	SP	H	L	W	P,PK,R,BU	F,N	N
N	M	E	G	Y	S	SP,S	H	M	W	R,B	U	N
N	H	E	G	W	I	Y	H	M	W	S,P,R,BU	F	N
M	H	E	G	B	S	Y	H	L	W	R,PK	F	T
N	H	E	G	W	S,F	S	H	M	W	R,S,PK,B	U	N
N	H	E	G	W	I	SP	H	M	W	F,R,PK	F	N
M	H	E	G	W	S,F	F	H	L	W	F,R,PK,M,B	F	N

Pink Powderpuff
Calliandra surinamensis

trees *(continued)*

Drought Tolerance	Common Name	Scientific Name	Invasive Plant	Natural Height Range	Nominal Height	Growth Rate	Na
❋	Lychee	*Litchi chinensis*	N	30–40'	35	M	
❋ ❋	Macadamia Nut	*Macadamia integrifolia*	N	15–30'	20	S	
❋ ❋	Magnolia, Southern	*Magnolia grandiflora*	N	60–100'	65	M	
❋ ❋	Mahoe	*Hibiscus tiliaceus*	Y	30–45'	40	F	
❋ ❋	Mahoe, Seaside	*Thespesia populnea*	N	35–45'	40	F	
❋ ❋	Mahogany	*Swietenia mahogani*	N	35–60'	45	F	
❋	Mango	*Mangifera indica*	N	40–60'	50	M	
	Mangrove, Black	*Avicennia germinans*	N	20–30'	25	M	
	Mangrove, Red	*Rhizophora mangle*	N	30-80'	40	M	
	Mangrove, White	*Laguncularia racemosa*	N	40–60'	50	M	
	Maple, Red	*Acer rubrum*	N	35–50'	40	F	
❋ ❋	Mastic	*Mastichodendron foetisdissimum*	N	45–70'	50	S	
❋ ❋	Milkbark	*Drypetes diversifolia*	N	30–40'	30	M	
❋ ❋	Millettia	*Millettia ovalifolia*	N	20–35'	25	M	
❋ ❋	Mimosa	*Albizia julibrissin*	Y	30–40'	35	F	
❋ ❋	Mimusops	*Manilkara roxburghiana*	N	15–25'	20	S	
❋ ❋	Mulberry, Red	*Morus rubra*	Y	30–45'	40	F	
❋	Norfolk Island Pine	*Araucaria heterophylla*	N	100–150'	125	F	
❋ ❋	Oak, Bluejack	*Quercus incana*	N	20–30'	25	S	
❋ ❋	Oak, Chapman	*Quercus chapmanii*	N	30–45'	35	S	
❋ ❋	Oak, Laurel	*Quercus laurifolia*	N	60–100'	80	F	
❋ ❋	Oak, Live	*Quercus virginiana*	N	50–60'	50	M	
❋ ❋	Oak, Myrtle	*Quercus myrtifolia*	N	10–25'	20	S	
❋ ❋	Oak, Pin	*Quercus palustris*	N	60–100'	80	M	
❋ ❋	Oak, Post	*Quercus stellata*	N	30–60'	45	M	
❋ ❋	Oak, Shumard Red	*Quercus shumardii*	N	80–100'	80	M	
❋ ❋	Oak, Turkey	*Quercus laevis*	N	40–50'	45	S	
❋ ❋	Oak, Water	*Quercus nigra*	N	60–100'	80	F	
❋ ❋	Ochrosia	*Ochrosia elliptica*	N	10–20'	15	M	
❋ ❋	Olive, Black	*Bucida buceras*	N	40–50'	45	M	
❋ ❋	Olive, Scrub Wild	*Osmanthus megacarpa*	N	15–20'	20	S	
❋ ❋	Olive, Spiny Black	*Bucida spinosa*	N	15–20'	18	S	
❋ ❋	Olive, Madagascar	*Noronhia emarginata*	N	20–30'	25	M	
❋ ❋	Orchid Tree	*Bauhinia* spp.	N	20–30'	25	F	
❋ ❋	Osage Orange	*Maclura pomifera*	N	50–60'	30`	S	
❋ ❋	Palm, Alexandra	*Archontophoenix alexandrae*	N	40–45'	40	M	
❋ ❋	Palm, Arikury	*Arikuryoba schizophylla*	N	10–15'	10	S	
❋ ❋	Palm, Bismarck	*Bismarckia nobilis*	N	30–60'	40	S	
❋	Palm, Bottle	*Hyophorbe lagenicaulis*	N	15–25'	20	S	

Redbud
Cercis canadensis

Cold Hardi-ness	Salt Toler-ance	Wind Toler-ance	Plant Type	Foliage Color	Flower Color	Flower Charac-teristics	Flowering Season	Light Require-ments	Nutritional Require-ments	Soil pH	Uses	Wildlife Value	Protected Species
	N	H	E	G	W	I	SP	H	M	W	R,PK,S,P,F	F	N
	N	H	E	G	W	I	SP	H	M	W	R,PK,S,P,B,M,F	U	N
	Y	H	E	G	W	S,F	SP	H	M	A	R,PK,S,P,B,M	F	N
	Y	L	E	G	Y/R	S	Y	H	L	W	PK,BU	U	N
	Y	M	E	G	Y/R	S	Y	H	M	W	PK,R,B	U	N
	M	H	E	G	G/Y	I	SP	H	L	W	R,S,PK,B,M,PL	U	N
	N	M	E	G	W	S	SP	H	M	W	F,PK,R	F	N
	Y	H	E	G	W	I,F	SP	H	L	W	BU	N	P
	Y	H	E	G	Y	I	Y	H	L	W	PK	N	P
	Y	H	E	G	G	I,F	SP	H	L	W	S,PK,P,R,BU	U	N
	N	M	D	G	R	S	W,SP	H	L	W	S,P,PL,M,B,R,BU	F,N	N
	Y	H	E	G	Y/G	I	SP,S,F	H	L	W	P,PL,M,S,R,PK	F	N
	Y	H	E	G	W	I	S	H	L	W	R,P,SP	F	N
	N	H	E	G	P	S	SP	H	M	W	R,PK,M,B	U	N
	M	L	D	G	P	S	SP	H	M	W	R,PK,M,B	U	N
	Y	L	E	G	W	I	S	H	L	W	R,B,PK,M,PL	U	N
	N	H	D	G	W	I	S	H	L	W	R,F,PK	F	N
	M	L	E	G	BR	I	SP	H	L	W	M,P,BU	U	N
	N	H	D	G	G	I	SP	H	L	W	R,PK,S,B	F	N
	M	H	D	G	G	I	SP	H	L	W	PK,R,M,B	F	N
	N	H	E	G	G	I	SP	H	L	W	S,R,PK,B	F,N	N
	Y	H	E	G	G	I	SP	H	L	W	S,B,R,PK	F	N
	M	H	E	G	G	I	SP	H	L	W	PK,R,S,B	F	N
	N	H	E	G	G	I	SP	H	H	A	S,R,B,PK	F	N
	N	H	D	G	G	I	SP	H	L	W	S,R,B,PK	F	N
	N	H	D	G	G	I	SP	H	L	W	S,R,B,PK	F	N
	N	H	D	G	G	I	SP	H	L	W	R,PK,B	F	N
	N	H	E	G	G	I	SP	H	L	W	R,S,PK,B	U	N
	Y	M	E	G	Y/W	I,F	S	M,H	M	W	R,PK	U	N
	Y	H	E	G	G	I	SP	H	M	W	S,P,PL,M,B,R	U	N
	N	H	E	G	W	I,F	SP	H	L	W	PK,R,PL,P,BU,SP	F	N
	M	H	E	G	G	I	SP	H	M	W	R	U	N
	Y	H	E	G	Y	I	SP	H	L	W	BU,S,P,PL,M,B,R,PK	U	N
	N	L	D	G	W,P,PU,Y	S	F,W,SP	H	M	W	R,P,PU	U	N
	M	H	D	G	Y	S	S	H	L	W	S,IH	U	N
	N	H	P	G	W	I	S	M,H	M	W	R,PK,B	U	N
	N	H	P	G	W	I	S	M,H	M	W	R,M	U	N
	N	H	P	B/G	W	I	SP	M,H	M	W	R,B,M	U	N
	M	H	P	G	W	I	S	M,H	M	W	R,PK,B,M	U	N

Sea Grape
Coccoloba uvifera

©Robin L. Cole/Colephoto

trees *(continued)*

Drought Tolerance	Common Name	Scientific Name	Invasive Plant	Natural Height Range	Nominal Height	Growth Rate	Nat
✽ ✽	Palm, Buccaneer	*Pseudophoenix sargentii*	N	10–15'	10	S	Y
✽ ✽	Palm, Cabbage	*Sabal palmetto*	N	45–70'	50	S	Y
✽ ✽	Palm, Canary Island Date	*Phoenix canariensis*	N	35–50'	40	S	N
	Palm, Carpenteria	*Carpentaria acuminata*	N	35–45'	40	F	N
✽ ✽	Palm, Cliff Date	*Phoenix rupicola*	N	25–30'	25	S	N
✽ ✽	Palm, Coconut	*Cocos nucifera*	N	60–100'	60	M	N
✽ ✽	Palm, Cuban Royal	*Roystonea regia*	N	50–70'	60	M	N
✽ ✽	Palm, Date	*Phoenix dactylifera*	N	60–90'	70	M	N
✽ ✽	Palm, Desert Fan	*Washingtonia filifera*	N	40–60'	50	M	N
✽ ✽	Palm, Fan, Chinese	*Livistona chinensis*	N	20–30'	25	S	N
✽	Palm, Florida Royal	*Roystonea elata*	N	60–125'	80	M	Y
✽ ✽	Palm, Florida Thatch	*Thrinax parviflora*	N	15–30'	20	S	Y
✽ ✽	Palm, GruGru	*Acrocomia totai*	N	25–35'	30	S	N
✽	Palm, Hurricane	*Dictyosperma album*	N	25–40'	30	S	N
✽ ✽	Palm, Key Thatch	*Thrinax morrisii*	N	15–30'	20	S	Y
✽ ✽	Palm, Latan, Blue	*Latania loddigesii*	N	20–50'	30	S	N
✽ ✽	Palm, Licuala	*Licuala grandis*	N	10'	10	S	N
✽ ✽	Palm, Macarthur	*Ptychosperma macarthuri*	N	20–30'	25	S	N
✽ ✽	Palm Manila	*Veitchia merrilli*	N	10–25'	15	M	N
✽ ✽	Palm, Montgomery's	*Veitchia montgomeryana*	N	25–40'	35	F	N
✽	Palm, Paurotis	*Acoelorrhaphe wrightii*	N	15–25'	20	S	N
✽ ✽	Palm, Pindo	*Butia capitata*	N	10-20'	15	S	N
✽ ✽	Palm, Pritchardia	*Pritchardia* spp.	N	10–25'	15	S	N
✽	Palm, Pygmy Date	*Phoenix roebelinii*	N	10–20'	15	S	N
✽	Palm, Queen	*Syagrus romanzoffianum*	N	40–45'	40	M	N
✽ ✽	Palm, Sagisi	*Heterospathe elata*	N	30–45'	40	S	N
✽ ✽	Palm, Senegal Date	*Phoenix reclinata*	N	25–35'	25	S	M
✽ ✽	Palm, Silver	*Coccothrinax argentata*	N	10–20'	15	S	Y
✽ ✽	Palm, Solitaire	*Ptychosperma elegans*	N	15–25'	15	S	N
✽	Palm, Spindle	*Hyophorbe verschafeltii*	N	15–25'	20	S	N
✽ ✽	Palm, Thatch	*Thrinax radiata*	N	15–25'	20	S	Y
✽	Palm, Toddy Fishtail	*Caryota urens*	N	40–60'	50	M	N
✽	Palm, Triangle	*Neodypsis decaryi*	N	10–20'	15	S	N
✽ ✽	Palm, Washington	*Washingtonia robusta*	N	50–80'	60	F	N
✽ ✽	Palm, Wild Date	*Phoenix sylvestris*	N	40–60'	50	S	N
✽ ✽	Palm, Windmill	*Trachycarpus fortunei*	N	20–40'	25	S	N
✽ ✽	Palm, Winin	*Veitchia winin*	N	40–65'	50	F	N
✽ ✽	Paradise Tree	*Simrouba glauca*	N	35–50'	40	S	N
	Peach	*Prunus persica*	N	10–15'	12	M	N

Silver Trumpet-Tree
Tabebuia caraiba

...d Hardi-ness	Salt Toler-ance	Wind Toler-ance	Plant Type	Foliage Color	Flower Color	Flower Charac-teristics	Flowering Season	Light Require-ments	Nutritional Require-ments	Soil pH	Uses	Wildlife Value	Protected Species
	Y	H	P	G	Y	I	S	M,H	M	W	R,PK	F	E
	Y	H	P	G	W	I	SP,S,F	H	L	W	R,PK,B,PL,M,P	F	N
	M	H	P	G	W	I	SP	M,H	M	W	R,PK,B,M	U	N
	N	M	P	G	W	I	Y	H	H	W	R,PL,P,M	U	N
	M	H	P	G	W	I	SP	H	M	W	R,PK,B,M	U	N
	Y	H	P	G	W	I	Y	H	M	W	R,PK,S,F	U	N
	N	H	P	G	Y	I	SP	H	M	W	B,PK,R,P	F	N
	Y	H	P	G	W	I	SP	H	M	W	PK,B	F	N
	M	H	P	G	W	I	SP	H	M	W	PK,M,B,P	U	N
	N	H	P	G	W	I	S	M,H	M	W	R,PK,M,PL,B	U	N
	N	H	P	G	Y	I	SP	H	M	W	PK,R,B,P	F	N
	Y	H	P	G	Y	I	S,F	H	L	W	SP,P,R	F	T
	M	H	P	G	W	I	S	H	M	W	PK,B	U	N
	M	H	P	G	W	I	SP	H	M	W	R,B,PK,M	U	N
	Y	H	P	G	W	I	SP	M,H	L	W	R,PK,M	F	N
	N	H	P	B/G	W	I	S	H	M	W	PK,M,B,R	U	N
	N	M	P	G	W	I	S	L,M	H	W	R,P	U	N
	N	M	P	G	W	I	S	M,H	M	W	H,PK,B,M,P	U	N
	M	H	P	G	W	I	S	M,H	M	W	R,PK,M	U	N
	N	H	P	G	W	I	S	M,H	M	W	PK,R,B	U	N
	M	H	P	G	W	I	SP	M,H	M	W	M,R,BU	F	N
	M	H	P	B/G	W	I	SP	M,H	M	W	F,P,R,B,M	F	N
	Y	H	P	G	W	I	S	M,H	M	W	R,PK,M	U	N
	N	H	P	G	W	I	SP	M,H	M	W	R,PK,M,B	U	N
	N	H	P	G	W	S	Y	M,H	H	W	R,S,PL,M,B	U	N
	N	H	P	G	W	I	S	H	M	W	R,PK,B	U	N
	M	H	P	G	W	I	SP	H	M	W	R,PK,B,M,BU	U	N
	Y	H	P	G	W	I	S	M,H	L	W	R,M,PK,PL	F	N
	N	M	P	G	W	I	S	M,H	M	W	R,PK,B,M	U	N
	M	H	P	G	W	I	S	H	H	W	R,PK,M,B	U	N
	Y	H	P	G	W	I	SP	M,H	L	W	R,PK,M	F	T
	N	H	P	G	W	I	SP	H	M	W	P	U	N
	N	H	P	B/G	W	I	SP	M,H	M	W	R,PK,B,M	F	T
	M	H	P	G	W	I	SP	H	M	W	PK,B,P	U	N
	M	H	P	B/G	W	I	SP	H	M	W	PK,B,M	U	N
	M	H	P	G	W	I	SP	M,H	M	W	R,PK,M	U	N
	N	H	P	G	W	I	S	M,H	M	W	R,PK,B	U	N
	M	H	E	G	W	I	SP	H	M	W	R,PK,B	F	N
	N	M	D	G	P	S	SP	H	M	W	R,PK,F	F	N

Bleeding Heart Vine
Clerodendron thomsoniae

trees *(continued)*

Drought Tolerance	Common Name	Scientific Name	Invasive Plant	Natural Height Range	Nominal Height	Growth Rate	Nat
❄❄	Persimmon	*Diospyros virginiana*	N	30–45'	35	M	Y
❄❄	Pine, Japanese Black	*Pinus thunbergiana*	N	50–70'	60	M	N
❄❄	Pine, Loblolly	*Pinus taeda*	N	80–100'	90	M	Y
❄❄	Pine, Long-Leaf	*Pinus palustris*	N	80–100'	90	M	Y
❄❄	Pine, South Florida Slash	*Pinus elliottii* var. *densa*	N	80–100'	85	F	Y
❄❄	Pine, Sand	*Pinus clausa*	N	60–80'	65	S	Y
❄	Pink-and-White Shower	*Cassia javanica*	N	40–50'	45	F	N
❄❄	Pink Powderpuff Tree	*Calliandra surinamensis*	N	8–12'	10	M	N
❄❄	Pittosporum, Rusty	*Pittosporum ferrugineum*	N	40–60'	45	F	N
❄❄	Plum, Darling	*Reynosia septentrionalis*	N	20–30'	25	S	Y
❄❄	Plum, Flatwoods	*Prunus umbellata*	N	10–15'	12	F	Y
❄❄	Plum, Guiana	*Drypetes lateriflora*	N	20–30'	25	S	Y
❄❄	Plum, Pigeon	*Coccoloba diversifolia*	N	25–30'	25	S	Y
❄❄	Plum, Tallowwood	*Ximenia americana*	N	20–25'	25	M	Y
❄	Podocarpus, Nagi	*Podocarpus nagi*	N	20–40'	30	M	N
❄	Podocarpus, Weeping	*Podocarpus gracilior*	N	15–35'	25	M	N
❄	Podocarpus, Yew	*Podocarpus macrophyllus*	N	25–45'	35	M	N
❄❄	Pongam	*Pongamia pinnata*	N	30–40'	35	F	N
❄❄	Ponytail	*Beaucarnea recurvata*	N	15–25'	15	S	N
❄	Princewood	*Exostema caribaeum*	N	20–25'	20	S	Y
	Privet, Glossy	*Ligustrum lucidum*	N	30–35'	30	M	N
❄❄	Red Bay	*Persea borbonia*	N	50–60'	55	M	Y
❄	Red Silk-Cotton Tree	*Bombax ceiba*	N	50–75'	60	M	N
❄❄	Redbud	*Cercis canadensis*	N	20–30'	25	M	N
❄❄	Royal Poinciana	*Delonix regia*	N	25–40	30	F	N
❄❄	Rubber Tree, Indian	*Ficus elastica*	Y	40–60'	50	F	N
❄❄	Sabucu	*Lysiloma latisiliqua*	N	20–30'	25	M	N
❄	Sandbox Tree	*Hura crepitans*	N	40–60'	50	F	N
❄❄	Sapodilla	*Manilkara zapota*	N	40–50'	45	S	N
❄	Sapote, Black	*Diospyros dignya*	N	30–40'	35	F	N
❄❄	Satin Leaf	*Chrysophyllum oliviforme*	N	30–40'	35	S	Y
❄	Sausage Tree	*Kigelia pinnata*	N	40–45'	40	M	N
❄❄	Screwpine	*Pandanus utilis*	N	20–30'	25	S	N
❄❄	Screwpine, Veitch	*Pandanus veitchii*	N	20–30'	25	S	N
❄❄	Seagrape	*Coccoloba uvifera*	N	15–30'	25	M	Y
❄❄	Seagrape, Big-Leaf	*Coccoloba pubescens*	N	60–80'	60	M	N
❄	Shavingbrush Tree	*Pseudobombax ellipticum*	N	20–30'	25	F	N
❄❄	Silk Cotton Tree	*Ceiba pentandra*	N	50–80'	75	F	N
❄	Silk Oak	*Grevillea robusta*	N	45–60'	50	F	N

©Robin L. Cole/Colephoto

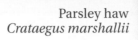

Coral Honeysuckle
Lonicera sempervirens

Parsley haw
Crataegus marshallii

Salt Tolerance	Wind Tolerance	Plant Type	Foliage Color	Flower Color	Flower Characteristics	Flowering Season	Light Requirements	Nutritional Requirements	Soil pH	Uses	Wildlife Value	Protected Species
N	H	D	G	G	I	SP	H	M	W	P,R,S,F	F	N
Y	H	E	G	BR	CONE	SP	H	L	W	R,PK,BU	U	N
N	H	E	G	BR	CONE	SP	H	L	W	PK	F	N
N	H	E	G	BR	CONE	SP	H	L	W	PK	F	N
M	H	E	G	BR	CONE	SP	H	L	W	PK,R,BU,B	F	N
Y	H	E	G	BR	CONE	SP	H	L	W	PK,S,R	F	N
M	M	D	G	R/P	S	SP,S	H	M	W	R,S,B	U	N
N	H	E	G	P	S,F	SP	H	M	W	PK,R,B,SP	U	N
N	M	E	G	Y	I	SP	H	M	W	R,PK,M,B,BU	F	N
Y	M	E	G	Y/G	I	SP,S	H	L	W	R,PK,B	F	N
N	H	D	G	W	I	SP	M	M	W	R,PK,P,BU,F	F	N
Y	H	E	G	?	I	F	H	L	W	P,R	U	N
Y	H	E	G	W	I	SP	H	L	W	R,PK,PL,M,B	F	N
Y	H	E	G	Y	I	Y	H	L	W	PK,R	F	N
M	H	E	G	G	I	S	M,H	M	W	R,PK,BU,B,P	U	N
M	M	E	G	G	I	S	M,H	M	W	R,M,B,P,BU	U	N
M	H	E	G	G	I	S	M,H	M	W	R,PK,BU,B,P	U	N
Y	H	D	G	P	S	SP	H	M	W	R,PK,M,B	U	N
M	H	E	G	W	S	S	H	M	W	R,PK	U	N
N	H	E	G	W	S,F	SP,S	H	M	W	PK,R	U	N
N	H	E	G	W	I	SP	M,H	M	W	R,P,B,PK,M	U	N
M	H	E	G	G	I	SP	H	L	W	R,PK,S,B	F	N
N	M	D	G	R	S	W	H	M	W	R,S	U	N
N	H	D	G	P,W	S	SP	H	M	W	R,PK,B	U	N
M	M	D	G	R,Y	S	S	H	L	W	PK,S,B,R	U	N
M	L	E	G	G	I	Y	M,H	M	W	PK	U	N
Y	H	D	G	W	I	SP,S	H	L	W	PK,B,M,R,P,PL	F	N
N	L	D	G	R	S	Y	H	M	W	None	U	N
Y	H	E	G	W	I	S	H	L	W	R,PK,F,S,P	F	N
N	H	E	G	Y/G	I	SP	H	M	W	F,R,PK	F	N
N	H	E	G	W	I	F	H	L	W	S,PL,M,B,R,PK	F	N
N	H	E	G	PU	S,F	Y	H	M	W	PK	U	N
Y	M	E	G	Y	I	Y	H	L	W	R,PK,M,BU,B	F	N
M	H	E	G,V	Y	I	Y	Light	M	W	R,PK,B,BU,M	U	N
Y	H	E	G	W	I	S	H	L	W	F,BU,PK	F	Y
Y	M	E	G	G	I	SP	H	M	W	SP	F	N
M	M	D	G	R	S	W,SP	H	M	W	R,P,S,B,M	U	N
M	M	D	G	W,P	S	SP	H	M	W	PK,R,B	U	N
N	L	E	G	O	S	SP	H	M	W	R,PK,B	U	N

©Betty Wargo/Colephoto

Cross Vine
Bignonia capreolata

Railroad Vine
Ipomoea pes-caprae

trees *(continued)*

Drought Tolerance	Common Name	Scientific Name	Invasive Plant	Natural Height Range	Nominal Height	Growth Rate	N
❋ ❋	Simpson's Stopper	*Myrcianthes fragrans*	N	20–30'	25	M	
❋	Snakewood	*Cecropia palmata*	N	40–50'	45	F	
❋ ❋	Snow-in-Summer	*Melaleuca decora*	N	15–30'	25	M	
❋	Snowflake Tree	*Trevesia palmata*	N	15–20'	15	M	
❋ ❋	Soapberry	*Sapindus saponaria*	N	35–45'	40	M	
❋ ❋	Soursop	*Annona muricata*	N	15–20'	15	M	
❋ ❋	Spanish Lime	*Melicoccus bijugatus*	N	40–50'	45	M	
❋ ❋	Sparkleberry	*Vaccinium arboreum*	N	20–30'	25	M	
❋ ❋	Stoppers	*Eugenia* spp.	N	15–20'	15	S	
❋ ❋	Strongbark, Bahama	*Bourreria suculenta* var. *revoluta*	N	20'	20	M	
❋ ❋	Sugarberry	*Celtis laevigata*	N	40–60'	50	M	
	Sweetbay	*Magnolia virginiana*	N	40–60'	50	M	
❋ ❋	Sweetgum	*Liquidambar styraciflua*	N	60–100'	70	F	
❋	Sweetsop	*Annona squamosa*	N	15–20'	20	M	
	Sycamore	*Platanus occidentalis*	N	70–150'	100	F	
❋ ❋	Tabebuia	*Tabebuia umbellata*	N	15'	15	S	
❋ ❋	Tabebuia, Golden	*Tabebuia chrysotricha*	N	35–50'	40	M	
❋ ❋	Tabebuia, Purple	*Tabebuia impetiginosa*	N	15–20'	15	S	
❋ ❋	Tamarind	*Tamarindus indica*	N	45–65'	50	M	
❋ ❋	Tamarind, False	*Lysiloma latisiliquum*	N	40–50'	45	F	
❋	Traveler's Tree	*Ravenela madagascariensis*	N	20–30'	25	M	
❋ ❋	Trumpet-Tree, Pink	*Tabebuia heterophylla*	N	15–30'	25	M	
❋ ❋	Trumpet-Tree, Silver	*Tabebuia caraiba*	N	20–30'	25	M	
	Tulip Tree	*Liriodendron tulipifera*	N	80–100'	85	F	
❋ ❋	Tulipwood	*Harpulia arborea*	N	30–50'	40	S	
	Tupelo, Black	*Nyssa sylvatica*	N	50–80'	65	M	
❋ ❋	Wax Myrtle	*Myrica cerifera*	Y	15–25'	20	M	
❋ ❋	West Indian Laurel	*Ficus perforata*	N	30–40'	35	M	
❋ ❋	Wild Dilly	*Manilkara bahamensis*	N	15–20'	15	S	
❋ ❋	Wild Lime	*Zanthoxylum fagara*	N	20–30'	25	M	
❋ ❋	Wild-Cinnamon	*Canella alba*	N	20–35'	25	S	
	Willow, Coastal Plain	*Salix caroliniana*	Y	20–30'	25	F	
❋	Ylang-Ylang	*Cananga odorata*	N	30–40'	35	F	
❋ ❋	Zelkova, Japanese	*Zelkova serrata*	N	50–60	60	F	

Carolina Yellow Jessamine
Gelsemium sempervirens

	Salt Toler-ance	Wind Toler-ance	Plant Type	Foliage Color	Flower Color	Flower Charac-teristics	Flowering Season	Light Require-ments	Nutritional Require-ments	Soil pH	Uses	Wildlife Value	Protected Species
	Y	H	E	G	W	I,F	Y	M,H	L	W	R,PK,M,B	U	N
	N	L	E	G	Y	I	S	H	M	W	PK	U	N
	M	H	E	G	W	S	S	H	L	W	R,S,M,B,PK	U	N
	N	M	E	G	W	I	S	M,H	M	W	R,PK	U	N
	Y	H	D	G	W	I	W,SP	H	L	W	PK,R,B	U	N
	M	H	E	G	Y	I,F	Y	H	M	W	R,F	F	N
	M	H	E	G	W	I	SP	H	M	W	B,R,PK,F	U	N
	N	H	D	G	W	I,F	SP	M	L	A	R,P,BU,SP	F	N
	N	H	E	G	W	I	SP,S	M,H	L	W	R,PK	F	N
	M	H	E	G	W	I	Y	H	L	W	R	F	N
	N	H	D	G	G	I	SP	H	L	W	S,P,PL,R,PK	F,N	N
	N	H	D	G	W	S,F	S	H	M	W	R,S,PK,M,B	F	N
	N	H	D	G	W	I	SP	H	L	W	R,PK,S,B	F	N
	N	H	E	G	G/Y	I	W,SP	H	M	W	F,R	F	N
	N	H	D	G	G	I	SP	H	M	W	PK,R,S,B	U	N
	M	M	D	G	Y	S,F	SP	H	M	W	R,PK,B,M	U	N
	M	L	D	G	Y	S	SP	H	M	W	PK,R,S,M,B	U	N
	M	M	D	G	PU	S	SP	H	M	W	R,PK,B,M	U	N
	M	H	E	G	Y/R	I	SP,S,F	H	M	W	R,S,PK,B	F	N
	Y	H	D	G	W	I	SP,S	H	L	W	R,S,B,PK,PL,M	F,N	N
	N	H	E	G	W	S	SP,S,F	M,H	M	W	R,PK	U	N
	M	M	E	G	P,W	S	SP,S	H	M	W	R,S,PK,B,M	U	N
	M	L	D	G/S	Y	S	SP	H	M	W	R,S,PK,B,M,PL	U	N
	N	M	D	G	Y/G	S	SP	H	M	W	R,PK,B	U	N
	N	H	E	G	G	I	S	H	L	W	S,R,PK,B,PL,M	F	N
	N	M	D	G	W	I	SP	H	L	W	S,R,B,PK	F	N
	Y	H	E	G	W	I	S	H	L	W	R,PK,BU	F	N
	M	H	E	G	G	I	Y	H	M	W	PK,B,R,S,M	U	N
	Y	H	E	G	Y	S	W,SP	H	L	W	SP,P,R	F	N
	Y	H	E	G	G	I	Y	H	L	W	PK	F	N
	M	H	E	G	W	I	S,F	H	L	W	R	F	N
	N	L	E	G	G	I	SP	H	L	W	PK	U	N
	N	L	E	G	Y	F	Y	H	M	W	PK,R	U	N
	N	M	D	G	G	I	SP	H	M	W	S,R,PK,B	U	N

Rangoon Creeper
Quisqualis indica

Virginia Creeper
Parthenocissus quinquefolia

©Robin L. Cole/Colephoto

vines

Drought Tolerance	Common Name	Scientific Name	Invasive Plant	Growth Rate	Native	Cold Hardiness	Salt Tolerance
❄	Allamanda, Purple	*Allamanda violacea*	N	M	N	S	N
❄ ❄	Allamanda, Wild	*Urechites lutea*	N	M	Y	T	M
❄	Allamanda, Yellow	*Allamanda cathartica*	N	F	N	S	N
❄	Bengal Clock Vine	*Thunbergia grandiflora*	Y	F	N	S	N
	Bleeding Heart	*Clerodendrum thomsoniae*	N	F	N	H	N
❄ ❄	Bougainvillea	*Bougainvillea spectabilis*	N	M	N	S	Y
❄	Calico Flower	*Aristolochia elegans*	Y	F	N	S	N
❄	Carolina Yellow Jessamine	*Gelsemium sempervirens*	N	M	Y	VH	N
❄	Ceriman	*Monstera deliciosa*	N	M	N	S	N
❄	Climbing Hydrangea	*Decumaria barbara*	N	M	Y	VH	N
❄	Coral Honeysuckle	*Lonicera sempervirens*	N	S	Y	VH	M
❄ ❄	Coral Vine	*Antigonon leptopus*	Y	F	N	H	N
❄ ❄	Creeping Fig	*Ficus pumila*	Y	F	N	H	Y
❄	Cross Vine	*Bignonia capreolata*	Y	F	Y	VH	N
❄ ❄	Flame Vine	*Pyrostegia venusta*	Y	F	N	S	N
❄ ❄	Garlic Vine	*Pseudocalymma alliaceum*	N	M	N	S	N
❄	Gloriosa Lily	*Gloriosa rothschildiana*	N	F	N	VH	N
❄ ❄	Grape, Muscadine	*Vitis rotundifolia*	Y	F	Y	VH	N
❄	Herald's Trumpet	*Beaumontia grandiflora*	N	F	N	S	N
❄	Jacquemontia	*Jacquemontia* spp.	N	M	Y	S	N
❄	Japanese Clematis	*Clematis dioscoreifolia*	N	M	N	VH	N
❄	Jasmine, Confederate	*Trachelospermum jasminoides*	N	M	N	VH	M
❄ ❄	Jasmine, Madagascar	*Stephanotis floribunda*	N	M	N	T	M
❄ ❄	Lemon Vine	*Pereskia aculeata*	N	M	N	T	Y
❄ ❄	Madagascar Rubber-Vine	*Cryptostegia madagascariensis*	N	M	N	S	M
❄ ❄	Mandevilla	*Mandevilla* spp.	N	F	N	S	M
❄ ❄	Marine Ivy	*Cissus incisa*	N	F	Y	VH	Y
❄ ❄	Mexican Flame Vine	*Senecio confusus*	N	F	N	S	N
❄ ❄	Night-Blooming Cereus	*Hylocereus undatus*	Y	M	N	S	H
❄	Passion Flower	*Passiflora* spp.	Y	F	N	S–H	M
❄	Pelican Flower	*Aristolochia grandiflora*	N	F	N	S	N
❄ ❄	Rangoon Creeper	*Quisqualis indica*	Y	F	N	H	N
❄	Rubber Vine	*Rhabdadenia biflora*	N	M	Y	S	Y
❄ ❄	Sicklethorn Vine	*Asparagus falcatus*	N	M	N	H	N
❄ ❄	Trumpet Vine	*Campsis radicans*	Y	F	Y	VH	N
❄ ❄	Virginia Creeper	*Parthenocissus quinquefolia*	Y	F	Y	VH	N
	Wisteria, American	*Wisteria frutescens*	N	F	N	VH	Y
❄	Wooly Morning Glory	*Argyreia nervosa*	Y	F	N	S	N

Flame Vine
Pyrostegia ignea

...t e	Foliage Color	Flower Color	Flower Characteristics	Flowering Season	Light Requirements	Nutritional Requirements	Soil pH	Uses	Wildlife Value	Protected Species
E	G	PU	S	S	H	M	W	T,GC	U	N
E	G	Y	S	Y	M,H	M	W	T,F,GC	U	N
	G	Y	S,F	SP,S,F	H	M	W	T,GC	U	N
E	G	W,BL	S	S,F	M	M	W	T,F	U	N
E	G	W-R	S	S	M	M	W	T	U	N
	G,V	R,P,W,O	S	Y	H	M	W	F	U	N
E	G	R/PU-W	S	S,F	M,H	M	W	T	U	N
E	G	Y	S,F	W,S	M,H	M	W	T,F	U	N
E	G	W	I	S	L,M	M	W	T	F	N
D	G	W	S	SP	M,L	M	A	T	U	N
	G	R/Y	S,F	SP,S	M,H	L	W	T,GC	U	N
	G	P	S	SP,S,F	H	W	W	T,F	U	N
E	G	G	I	S	M,H	L	W	F,M	U	N
	G	R/Y	S	SP	M	M	W	T,F,M	U	N
	G	O	S	W,SP	M,H	M	W	T,F,M	U	N
	G	L,P,W	S,F	SP,S,F	H	L	W	T,F	U	N
D	G	R/Y	S	SP,S,F	M,H	M	W	T,F	U	N
D	G	Y	I	SP	M,H	L	W	T,F	F	N
E	G	W	S,F	SP	M,H	M	W	T	U	N
E	G	W	S	SP,S,F	M,H	M	A	T,F	U	N
D	G	W	S,F	S,F	H	M	W	T,F	U	N
E	G	W	S,F	SP	M,H	M	W	T,F,GC	U	N
E	G	W	S,F	S	M,H	M	W	T,F	U	N
E	G	Y	S	SP,S	H	L	W	T,GC	F	N
E	G	L	S	S,F	H	M	W	FT,F	U	N
E	G	P,R	S	S	H	M	W	T,F	U	N
D	G	G	I	S	M,H	L	W	T,F	U	N
E	G	O	S	SP,S,F	H	M	W	T,F	U	N
S	G	W-Y	S,F	S	M,H	L	W	F,M	F	N
E	G	B,W,R,PU	S,F	S,F	M	M	W	T,F,GC	F	N
E	G	PU-W	S,F	S,F	M,H	M	W	T	U	N
E	G	W/R/P	S,F	S,F	M,H	L	W	T,F,GC	U	N
	G	W/Y	S	Y	H	M	W	T,F	U	N
	G	W	S,F	W	L,M	M	W	T,F	F	N
D	G	O	S	S	M,H	L	W	F,T,M	U	N
D	G	W	I	S	M,H	L	W	F,T,M	U	N
D	G	PU	S	SP,S	H	M	W	F,T	U	N
E	G	P,PU	S	SP,S,F	H	M	W	T	U	N

Appendix B –
Garden Products Suppliers

Local

Check in the garden and plumbing departments of your neighborhood nurseries, builders' supply stores, discount and department stores.

Idea Factory, Inc., 2023 Country Drive, Plano, IL 60545. Makes Help™, a micro-biological spray for houseplants, fruits and vegetables, flowers, trees and lawns. If local stores don't stock it, have them call 1-800-886-4332 to order.

Rain Bird Inc.
    Irrigation and drip watering supplies. Call 1-800-247-3782 for a dealer in your area.

Mail Order

Association of Florida Native Nurseries, P. O. Box 434, Melrose, FL 32666-0434.
    Web: members.aol.com/afnn Send $5.00 for a copy of their annual *Native Plant & Service Directory*. Plants are listed by common and scientific name, and are cross-referenced to member nurseries.

Brundy's Exotics, P. O. Box 820874, Houston, TX 77282-0874
    Tropical plants. Send $2.00 for catalog.

Burpee Seed Co., 300 Park Avenue, Warminster, PA 18974.
    Web: www.burpee.com Phone: 1-800-333-5808
    A classic catalog for flowers, vegetables, some trees, shrubs, fruit, supplies.

Circle One International, Inc., 16209 Flight Path Drive, Brooksville, FL 34609.
    Web: www.circle-one.com Phone: 1-800-780-1215
    Organic garden products, including biological controls and fungal inoculants.

Daylily Discounters, One Daylily Place, Alachua, FL 32615

Easy Gardener, Inc., Box 21015, Waco, TX 76702-1025 Web: www.easygardener.com
    Phone: 1-800-327-9462 Anti-transplant sprays, mulch cloth, many other garden products.

ECHO, Inc. (Educational Concerns for Hunger Organization), 14730 Durrance Road,
    North Fort Myers, FL 33917 Web: www.xc.org/echo/ Phone: (941)543-3246
    Has a very unique seeds list; send $2 and a large SASE for a copy. If you are in the area, take a fascinating tour of their facility, including the ECHO nursery.

The Fig Tree Nursery, P. O. Box 124, Gulf Hammock, FL 32639. Figs, grapes and other fruits.

Floralabs, 6857 Olsen Road, Pensacola, FL 32506

Florida Keys Native Nursery, Inc., U.S. 1 and Mile Marker 89, Tavernier, FL 33073
    Mail: 102 Mohawk Street, Tavernier, FL 33070 Phone: (305)852-2636
    Native trees and shrubs.

Gardens Alive!, 5100 Schenley Place, Lawrenceburg, IN 47025 Phone: (812)537-8651
    Web: www.gardens-alive.com Organic garden products including natural controls, composting aids and soil amendments.

Gardener's Supply Company, 128 Intervale Road, Burlington, VT 05401-2850
    Web: www.gardenerssupply.com Phone: 1-800-863-1700
    Anti-transplant sprays, irrigation equipment, many other garden products and supplies.

Gurney's Seed & Nursery Co., 110 Capital Street, Yankton, SD 57079
   Web: www.gurneys.com Phone: (605)665-1671. Seeds, plants, and gardening supplies.
H. B. Hastings, P. O. Box 115535, Atlanta, GA 30310. Seeds and plants, especially southern
   varieties, and some supplies.
J. L. Hudson, Star Route 2, Box 337, LaHonda, CA 94020. One of my favorite sources for hard-
   to-find seeds. Send $1.00 for a catalog brimming with information.
Kilgore Seed Company, 1400 West First Street, Sanford, FL 32771
   Many hard-to-find southern seeds like chuffa and special peanut varieties.
A. M. Leonard, 6665 Spiker Road, Piqua, OH 45356. Web: www.amleonard.com
   Phone: 1-800-543-8955 Anti-transpirant sprays.
Mellinger's Inc., 2310 W. South Range, North Lima, OH 44452-9731
   Web: www.mellingers.com Phone: 1-800-321-7444
   Good catalog for all kinds of gardening supplies.
Mail-Order Natives, P. O. Box 9366, Lee, FL 32059 (850)973-4688
   Web: www.mindspring.com/~plants/natives.catalogue.html
Park Seed Co., 1 Parkton Avenue, Greenwood, SC 29647-0001 Web: www.parkseed.com
   Phone: 1-800-845-3369 Seeds, plants and supplies.
Raindrip, Inc., 21305 Itasca Street, Chatsworth, CA 91311
   Web: www.raindrip.com Phone (818)718-8004 Drip irrigation equipment.
Smith & Hawken, 25 Corta Madera, Mill Valley, CA 94941
   Web: www.smith-hawken.com Phone (415)383-2000
   Source of Mosquito Dunks (item #2327, $11) and many other garden supplies.
Solutions, P. O. Box 6878, Portland, OR 97228 Phone: 1-800-342-9988
   Also has Mosquito Dunks (item #8648; $12 for one package of six dunks, $22 for two
   packages). Has a catalog, but Mosquito Dunks aren't listed in it.
Southern Seeds, P. O. Box 803, Lutz, FL 33548 Phone: 813-357-3354
   Special plant varieties for Florida. Send $2 for a catalog (refunded if you order).
Spray-N-Grow, P. O. Box 2137, Department D, Rockport, TX 78381
   Web: www.spray-n-grow.com Phone: (512)790-9033
   Micro-nutrients and bio-activators. Call for a free newsletter.
Thompson & Morgan, Inc., Box 1308, Jackson, NJ 08527 Phone: 1-800-274-7333
   Many specific colors and varieties of flowering plants, also some vegetables. An excellent
   catalog to have for reference.
Tomato Growers' Supply Co., P. O. Box 2237, Fort Myers, FL 33902 Phone: (941)768-1119
The Urban Farmer Store, 2833 Vincente Street, San Francisco, CA 94116
   Web: www.3000.com/urbanfmr/ Phone: (415)661-2204
   Irrigation equipment. Call for a free catalog.
Wayside Gardens, One Garden Lane, Hodges, SC 29695
   Web: www.waysidegardens.com Phone: 1-800-845-1124
   Special varieties of trees, shrubs and perennials.
Worm's Way Indiana, 3151 S. Hwy 446, Bloomington, IN 47401
   Web: www.wormsway.com Phone: 1-800-274-9676
   Has Hydretain™ water-retaining gel and other products. Also has an office in Tampa, but
   write to Indiana for their catalog.

Magazines:
Florida Gardening, P. O. Box 500678, Malabar, FL 32950. Web: www.floridagardening.com
   Phone: (407)951-4500. "Florida's own home gardening magazine", published six times a year.
The Palmetto, quarterly magazine of the Florida Native Plant Society, P. O. Box 6116, Spring
   Hill, FL 34611. Web: www.flmnh.ufl.edu/fnps/fnps.htm Phone: (727)856-8202.

Bibliography

Ball, Ken, Ann Reilly, and Gary O. Robinette. 1990. *Taylor's Guide to Water-Saving Gardening.* Boston, MA: Houghton-Mifflin.

Bell, C. Ritchie, and Bryan J. Taylor. 1982. *Florida Wildflowers and Roadside Plants.* Chapel Hill, NC: Laurel Hill Press.

Binetti, Marianne. 1990. *Tips for Carefree Landscapes.* Pownal, VT: Storey Communications.

Brandies, Monica Moran. 1993. *Florida Gardening: the Newcomer's Survival Manual.* Wayne, PA: B. B. Mackey Books.

Broschat, Timothy K., and Alan W. Meerow. 1994. *Betrock's Reference Guide to Florida Landscape Plants* (second edition). Pembroke Pines, FL: Betrock Information Systems.

Chaplin, Lois Trigg, and Monica Moran Brandies. 1998. *The Florida Gardener's Book of Lists.* Dallas, TX: Taylor Publishing Company.

Creasy, Rosalind. 1982. *The Complete Book of Edible Landscaping.* San Francisco: Sierra Club.

DeFreitas, Stan. 1993. *The Water-Thrifty Garden.* Dallas, TX: Taylor Publishing Company.

Edson, Seton N. 1963. *Florida Garden Soils: 500 Questions and Answers.* Gainesville, FL: University of Florida Press.

Ellefson, Connie, Tom Stephens, and Doug Welsh. 1992. *Xeriscape Gardening: Water Conservation for the American Landscape.* New York: Macmillan.

Garner, Allen, John Stevely, Heidi Smith, Mary Hoppe, Tracy Floyd and Paul Hinchcliff. 1996. *A Guide to Environmentally Friendly Landscaping: Florida Yards and Neighborhoods Handbook.* Gainesville, FL: University of Florida Institute of Food and Agriculture Sciences, Bulletin 295.

Haehle, Robert G., and Joan Brookwell. 1999. *Native Florida Plants: Low-Maintenance Landscaping and Gardening.* Houston, TX: Gulf Publishing Company.

Huegel, Craig N. 1995. *Florida Plants for Wildlife: A Selection Guide to Native Trees and Shrubs.* Orlando, FL: Florida Native Plant Society.

Knox, Gary W. Undated. *Drought Tolerant Plants for North and Central Florida.* Gainesville, FL: University of Florida Institute of Food and Agriculture Sciences, Circular 807.

MacCubbin, Thomas. 1997. *Florida Home Grown: Landscaping* (revised edition) Oviedo, FL: Waterview Books.

Mackey, Betty Barr, and Monica Moran Brandies. 1992. *A Cutting Garden for Florida.* Wayne, PA: B. B. Mackey Books.

Milne, Murray. 1979. *Residential Water Re-Use.* Davis, CA: University of California/Davis.

O'Keefe, John M. 1992. *Water Conserving Gardens and Landscapes.* Pownal, VT: Storey Communications.

Ortho Books, Editors of. 1993. *All About Ground Covers,* San Ramon, CA: Ortho Books.

—, *Gardening in Dry Climates.* 1989.

—, *Improving Your Garden Soil.* 1992.

—, *Landscaping with Wildflowers and Native Plants.* 1984.

Perry, Mac. 1996. *Mac Perry's Florida Lawn and Garden Care* (fourth edition). Miami, FL: Florida Flair Books.

Postel, Sandra. 1992. *Last Oasis.* New York: W. W. Norton.

Ruppert, Kathleen C., and Robert J. Black, editors. 1998. *Florida Lawn Handbook: An Environmental Approach to Care and Maintenance of Your Lawn* (second edition). Gainesville, FL: University Press of Florida.

Schaefer, Joe, and George Tanner. 1998. *Landscaping for Florida's Wildlife: Re-creating Native Ecosystems in Your Yard.* Gainesville, FL: University Press of Florida.

Suncoast Native Plant Society, Inc. 1997. *The Right Plants for Dry Places: Native Plant Landscaping in Central Florida.* St. Petersburg, FL: Great Outdoors Publishing Company.

Sunset Books and *Sunset* Magazine editorial staff. 1989. *Waterwise Gardening: Beautiful Gardens with Less Water.* Menlo Park, CA: Lane Publishing.

Sunset Magazine editorial staff. 1990. "80 Little Things and One Great Big Thing You Can Do to Save Water in the Garden". *Sunset,* May 1990.

Sunset Magazine editorial staff. 1991. "Dealing with the Drought." *Sunset,* April 1991.

Taylor, Walter Kingsley. 1992. *The Guide to Florida Wildflowers.* Dallas, TX: Taylor Publishing Company.

Taylor, Walter Kingsley. 1998. *Florida Wildflowers in Their Natural Communities.* Gainesville, FL: University Press of Florida.

Van Atta, Marian. 1991. *Growing and Using Exotic Foods.* Sarasota, FL: Pineapple Press.

Wasowski, Sally. 1992. *Requiem for a Lawnmower.* Dallas, TX: Taylor Publishing Company.

Wasowski, Sally, and Andy Wasowski. 1994. *Gardening with Native Plants of the South.* Dallas, TX: Taylor Publishing Company.

Xeric Landscaping with Florida Native Plants. 1991. San Antonio: FL: Association of Florida Native Nurseries.

Xeriscape Plant Guide. Undated. Palatka, FL: St. Johns River Water Mgmt. District.

Xeriscape Plant Guide II. Undated. West Palm Beach, FL: South Florida Water Mgmt. District.

Xeriscape Plant Guide. Undated. Brooksville, FL: Southwest Florida Water Mgmt. District.

Index